THEE

&

me

Janeece England

DEDICATION

To our daughter, Rebekah Joy, our son-in-law, Jake, and our granddaughter, Trinity.

.... praying you have as fulfilling a life in the Lord as we have been blessed to enjoy. For all your special occasions when our chairs remained empty, we thank you for sharing us with the world outside Indiana.

A special thanks to Elvina McEwen who read through 17 years-worth of newsletters, e-mails, and correspondence in choosing which stories and material to include in this book. As Elvina said while working feverishly to finish this project, "I'm not possessed, just obsessed."

CONTENTS

MINISTRY BACKGROUND

Janeece (Holt) England, a native of Oblong, Illinois, and Steve England of Bethel, Ohio, met at Kentucky Christian College, now Kentucky Christian University. In 1972, they were married during semester break their senior year. They have one grown daughter, Rebekah Joy, a granddaughter, Trinity Jade, and son-in-law, Jake Liles. The Englands served a combined thirty years in three local ministries, all in Indiana. Together, they led church members on short-term mission trips to India, China, Mexico, St. Croix, and Jamaica to help missionaries supported by the church.

In 2002, Karen and Ben Pennington, missionaries to Zimbabwe, asked them to assist with the on-going of their mission work in Masvingo, Zimbabwe while they returned to the States on furlough. The Englands thought this trip was a one-time request for five months. God had other plans for them which took them to Guinea, India, China, South Africa, Italy, Tanzania, Hong Kong, and Czech Republic. Seventeen years later, Janeece is booked through 2021 and presently preparing for her thirty-fifth MRS (Missionary Relief Services) assignment.

Steve and Janeece England

ABOUT THE BOOK

THEE & me is the story of how an extraordinary God used an ordinary couple as relief missionaries to touch the lives of people whose language they could not speak to further His Kingdom.

These stories have been gleaned from MRS Newsletters and e-mail correspondences.

May these memories bring a smile, encouragement, and inspire you to live the life to which God has called you.

Want additional copies of *THEE & me*? Order additional copies from Amazon. www.amazon.com Janeece England - THEE & me

Need a mission speaker for your local church? Have questions or know career missionaries who wish assistance with their work while on furlough?

E-mail address: vsengland1973@yahoo.com

Snail-mail: P.O. Box 52, Staunton, IN 47881

Acknowledgements

All Scripture quotations, unless otherwise indicated, are taken from the **Holy Bible, New International Version (NIV®)** Copyright © 1973, 1978, 1984 *International Bible Society*. Used by permission of *Zondervan*. All rights reserved.

Scriptures marked "(CEV)" are taken from the **Contemporary English Version** © by *American Bible Society*. Used by permission.

Scripture quotations marked "(ESV)" are taken from the ESV® Bible (**The Holy Bible, English Standard Version®**.) Copyright © 2001 by Crossway, a publishing ministry of Good News Publishers. Used by permission. All rights reserved.

The Message, copyright © by *Eugene H. Peterson,* 1993, 1994, 1995, 1996 used by permission of *NavPress Publishing Group*.

Scripture marked "(NLT)" are taken from the **Holy Bible, New Living Translation (NLT)**, copyright © 1966. Used by permission of *Tyndale House Publishers, Inc.*, Wheaton, Illinois 60189. All rights reserved.

Scripture quotations marked "(NKJV)" are taken from the **New King James Version®**. Copyright © 1979, 1980, 1982 by *Thomas Nelson, Inc.* Used by permission. All rights reserved.

Scripture quotations marked "(KJV)" are taken from the KING JAMES VERSION (KJV): KING JAMES VERSION, public domain.

2002

Our First Adventure in Zimbabwe: Stranded in the Game Reserve

We went to Bulawayo and stayed overnight with Ivan and JoAnn Martin to pick up Sunday School literature and Holiday Bible School craft patterns (VBS). Since Bulawayo is halfway to Victoria Falls, we journeyed on to see one of the Seven Wonders of the World.

Victoria Falls was awesome! The Bible describes God's voice as "The sound of mighty waters." If it was louder than the falls, it is no wonder the Israelites were frightened. Rainbows were all around us. I took a picture of Janeece standing in the middle of one. It was a reminder that God promised never to leave us nor forsake us if we trust and obey Him. We even saw the rainbow going into the ground. Janeece said we found the end of the rainbow here in Africa.

The next day, Janeece went white water rafting on the Zambezi River. She heard stories about how good the Class Five rapids were, plus there were hippos and crocodiles in the river to add to the excitement.

Since water is not my thing, I wanted to stay on dry land where it was safe and not so exciting! I decided to drive the trails in the National Game Reserve to see the African wildlife. After that I would eat lunch then it would be time to pick Janeece up from rafting.

The drive started out promising as I saw monkeys, impalas, and a kudu. But after two hours of seeing little, I decided to take Chubu Loop for 11 kilometers (km) until it rejoined the main road. The sign said that it would rejoin the main path in 11 km. I thought since it was hotter that the animals would be away from the river in the shade and this loop led away from the river. The route looked promising, so I took it.

Many times in life we leave the path of Christianity because the side roads look so promising and full of excitement. We promise God it is only for a little time and we will soon return to Him.

The path or road I took was surrounded by grass which was soon taller than the truck. The grass ended, but now I had to climb a hill with loose gravel and boulders to dodge. Soon the truck's rear wheels were throwing gravel as it slipped up the hill. On one occasion I thought the truck might roll over on its side.

After nine km of bad terrain I considered turning around, but there were no promising places to do so. It was only two more km to where I was to rejoin the main road so why backtrack. I pressed forward.

The road became sand and soon I was going down a large hill that almost immediately went upward. I shifted gears and that was it. The truck was stuck. It was 1:30 p.m. I later learned I was on a path that only the canoe company used, on occasion, to pick up people who had been canoeing. I was frustrated and upset at myself for leaving the main path in search of more adventure.

There were just small grains of sand holding the truck fast. Only one small sin will keep us out of heaven as no sin is allowed.

I found a sturdy stick to dig and put more sticks by the wheels to try to get out, but no luck. I thought, okay, I will walk out the direction I was headed but soon the heat was too much, and I went back to the truck. At the truck, I tried calling on the missionary's cell phone. I had phone numbers, but no signal. I tried digging again, but no luck. I settled down in the seat and thought, I have all the suitcases, money, identification papers, sleeping bags, and ice chest, so I could spend the night here. About 3:30 p.m. the flies, gnats, and insects decided they liked me. So I sprayed myself with insect repellent. I think it just attracted more. I felt it was like the plagues of flies and gnats of Egypt only on a smaller scale.

I decided then if I were going to make it out I would have to walk out on my own with the Lord's help. I knew it was at least 15 km back (9.3 miles) to the main road where I turned off. Surely someone would be looking for me when the park closed at 6 p.m.

I waited until 4:30 p.m. for the shadows to come and armed myself with two water bottles, a flashlight, a black windbreaker, and my sturdy sand digging walking stick and set off to be rescued.

The first two hours went by with the sight of an occasional bird and kudu. I walked, tripped, and stumbled over the same rugged terrain that I had driven over that morning. I did not really think about animals, as I had seen hardly any all day. Finally, I reached the main road in the park at the Zambezi River Drive where I had turned off earlier in the day. The signpost said 28 km to the gate (just shy of 18 miles). I was hoping on a rescue soon as all the signposts told people to stay in their vehicles because of the wild animals in the park and here I was on foot.

So many times in life the devil gets us to take side trips off the straight and narrow. We decide to set out on our own power and get into a sticky situation. The Bible warns us to stay with Christ. We soon are lost in sin and pray for rescue.

The full moon came up shortly after sunset, which helped me along the rugged road. My guardian angel and I were on our own.

As 8 p.m. approached, the area became alive with animal sounds. The animals were coming out of the shade and heading for the Zambezi River for a drink. I heard a very loud crashing sound on my left. I turned on the flashlight. It was a herd of elephants breaking

3

down trees as they walked to the river. Picking up the pace, I heard something on my left maybe thirty feet away. On came the flashlight again and the light revealed a bull elephant. I left the light on him as I tried to walk by, but I soon saw his ears stand straight out, his head shaking, the trunk go up and with a very loud trumpet call he was charging me!! Off I went zig-sagging and telling the Lord I did not want to die in Africa by an elephant. I thought if I were to die I wanted to die facing the elephant. What difference it would make I do not know. I turned to face him and with my stick raised I yelled at him to get out of here. Really original, but what do you yell at a charging elephant? He turned and walked away. This took seconds and a few feet, but it seemed like hours and miles. (A professional guide told me later, elephants do not like lights in their eyes and it was just a mock charge to get me to leave. If this was his intention, he did a good job! You are supposed to stand your ground, clap your hands and yell to stop a charging elephant, so they tell me.)

The elephant's trumpet was loud and clear. Are we with the Lord's message? We need to make Christ's message loud and clear. I used to make fun of Peter's short prayer, "Lord, save me!" Mine was not much better.

I found some trees and bushes to crouch in and when it seemed the elephants were closer to the river, I quietly walked on. All the time I was walking, I was scaring up animals and watching shadows scatter and hearing hooves. I was rationing my water consummation by forcing myself not to drink until a certain place or so many minutes went by. Soon I had elephants on each side of me again. This herd had about twenty in it and their leader just shook his head and sounded his trumpet signal for me to leave, so I went under another tree for a while. I was lost, and no one was looking. I could see lights on houses, people talking on the other side of the river, but I could not attract their attention with my torch or shouts.

Luke 19:10 "The Son of Man has come to seek and save those who are lost." (NIV) *Are we listening and searching?*

Back on the road I heard all the animal sounds as they called to each other and fought among themselves. I prayed that I would not be the next victim. I was tired as it was about 11 p.m., so I found a rock to lie down on to sleep for the night. But after ten minutes of sleep I decided that was not a good idea, since elephants and other animals travel on that path. I had tripped over several piles of elephant dung while I was walking.

As animals were scattering on my approach, my next encounter was with either sables (elk like animals with horns which will leave unless cornered and then will be aggressive) or cape buffaloes (they are the meanest animals I was told and will kill). Sometimes if you sneak up on them they will scatter, but you should not stay there as they will return. When I saw black with horns as they scattered, these old legs went a flying down the road. Nothing came after me.

I had finished one water bottle and still had eight miles left to go. Soon I laid down in the road for a minute but thought snakes might like to cuddle up with my warm body on the road. I did not like that idea so off I went again. As the miles grew fewer my confidence went up and my feet got sorer. After ten hours of walking and jogging, I saw the gate entrance at 2 a.m. I thought I would be welcomed, instead the night guard got on his radio and called for help. Three more men arrived quickly and ordered me to lay down my walking stick, as they did not want me to attack them. I hated to part with the stick as it had been with me during my ordeal. It upset me the next day when I saw it had been used as firewood for the night watchman.

I asked for water but no, I had to answer questions. Who was I? Where did I come from? Were there others with me? What was I doing in the park after 6 p.m.?

The guard on duty during the day had checked me out not wanting to go looking for me. The night guards said I could not have possibly walked that many kilometers or be Steve England as he had checked out that afternoon. Finally, at 3 a.m. they allowed me to go to a lodge for a drink and to sleep with the promise they would help me get the truck unstuck at 7 a.m. Not the welcome I had expected. The people who should be concerned about the lost person did not seem to be so.

My feet were tired and blistered. I took a bath and could not believe all the bugs floating in the tub that had hitched a ride on my body. I emptied the tub and refilled it for another bath wanting to make sure all unwelcomed guests were gone. I went to bed, but my dreams of elephants did not allow for a long nap.

The manager of the lodge came at 7 a.m. and walked with me to the road. I thought I was going to get the truck. Then he told me to walk to town to find help, neither he nor his men were going to help me. So I walked to the front gate. The lady registrar came out to ask me more questions. I'd had it! When I told her who I was, she said Janeece had been there the evening before looking for me, but no one knew anything about a missing person. She offered me tea and bread from her own lunch. She called and found Janeece and allowed us to talk. It was great hearing Janeece's voice. The rafting company had driven her around town on their own looking for me. The rafting company offered to come and pull the truck out after they returned from rafting that day. I continued to talk to the park people and finally the warden said they would help. Finally, at 10 a.m. two men came with a four-wheel drive truck and off we went. They could not believe where I drove (it was a forty-minute drive) and how far I had walked. It took about five minutes to get the truck unstuck.

Soon I was in town picking up Janeece. I had been missing for eighteen hours! It was good to be reunited with Janeece, the love of my life of thirty years! (Her side of the adventure needs to be heard also.)

I was told by many guides and people who operate safaris that I was lucky to be alive and had to be a strong person to walk over 43 km (27 miles) in rugged terrain with wild animals. Just a couple of months earlier in the same park a photographer was mauled to death by a lion while he was out of his jeep shooting pictures. Later we learned on the Discovery Channel that the Zambezi River Valley was number three on the most dangerous places on earth for wild animals. (I have been asked if I took any good pictures during my walk. NO!)

Most Americans have told me I should have stayed with the vehicle. I know I should have, and I wanted to, but something told me to walk out. In Zimbabwe you are not considered missing until after seven days. Since the park had checked me out that meant no one had to look for me. The earliest anyone would have started would have been seven days later. It was by prayers and the power of God I am here today!

I did not receive my guardian angel's "resignation papers"! Though I was not killed or injured by a wild beast, please remember that each day many people are.

1 Peter 5:8 "Be careful! Watch out for attacks from the devil, your great enemy. He prowls around like a roaring lion looking for some victim to devour." (NLT)

As we watched two lions on the prowl, a few days later, every animal in the area barked out warnings to other animals. Even if the other animals were not the same species or may be enemies to each other, the lions were a greater danger. May we do the same and warn everyone about Satan and hell.

Remember: Your eternal future depends upon which path you take!

POSTSCRIPT BY JANEECE: After Steve "fetched me," we walked two blocks to Wimpy's (Africa's version of McDonalds), as neither of us had eaten for almost twenty-four hours. When we bowed our heads to pray for the food, all we could do was hold hands and cry. If you were to ask me what the worse day of the assignment was, this was the day! If you were to ask me what the best day of this assignment was, this was that day also!

The power of God's watchful care over us was so strong, so real, and His presence so close, neither of us could say a word. We just sat there in awe of Him and what He had just done for us. Let me tell you, the power with which God parted the Red Sea, stayed the mouths of lions, and kept a fiery furnace from consuming three men, this power has not diminished one little bit!

April 2002 - Masvingo, Zimbabwe

By the time you read this, we will be on our way to Zimbabwe, Africa. PRAISE THE LORD! We left Indiana on April 12th, just as our daffodils bloomed and our tulips were blossoming. We arrived in Zimbabwe as they began their winter season. This will be a year without a summer for us. Oh well, that will just help us appreciate next spring and summer even more.

God has surely blessed our missionary efforts through you. Thank you for allowing Him to use you in this way. We should have known, with everything going so smoothly, the devil was bound to try and interfere. Just twelve days before we were to fly out of the USA, Steve was diagnosed with a bulging disc in his lower back. Our first thoughts were concerning our four suitcases, weighing seventy pounds each, plus carry-ons that we would physically have to wrestle four different times, as well as twenty hours in a small, cramped airplane seat. Nothing happens but what God is in control, and He is in control of this situation as well.

June 2002 - Masvingo, Zimbabwe

The sunsets are beautiful here but are almost over as soon as you see them. One evening while we were leaving the local hospital (visiting a church member who had just given birth), Janeece remarked how beautiful the sunset was. The sun was sitting as a big red ball with a wisp of a cloud in the middle. We drove down the road to where we could get a great photograph, but in those two minutes the sun had disappeared below the horizon.

In Masvingo we were blessed to meet a family whose son-in-law was a coffee grower/exporter. He gave each family who participated in a church service a fresh bag of coffee. The next week, they had to leave their farm, as it was going to be taken over by the war vets. The family was not to take anything from their home or farm except their clothes. We have not heard from them since.

The area Friday night youth met at Masvingo Christian Church and baptized 23 of its members July 20th. Theo, one of the youth sponsors and elder at MCC, did the baptizing in the icy waters! After the 21st person was walking out, he was told there was one more. The candidate turned the corner and it was his wife, Marion! She decided to be immersed because she had just been sprinkled as an infant. There was a celebration in Heaven as the angels rejoiced, as well as did the youth group. Theo had pulled the plug to drain the baptistery when he heard another teen stating he wanted to be immersed also. Quickly the plug went back in and another soul was added to the Kingdom. In these days of trouble, the Lord's church is alive and well in Zimbabwe!

Almost every day we see God's hand working in the lives of these people. We know it is not because God takes a more active part in Zimbabwe. Perhaps OUR eyes are more focused.

July 2002 - Masvingo, Zimbabwe

Already Africa feels like home even though we have been here only two and a half months.

While everyone at home is enjoying a hot and warm summer we are in winter! We have only had a few COLD days. I have to force myself to wear earrings and necklaces as they are like chunks of ice on your body. We wait until the last possible moment to use the toilet. I just know one of these mornings I won't be able to get back up because of being stuck to the commode and I will pull all my skin off if I do! Everything even freezes in the refrigerator, which we have set at the highest possible setting. Have you ever tried to drink frozen milk, spread frozen mustard, or warm up frozen leftovers? They tell us later in July it gets even colder! I took a spare sweater (very heavy) to church, which I was waiting to put on until I really needed it. I was cold then but knew I would get even colder during the sermon so I would put it on then. Lo and behold, during the song service, the lady behind me asked if she could borrow my sweater for a friend since I was not using it. How could I refuse? I was grateful she felt she knew me well enough to even ask to borrow it. Later, during the sermon, I didn't feel so grateful.

As you have read of my (Steve's) "elephant charging adventure" in the National Park, I was asked to share that adventure three different times, first, with the Senior Saints at the Pioneer Lodge (assisted living, old age retirement home), second, with the Celebration Service at Masvingo Christian Church and third, I had a write up about it in the local newspaper, "The Mirror." Now in town when people see me they say, "I know you!" or "Are you the one?" The price of fame is too much! Ha! One remark made after my adventure was by my brother. He e-mailed stating my mom was not happy with my adventure. He said he told her that thirty years of marriage ought to have prepared Steve for anything! (Now Janeece is looking for him!)

One Saturday we drove to the Great Zimbabwe ruins just outside of Masvingo. The ruins are the remains of the Shona Empire from the 12th to 14th century. The Shona Empire at that time covered an area that included modern day Botswana, Mozambique, Zimbabwe and part of South Africa. The king's palace was on top of a granite hill with a commanding view of the area. The passageways were very steep and narrow between granite boulders in some parts. The story goes that each visitor who came to see the king had to bring three granite blocks up the hill. These were used to build the huge granite wall on top of the hill.

The king's wives (200 or more) and children lived in the village at the base of the hill, each in an enclosure with a granite wall and the whole area surrounded with a granite wall. These walls were made without any mortar and are very uniform. When the king wanted a wife to come and visit him, he would go to the cave on the hill. Facing the cave, he would call her name and they could hear the name down in the village. The wife would make the trek up the hill. While Janeece and I were on the hill, we could hear people's voices down below the hill. You will never guess which one of us had to climb to the very top of the granite boulder!

We got to see the Birchenough Bridge, which is a huge suspension bridge out in the middle of nowhere. Mr. Birchenough wanted the very best bridge, so he commissioned an engineer by the name of Freeman from London to design and build it. Everything was made in London and then shipped to Zimbabwe. As they were putting in the center span (the last section to be assembled) they discovered it did not fit. The supporting pins would not go in place. There was a gap of one and one-half inches on each side. They told Mr. Freeman that he had made a mistake in his calculations. He asked them what time it was and was told 10 a.m. He suggested they try the pins at noon, as that was the time he had calculated for the placing of the last span and the placing of the pins. At noon they tried again, and the pins fit perfectly. Mr. and Mrs. Birchenough's ashes are in the towers on each end of the bridge.

We went to Harare, (the capital city) about a three-hour drive north, to see Tony Phillips, a member of Masvingo Christian Church who had surgery. Since it was a long drive, we spent the night at Kathy McCarty's flat. For supper, we decided to try a pizza from Pizza Inn. Our choice was the seafood pizza with shrimp, mussels, and squid on it. As we ate the first piece Neece said it was hot but yet cool at the same time. I discovered the cool taste was the shrimp as they were still frozen. Pizza Inn put frozen shrimp on the crust and cheese over it and then baked it, but some pieces did not thaw! (However, the pizza was done in ten minutes as the sign boasted!) We belched it for hours. No more seafood pizza but we are ready to try their banana and ham next time in town!

Instead of the "land of the rising sun," Zimbabwe is the "land of rising inflation." The rate of inflation, as of June 2002 was 116 percent. Many are predicting it will be 200 percent by the end of the year. Prices climb daily, with shortages commonplace. There are shortages of maize (cornmeal), flour, sugar, salt, and even medical clinics are running out of medicines.

There is a shortage of food causing starvation. Most families are down to one meal a day, which is supper, and yet the village congregations are joyful. We paid $90 (Zimbabwe dollars) to mail a letter to the States when we first came. Now we pay $180. A can of Pepsi was $90. Now it is $123. Many people are leaving Zimbabwe for other countries, especially younger Zimbabweans ("European" and African). It is estimated that there are 700,000 Zimbabweans just in the city of London, England, alone! Many are Christians. What a mission opportunity!

To save money, the power company turns off electricity during peak hours. (They owe $35,000 US dollars!). It can be minutes or even hours that the electricity is off. One Friday night it went off for two hours, so we had baloney sandwiches by candlelight. It was actually quite romantic!

Stoplights are called "robots" in Zimbabwe. In Harare, many times on a robot (stoplight) all three lights will be out and then it is a guessing game, "Do I go, or do I wait?" Night driving is so dangerous. Many will not drive then (or very far) due to the high number of accidents that occur during the dark. One evening a bus loaded with students returning from a soccer match in Harare collided head on with a transport truck. Thirty-seven people were killed. Because of the fire following the accident, many bodies were unable to be identified. Now there are only eight left to be claimed. In a two-week period of time, 56 people died in similar accidents in Zimbabwe alone. Many families, already struggling to make ends meet because of the high inflation rate, are left with no "bread winner" at all in the family or, (as in the case with the students) families who have put every cent they have into sending their child to school (sometimes causing them to only have enough food for one meal a day) only to have them die months before graduation. Hopes of that child sustaining the family are gone in a second. Many families know their loved one was killed and is at the funeral home, but they fail to claim the body because they cannot afford to bury them. Those bodies will be buried in a mass grave, we have been told.

Our problems seem so small compared to the ones people face daily here in Zimbabwe. Please pray for Zimbabwe and us. We think the

Zimbabweans are spiritually deeper and more mature in their faith because of the tremendous daily trials they endure. These trials seem to increase every day. The only hope and true peace they have is what is drawn from their individual trust in God and His promises to us.

September 2002 - Masvingo, Zimbabwe, Terre Haute, Indiana

In the Sunday school class Janeece has been helping teach there is a little African boy named Nigel, (Nye-gel). She was told he never reads or pays attention. In fact, his name is the only one "carved" in pencil on the wooden tabletop. The last time she taught, when it came time to fill in the worksheets, she put her Bible away and asked Nigel if she could share with him. The others were able to work pretty much on their own with very little coaching from her, so Nigel and Janeece worked on his paper, looking the answers up in the Scriptures together. He seemed very diligent. The next Sunday, Steve preached at Rujeko so someone else taught the class. The following week, that person called to say Nigel had read out loud, listened intently, and tried to do his worksheet. Janeece was elated! Nigel isn't just "putting his time in" at church.

People have asked if we were afraid to go to Africa? NO WAY were we afraid. God's hand was too evident. We should be afraid to come home to no jobs, no income, no physical security. We're actually anxious to see what God has in store for us. Our future is uncertain, as we have been unable to find a ministry for when we return to the States. (via internet) We have seen Him work so many times in so many lives, we can't wait for Him to continue working in ours. We'll just leave that in God's hands!

Our return trip from Zimbabwe started just fine at the Harare airport. A lady from British Airways asked if we were flying straight through to America. We said, "Yes." She directed us to the correct line and gave us a paper to fill out. We did not understand a question on it. We asked her what it meant and why we were the only ones given the paper. She said only Americans fill them out since 9/11 as it was mainly for next of kin. Now, that makes you feel safe!

As we waited at the gate for boarding, another British official came up to Janeece (calling her by name) and asked if her husband was with her. They came to where I was seated, and the official asked for our boarding passes as she was upgrading us to first class for the first part of our trip at no extra charge! Janeece asked her who we should thank for the upgrade. She said her supervisor selects people to upgrade when world class is not full, and they had overbooked economy class. Her supervisor was the lady who had given us the 9/11 form. We did not mind the extra leg room at all, but when we changed planes at London, it was back to reality.

We were greeted by friends and our daughter, Rebekah, at the Indianapolis airport. Two Sunday School classes had stocked our shelves with groceries, and neighbors had mowed and weeded our yard and watched over the house and vehicles while we were in Zimbabwe. It made "homecoming" an even greater blessing for us.

We continue to see God's hand working in our lives. Within the first weeks of our arrival home, Steve had three contacts in one day concerning job opportunities. There was a telephone interview with a pulpit committee for the Senior minister's position, and an interview for a State Correctional officer position. The third opportunity was a request to return to Africa to serve in a relief missionary capacity from January to July 2003.

A carnal spiritual battle was fought within us for many days as we wrestled between having families close, the security of a regular paycheck, paid medical, dental and eye care, retirement benefits, etc. or returning to no pay check, uncertain financial support, no insurance, no security (as the world defines it). After much thought and prayer, we decided to step out in faith and return to South Africa to oversee the mission work of Brion and Joyce Morris. It will be in Johannesburg, (size of Chicago) South Africa, and will consist of preaching, teaching, hospital calls, youth groups, special church functions, and general pastoral duties.

Please continue praying for the farmers, the mission, us and the nation of Zimbabwe.

Steve and children in South Africa 2003

Hugs and kisses are the same in every language. 2007

2003

February 2003 - Johannesburg, South Africa

During our last trip to Africa, we met a Chinese lady and her 15-year-old daughter. The mother works in Africa while the daughter stays in Beijing, China with grandparents. The mother told us that she was a Buddhist and her daughter had no religious ties. As a Buddhist, the mother believes good works will get you an eternal reward. After talking for a while, we said we would send them a Bible to read. The daughter wrote from China telling us she received the Bible. Pray the Lord may give an increase.

After $10,000 worth of expenditures in the emergency rooms (the last one on Christmas night), hospitals, cat-scans, ultrasounds, scans, x-rays, barium swallows, EKG's and blood tests, the doctor's office called 11 days before we were to leave the country to tell us the last blood test showed I (Janeece) had a bacteria that comes from contaminated food or water. This they believe I got in the good ole' USA (NOT Africa) which should further reassure anyone concerned about our physical health while there. The insurance coverage we had while in the States finally decided it was not a pre-existing condition (before it was even diagnosed). What a blessing when we were told it would be covered! The doctor's office even gave me the sample pack medicines needed for the ten-day treatment which should cure the bacteria ONE DAY BEFORE WE WERE TO BOARD THE PLANE FOR AFRICA! God's perfect timing.

A doctor gave Steve 16 months' worth of the daily medicine he is taking. Had we purchased it from the pharmacy, it would have cost over $2,500. Praise God!

The weekend before leaving for Africa, we took Janeece's sister and her husband to the Indianapolis airport to board a plane. While there we learned that with the new cargo luggage x-ray machines, our camera, floppy discs, etc. would have been ruined being packed in luggage that was to go in the belly of the plane. They also told us to take our medicine and valuables out of suitcases (which were not to be locked) and put them in our carry-ons. We would never have known this had we not been at the airport that day. Again, God's hand at work.

We arrived in Africa on a Wednesday with Bible Study that evening at a member's flat (apartment). It was a challenge to stay awake as we'd only been in bed for one and one-half hours in three days!

Northside Christian Church has many extremes: baby Christians, mature Christians (50 years-in-the-faith Christians), white Africans, black Africans, Lutherans, Catholics, the very poor and the very rich. Three families work with Southern Bell Corp. as top executives and one CEO. At first, the SBC group was a bit intimidating, but they hug on the poor as well as the rich and seem to have no prejudices. Janeece's Ladies Bible study on Thursdays alternates between two of their homes. Their company has bought up many elite homes in a very secured, walled and monitored subdivision which has a gate where you have to answer many questions. If the resident doesn't leave your name at the gate, they don't let you in. The company also furnishes bodyguards (who carry guns!) for each wife who not only accompany her everywhere but drive her there as well. They have signed agreements stating the wives will not go anywhere without the bodyguards. The first time I met them was at our Ladies Bible study. One of the ladies forgot her purse in the car and used her cell phone to call the bodyguard (parked outside) to bring it to her. He was a big, muscle-bound man carrying this tiny little purse two feet in front of him like it was a bomb! Oh, the things these bodyguard/drivers get themselves into.

We invited all the Africans in church to come to our house for lunch one Sunday. They eat pap, which is the same thing as sudza in

Masvingo. We call it corn meal except theirs is white. They don't put anything in it just boil it in water. It doesn't have that much nutrition but helps fill their stomachs cheaply. One of the ladies said she would do the cooking if I (Janeece) got the food. I had her give me a grocery list. It was just mealie meal (for the pap), boerewors (like our fat sausage links) for the men to braai (grill) and coke. We also got a watermelon for dessert. Several of the people were not able to come, but it was so enjoyable visiting with the people who did come.

Steve left up the volleyball net from youth group two days before, so some people played volleyball. Others tried their skills with the hula-hoop. Later in the afternoon as we were transporting some of them home and to taxi ranks, there was a big thunderstorm which brought pea-size hail. It rained hard the rest of the afternoon. Needless to say, after everyone left we fixed some good ole' American food - peanut butter and jelly sandwiches!

March 2003 - Johannesburg, South Africa

Last week, we left home at 4 a.m. to take a kombie (VW van) load of Africans from the church to attend an African village funeral. The deceased was a sister to Phillip, one of the Africans who attends Northside Christian, the church with which we are working. Out of the blue, in the middle of the service (being translated for our benefit) after several family members spoke of the deceased, we were asked to say something about her as well! We had never even met her! Don't think that wasn't a hoot!

We've attended and taken part in many funerals in Africa, but this was the first village funeral for us. Steve ended up being a pall bearer, so they wouldn't drop the coffin. He just jumped in and helped. It was either that or have the body dumped on his lap. The family rented a bus to take people to the cemetery. We took a kombie full including some of the family.

The shining, wooden casket was set on canvas straps connected to the sides of a silver brace positioned over the grave which was used to lower the coffin. It looked like those used in America. A family member wiggled under the coffin and dropped into the grave. He carried with him a mat made of reeds which the mother had used during the service to sit on the ground at the head of the coffin. He also had a brand-new fleece blanket that he spread out in the bottom of the grave on which the coffin would rest. Another new blanket was already spread over the casket. We were told sometimes pots and pans are also buried with the deceased.

Scripture was read and the bishop, a man with a long flowing robe with a collar, spoke in Afrikaans for two or three minutes. Then the men started singing in a beautiful low voice as they began filling the grave after the family had each thrown a handful of dirt into the grave.

Just as love is a universal language, so is grief. We didn't need a translator to tell us what they felt, or what they were going through. We were thankful to be of help, as little as it was.

After the funeral the family fed over seventy people who had attended the service. We ate inside the tent where the service was held. The immediate family ate on the floor inside the house. Everything in the house, including furniture, wall hangings, etc. was placed in one room with a board barring the doorway so no one could enter. We were told when anyone dies, all the family members come to their home and take all the deceased's possessions even if the husband or children are still living there.

Before returning to Johannesburg, we asked if we could have prayer with the mother. Her son, Phillip, led us into the house. It was completely bare. He led us past his mother, aunt, sister, and grandmother who were sitting on the floor and into an adjacent room. There were four chairs and a very small table that had four empty glasses, a pitcher of Orus (brand name of an orange drink mixture) and a plate with four scones (sweet biscuits) that had been set up just for us. We were so humbled to be treated so special that we never even thought about the water used to make the Orus. (It later caused problems for us, but not until we were back home and near a modern bathroom! Thank you, Lord! We are fine now.)

That day, Steve helped bury Phillip's sister in an earthly grave. The next Sunday, Steve buried Phillip in a watery grave - the watery grave of baptism. When Phillip's time on earth has ended, he will not need to be buried with a mat and thick blanket. His life will be in the warm hands of His Heavenly Father.

June 2003 - Johannesburg, South Africa

We are doing fine but we can't say as much for our clothes. Some of them seem to be disintegrating. We have been told not to leave them very long on the clothesline as the sun's ultra violet rays are stronger here and break down the fabric quickly. We were also told the smog and chemicals in the air over the city sometimes give a person what is known as " Joburg's throat." Being from the country, I just thought it was a cloud resting on top of the city. That cloud is actually the smog!

We are anxious to see family and friends in the States but dread having to leave the African family God has made for us over here. They are such dear, dear people and have opened the doors of their lives and allowed us to become a part. One African wrote us, "You have not been in Africa for long time, but you fit to be with African people." Needless to say, they have grown in our heart.

2004

May 2004 - Terre Haute, Indiana

In less than two months, we will once again be ministering in Africa with the Masvingo Christian Church alongside Mike Coetzer who serves as the associate minister. We will be filling in for Ben and Karen Pennington who have served as missionaries to Zimbabwe for 28 years! When they first went to Zimbabwe it was under British rule and was called Rhodesia.

Our duties will consist of preaching, teaching, and encouraging the people at Masvingo and in the surrounding rural areas. Because of the political situation and the economy, there is much stress and depression. Therefore, it will be a people intensive situation.

Before going to Zimbabwe, our bodies were in need of some minor repair. Janeece's neck was still stiff and sore from our car accident in November 2003. She also had a chipped bone in one of her fingers and had another bout of H. pylori, caused by a bacteria that came from contaminated food or water while in the States and NOT Africa. Steve was feeling sluggish, so he went to the doctor for a physical. The results showed his cholesterol was high and his thyroid was only working ten percent of capacity! Janeece's finger is healing nicely and tests reveal her H. pylori is cured. Steve's cholesterol is already back to normal and the thyroid medicine he is now taking has him feeling like a different person. So, we are almost ready to go.

However, it is with mixed emotions that we leave as our only child, Rebekah and her husband, Michael, announced that their first baby (our first grandchild) is due to be born December 24th. Our assignment will not be completed until February 28, 2005. We celebrate in their joy, but it will be a little harder telling Rebekah goodbye this time.

September 2004 - Masvingo, *Zimbabwe*

When we first arrived, we exchanged $100 in US currency for half a million Zimbabwean dollars! The exchange rate was one US dollar for 5373.94 Zimbabwean Dollars. They don't mess with (or don't have) change or small bills so we didn't get all we were supposed to. Even though I felt we were "short-changed," I still felt like a millionaire... that is until we got to the market! A dozen eggs sold for $7,000, a loaf of bread was $2,500, one banana was $250, diesel was $3,00 a liter and a bottle of coke was $1,200. Prices increased daily. Even though the exchange rate has increased, it does not keep pace with the spiraling cost of inflation at 400 percent. Just think of the nationals who do not have American dollars to exchange or pensioners on fixed incomes. How do they manage? (And I remember complaining when gas increased by 25 cents in the States.) Now we are facing fuel shortages as people are queuing (lining up) to get what little fuel remains. The government promises more fuel this week when they get foreign exchange to pay for it.

THE "BIG A" - After finishing a delicious meal in the home of one of the more affluent members of Masvingo Christian Church, our hostess leaned across the table and whispered, "You know our cook hasn't been feeling well lately. We are lucky to have him cook for us today. He only has the strength to work three days a week now. He has the 'Big A' you know." I looked at her puzzled. She added, "AIDS". We cling to God's promises: **"Whoso putteth his trust in the Lord shall be safe." Proverbs 29:25** (KJV)
"In God have I put my trust: I will not be afraid what man can do unto me." Psalm 56:11 (KJV)

November 2004 - Masvingo, *Zimbabwe*

Diesel is one of several items that has been in short supply in Masvingo. I needed to "top off" the tank on the truck plus fill some spare containers but no diesel was to be found. One day a station had diesel but when I saw the queue of buses, lorries (semis), and bakkies (pick-up trucks) with 50-gallon drums in their beds to be filled along with their fuel tanks, I decided I could wait for another day. By Friday, our need for diesel had greatly increased.

The Friday Men's Prayer starts at 6 a.m. I drove to church to stop at the service station hoping to get diesel then. No one had any diesel. At 9:30 a.m. I had a meeting with the rural evangelists and decided to check the stations once again. No diesel. On the way home, I stopped, still no diesel. As I drove home, I noticed a lady from the church walking to town in the hot sun with her eight-month-old son.

It was the opposite way I was going but I gave them a lift using more of the precious fuel. After letting them off, I started home driving past the service station that 15 minutes earlier had no diesel. There was now a tanker delivering diesel. Quickly, I queued and was the third person to get diesel. OUR GOD DOES PROVIDE! If I had just waved and gone on home I would not have gotten the diesel. What answers to prayers are you missing by *"just waving"* as you continue in the opposite direction?

Before we left the States on July 26, 2004, I (Janeece) was cleaning out a mission folder I have had for YEARS! In it I found a letter dated July 21, 1971 from Dick Smith in Fort Victoria, Rhodesia, Africa. He wrote it in response to an inquiry by me to serve as an intern in Rhodesia, Africa, for three months between my junior and senior years at Kentucky Christian College for which I would get college credit.

That year, KCC started a singing group (now called Destiny) that would travel to churches and camps all summer doing PR for the college. It paid half of the next year's tuition, books, room, and board. In those days, most scholarships could not be used for private colleges, which included Christian colleges. Regardless how good my grades were, not one penny could be used to pay my college bill at KCC. Dad had to pay it all out of his own pocket. However, Dad had two of us in college at the same time. My older sister, Andrea was two years ahead of me in school. That put both of us in college at KCC at the same time for two years. Financially I couldn't pass up being part of the college's traveling singing group, so I did that instead of the mission internship.

In the 1980's the Rhodesians won their independence from Great Britain and changed their country's name to Zimbabwe. Fort Victoria is now known as Masvingo. Guess where Steve and I are living? Masvingo, Zimbabwe! Not only are we in the same town where I would have spent my internship, but the house in which we are living is the house Dick Smith helped build and in which they lived! The people with whom we are now working are the same people to whom the Smith's ministered 34 years ago when I wrote that letter of inquiry! The Scriptures tell us, **"Delight yourself in the Lord and He will give you the desires of your heart." Psalm 37:4** (ESV)

Ever since I was in fifth grade, when asked what I wanted to do when I grew up, I always said, "Go to Bible College, marry a preacher, and be a missionary to Africa." I guess I can say all my life's ambitions and goals I had set for myself over 40 years ago have now been realized. I swam in a river with elephants while sitting on top of one. I have walked through the bush alongside of lions being re-introduced to the wild. I have fed wild vervet monkeys who would take pieces of bananas from my shirt pocket. I have shared meals with fellow African Christians sitting on the dried cow dung floor of their smoke-filled, sun-dried, mud brick, round huts with grass thatched roofs.

God has truly been merciful to me. As I watch the African people walk past, as I cook goat, eat sudza, chicken feet, and tripe, as my heart is melted by the earnest and humble prayers of these Zimbabweans, I think how blessed my life has been... how good God is! How great it is as a Christian to be living and working among my sisters and brothers in Africa! (Thank you Mom, for allowing me the freedom to do so.) Thank you for helping make this mission trip possible through your support both financially and prayerfully. I am a peasant, living the life of a king.

December 2004 - Masvingo, *Zimbabwe*

We had a very blessed and fulfilling Christmas. We got up at 4:30 a.m. Christmas Eve and drove to Mucheke Old Folks Home where we made tea and lunch for 29 people. We had found that no one was furnishing any special meals for them on Christmas Eve, so we decided to do it ourselves.

Our Christmas Eve meal consisted of rice, relish, and chicken feet, and each resident was given a packet of homemade cookies with their tea. I was smart this time and bought four sacks of chicken feet that had already been skinned. I still forgot to take the "toenails" off, but no one complained. I think I have acquired a taste for the African meal as I now find it delicious! Maybe getting to eat it with your hands and licking your fingers afterwards helps add to the flavor. I tried making it on my own at home, but it just didn't taste the same. The Africans say food cooked over an open fire is better. I believe them now!

Steve abstained from eating which was probably wise. He had an upset stomach the next day, but at least he couldn't blame the chicken feet for it. He did try chewing the fruit picked off a tree the Zimbabweans refer to as "African gum." He spit it out after the first two chews, but it couldn't have made him sick because I chewed almost a whole African gum fruit with no ill effects. The fruit is also referred to as a "snot ball" which pretty well describes its texture. We did not join the residents in tea but brought bottled water which we kept in the truck so they wouldn't think we were too good to drink their water.

Between tea and lunch, Steve gave a short sermon which was translated into their Shona language. We enjoyed the Christmas carols in Shona. When we asked what songs they wanted to sing, one lady from South Africa originally, wanted everyone to sing the song she knew and started singing it. No one joined in because it was in the Ndebele language and no one knew it, but I recognized the tune. It was the doxology! So I sang it in English while she sang it in Ndebele. Her eyes just twinkled as she sang while looking at me across the room. In that moment, I felt as close to God in the dirty, hot little room as in any worship service in the States. Even though I could not understand their speech, an instant bond was formed. It is surprising how music can draw people's spirits together, yet why should that surprise me? Music has been called "the language of angels." Now I know why.

We stopped by Pioneer Lodge (an old folks' home in Masvingo) and brought two loads of the senior residents to our home for a Christmas Tea. I made a peach cobbler from fresh peaches which are coming on now. It was the first time any of them had ever had cobbler. I made enough for each of the guest to be able to take a big piece of cobbler back to the lodge for their afternoon tea. (Having tea is a big thing here. I think it's a cheap way to fill their stomachs.) I got so tickled at how everyone wanted to talk at the same time. I've learned to sit in the corner where I face all of them at the same time. When two individuals are trying the talk to me at once, I can look at both of them at the same time. One little lady in a wheelchair, kept complaining that one of the other ladies was doing all the talking. Since she was hard of hearing, her whispers could be heard to the other side of the room. The little lady dominating the conversation was so busy talking she never heard any of the derogatory remarks. Thank goodness!

Teaching Janeece how to play a drum made from a hallow log and animal skin to which women danced and sang praises. Zimbabwe 2007

Janeece during worship service accompanying the congregational singing at Northside Christian Church in Johannesburg, South Africa. 2003

2005

January 2005 - Chiredzi, Zimbabwe

We just got back from Chiredzi where Steve preached yesterday. On the way home, at one of those infamous, moving police roadblocks, we were once again stopped by a policeman. The heavily loaded semi-truck and trailer in front of us had been given the signal to stop, but he just slowed down and continued driving. Drivers have been shot for doing this. We thought perhaps we had just misread the signal. The policeman immediately came to the next vehicle which was us and excitedly asked us - TOLD us he wanted a ride. Being 20 km from Masvingo, we thought that was where he was going. Instead, they wanted us to chase the semi-truck. Steve looked at me and before we knew it the policeman was not only climbing in the truck bed but had hollered (in Shona) to another man who we assumed to also be a policeman who pulled out a hidden AK-47. Of course, we had no idea what would happen when we caught up to the semi and not wanting to be in the middle of whatever it would be, Steve was not driving fast. To keep "our uninvited passengers" from realizing this, Steve hit all the potholes which threw the policemen around and hopefully kept them from "taking aim" if we did get into shooting range. Steve would slow down to pull in behind every semi that was stopped on the side of the road. The policeman barked something in Shona and banged on the cab for Steve to proceed. We came upon the rogue semi parked on the side of the road. When he saw us coming the driver quickly climbed back into his cab and started to drive off. The policeman hollered for us to stop as we drove up beside him. We were now side by side with his door three feet from mine, both vehicles still moving forward with no signs of stopping. The officer continued shouting and waving his rifle as I looked into the eyes of the man trying to drive away. Chills

29

ran through me as our eyes locked. It was like time stood still and no one else was there. His look reminded me of the stone-cold stare in the eyes of the pet lion cub that had playfully stalked me three years ago. I was thankful for the thump on the cab roof which brought reality back to life. Steve stopped. The two officers jumped out. The semi continued edging ahead. Both shouting policemen were running to get in front of the moving semi, threatening the driver by waving their rifles. Steve saw his chance to remove us from this havoc and drove back onto the road and away we went.

The last we saw in our rearview mirrors was the policemen climbing into the passenger side of the cab of the rogue-semi which was still moving forward. I could tell the semi driver was not Zimbabwean, so he probably did not understand the policeman's command to stop at the road block. I'm thankful we were "prayed-up-to-date!!" and were covered by your prayers as well. People have asked us what we want them to pray for. This is one incident I doubt we could have even imagined putting on that prayer list!

Proverbs 29:25 "Whoso putteth his trust in the Lord shall be safe." (KJV)

February 2005 - Chiredzi, Zimbabwe

"Now to Him who is able to do immeasurably more than all we ask or imagine, that is at work within us, to Him be glory... for ever and ever!" Ephesians 3:20 (NIV)

The less we worry about how we will survive tomorrow, the more we see God's hand directing our plans and His power at work in our lives.

To think just months ago we only had $200 in the MRS account and only one single commitment for continued monthly support. Thanks to the response for additional funds, we will be accepting the call to work with Chiredzi Church of Christ through May 2005.

Missionaries of our brotherhood who also have an orphanage, school and hospital ministries started the **Chiredzi** church over thirty years ago. We traveled to Chiredzi in late November for a meeting with John Mark and Leann Pemberton and members of Chiredzi Church of Christ to discuss possible plans for 2005. We have been sharing duties between Masvingo and Chiredzi since January 2005.

Our first Sunday to preach at Chiredzi was January 2, 2005. As we loaded up in Pemberton's truck to drive to Chiredzi, it would not start. The battery was dead. We had to unlock four door locks and two padlocks to get the Pennington's car keys in order to jumpstart the Pemberton's truck.

As we entered the town of Chiredzi, we were not sure of the church's location. We asked two young ladies walking along the side of the road. They said they were part of the worship team that morning! Thank you, Lord.

Returning to Masvingo, we were stopped at four different police roadblocks. The first asked us to get out of the truck as they searched for hidden weapons. One officer asked us to tell him where the weapons were hidden to speed up the process. We were searched for any illegal items at the next roadblock and once again had to exit the vehicle. The final roadblock was about two miles from home. We were asked many questions including from where we were coming to where we were going. The roadblocks themselves are not as much a problem as the time sitting in queue and fuel wasted inching forward.

March 2005 - Chiredzi, Zimbabwe

I'm a little anxious concerning our five-hour trip to Harare airport the day before their elections. Our flight leaves so early that morning, we are forced to go up the day before to avoid driving in the dark. Harare is not only buzzing with politickin' being the capital city, but it is also where President Mugabe lives. All through the year certain roads are barricaded between 6 a.m. to 6 p.m. EVERY DAY to shore Mugabe's insecurities. A few months back a lady was shot for driving on one of the barricaded roads. I can't even imagine what it will be like now. We were stopped at four road blocks in the short two-hour drive between Chiredzi and Masvingo two months ago and got to drive "rifle-waving police" in a truck chase another time.

I can't help but wonder what awaits us next week.

Last week, one of the "European" (white) ladies in my Bible Study told of having to use the mace she had in her purse to stop a would-be attacker in town earlier that week. It was in the middle of the day on one of the main streets with people standing around watching, but no one offered a finger to help. I always carry my grandpa's pocketknife in my purse. (I even forgot and carried it into the US Embassy when we voted in the presidential election. That was a hoot! Steve wasn't very happy with me.)

I've got to stop thinking about it and force it out of my mind. Nothing will happen that isn't in God's plan for us. We'll just have to allow gobs of extra time for roadblocks. Being "European" and having lots of luggage will make us prime candidates to be searched at every roadblock. It was bad enough at the Zimbabwe/South Africa border. Our hands got to shaking so badly, Steve had to put his in his pockets. I laid mine on the counter pretending to protect passports.

We're kind of doing what the song in the musical, *The King and I* says, "Whenever I feel afraid, I hold my head erect and whistle a happy tune so no one will suspect I'm afraid... And when I fool the people I feel, I fool myself, as well."

I'm looking at this all wrong. Think of the adventure that may be in store for us and how great it will be to see the awesome power of God work through these little "inconveniences!" Besides, Jesus said, **"Don't worry about tomorrow. Sufficient for the day is the evil therein."**

Since our first trip to India in 1975 I think my favorite hymn which was so comforting then and now is *"Anywhere with Jesus I Can Safely Go".* If we didn't believe that, we sure wouldn't be here now!

With the recent political violence and continued economic collapse, we have been praying especially hard for Zimbabwe and the missionaries serving there. Having lived in Zimbabwe ourselves for a combined total of three and one-half years, (not all in the same stretch) we know exactly what hardships they are facing. In 2002, just before that presidential election, our visas needed to be renewed. Of course, only INVITED foreign observers are allowed to be in the country during the elections. All other foreigners, who did not need to be there, were not being granted permission to stay. Americans are right there on the very top of President Mugabe's least favorite peoples list along with the British. The government only renewed our visas for a week which expired the day before the 2002 presidential elections.

Driving between our preaching points in Masvingo and Chiredzi, about a two-hour drive, we would be stopped at four to five police roadblocks with us having to get out of the vehicle each time for them to search. They were mainly checking for weapons that they thought would be used by the opposition party, MDC, during the elections.

At that time, we were driving the 4x4 truck belonging to the missionary for whom we were relieving in Chiredzi while they were in the States on furlough. Their friends in Zimbabwe had people coming who needed a 4x4 to drive on safari. Our truck was traded with them a week before our visas expired. The truck we got was a brewery truck with large beer emblems on both doors. It had no canopy over the back, like the 4x4, to keep our luggage dry during the five to six-hour drive to the airport when we left. It was the rainy season. We also knew with the paranoia of the government towards perceived opposition, especially the day before PRESIDENTIAL elections, we would probably be stopped at every police roadblock between Chiredzi and Harare. Without the protection of the canopy, our clothes, Bibles, printed lesson materials, sermon outlines, Bible studies material, seminar info, etc. would all be soaked. To say the least, we were not happy campers especially for a preacher to be driving around town in a beer truck!

We left for the airport the day before the elections, the day our visas expired. Never knowing how long one would be at a roadblock, we left at 3 a.m. It was raining hard when we were pulled over at the first of many roadblocks. We could just envision the slow, methodic pace at which our American luggage would be torn apart looking for non-existent weapons. To our amazement, the policeman smiled and waved us on. We could hardly believe our eyes!

We experienced the same event at every roadblock. NOT ONCE were we stopped at any of the police roadblocks! It wasn't until the last roadblock that we realized why we were being waved through all of them, when the policeman pointed to the beer emblem on the side of the truck, smiled and waved us on!

The police must have been beer-drinkers. Recognizing the brewery's emblem, they waved us through every roadblock. We were not stopped one time nor did we have to open our suitcases in the rain one single time.

God had this all worked out. What seemed to be an embarrassment to us, was actually God's plan at work for us.

God is the Master Designer. What is happening in Zimbabwe, He will some way, unknown to us, use for His glory. You can be sure of that! Already, the churches in Zimbabwe are the strongest churches of any we have ever had the privilege with which to work...and they continue to grow! When EVERTHING else is grinding to a halt in Zimbabwe, the church is still growing! Just like the first century church did during their persecutions.

It seems that every great calamity that enters our life is usually followed by an even greater blessing from God. If this remains so, just think of the blessing that awaits the Christians in Zimbabwe....

"Hold on My child, joy comes in the morning...."

The people here at Chiredzi are just like those at Masvingo in being kind-hearted, loving, and caring for each other as well as graciously accepting us as their own. On Sundays we stand at the back of the church by the main entrance through the beginning of the song service to greet late comers which is at least one-third of the congregation. One Sunday three very young children of a church family dropped the hands of their parents who were walking them into church and came running to give us hugs. As I said, they accept us as their own.

We used the last of our raisins and chocolate chips in our "care package" from home to make homemade cookies to take to the orphans at Hippo Valley Christian Village and Chiredzi Christian Children's Home. We gave them out after having devotions. At the village, we were immediately greeted by a group of pre-school children. It was evident many of them were suffering from AIDS. The matron asked if I (Janeece) knew the age of one of the boys. I thought he was four-years-old. Turned out, he was twelve-years of age!

One of the five-year-old girls stood on a piece of wood to be able to reach the bottom of a double-tubbed sink located outside the dorm where she was busy washing her clothes by hand. Walking back to the truck, the children fought with each other just to hold my hand. I was ashamed of myself thinking I might "catch" something from them. I thought of the lepers who continually reached out to Jesus. He wasn't afraid to touch them... Why was I hesitating?

Just before our visa extensions were denied in Zimbabwe, we received a request to do MRS work in Alberton, South Africa for veteran missionary, Alice Fishback who is returning to the States on furlough to assist with her 99-year-old mother. Alice has been a missionary in Africa for 30 years. It was an honor to meet yet another person about whom we had studied in Missions class in college. Alberton is located just outside of Johannesburg where we met Miss Fishback while doing MRS work in 2003. The Alberton Church is an English-French speaking congregation.

Alice has requested we come from June 2005 through the end of the year. This will only give us eight weeks at home to see family, visit churches, raise support for the work, and spoil a granddaughter whom we have yet to meet.

August 2005, Johannesburg, South Africa

I spoke at a Ladies Day this week. It was held in one of the local churches closer to the "not-so-nice/not-so-safe" parts of Johannesburg. Kimberly Road Church of Christ was only to be a fifteen-minute drive from our house. Registration was at 8 a.m. and tea started at 8:30 a.m. I left home at 8 a.m. I was to speak at 9:30. I finally pulled up beside the church at 9:40 a.m.! Ugh!

The street I planned to take did not have an exit from the one I was traveling on as shown on the map. Before I was able to exit the "concrete highway" (as they call the interstate), I got into what looked like a double four-leaf clover maze of exits. Usually one can see the exit and entrance ramp before leaving the highway one is traveling. Not here. I took the first exit I came to, not knowing how much farther I'd have to drive to get to the next exit, but I was still in the center of all these highways. I kept taking exits which were located within feet of each other until I got into a business area where I could pull off and "find myself" on the map. There were no street signs, but I found the name of one of the stores had the "subdivision" in the name of the store. It was still early, and stores were just beginning to open, so I found a "European" couple in a parking lot and asked them. They couldn't even tell me what street I had just exited but warned me to be very careful of the neighborhood where I was going. It was very unsafe, so I should be extremely careful and keep my doors locked. I re-entered the "concrete highway" until I came to an exit that named a street. The problem here in South Africa is the exit signs usually do not have the street names on them but the name of the biggest city to which that street will eventually take you. Some of those cities are hundreds of kilometers away, meaning that you have to know the geography of South Africa!

I pulled off on the shoulder to find myself on the map. By this time, I was in rush hour. Traffic and the big lorries (semi's) would make the little Toyota I was driving shake violently when passing, while I sat still on the side of the highway reading the map. I continued with this procedure, gradually working my way closer to Kimberly Road Church, since I couldn't read the map while driving.

Eventually, I was "in the thick" of things again with no shoulder on which to park. I came to the area where the map showed an exit (but there wasn't one) and took an exit at random. Some of the street names were beginning to sound familiar. I could see I definitely did NOT want to stop and ask directions or even stop the car but eventually found a place where I didn't see anyone "loitering." I stopped to read the map and found I was within a kilometer (a half mile) of the church! I mapped the route out in my head and took off again.

Unfortunately, the street, which would have led straight to Kimberly Road, was a one-way street and it wasn't going "my" way! The alternate street was blocked off by police and orange cones (like found at construction work on roads in the States). There were many streets being blocked by the police that morning, all in the area I needed to go. To add to this, Africans place some of their directional signs with arrows pointing out the turn past the actual turn instead of being just before the turn.

At one point while driving and looking for a street sign (many of the street names are not on signs attached to poles but are painted on the curbs close to the intersections), I drove across a manhole cover. (I assume that is what I heard as I never saw it.) It drew my attention to the middle of the road where three meters (nine to ten feet) on down the road was a big, deep manhole with no cover. It was followed by two more uncovered manholes. A detached car bumper was stuck in one of the manholes which was so deep that less than half the bumper was visible. I could only imagine what damage a car could occur by running over one of them. I decided the hole was so big that the car's entire tire would have been swallowed and the car stuck, if not flipped.

I prayed a silent prayer of thanks that the first manhole I ran over had a cover and thought of the possible consequences of being on foot in this area. Then I remembered I never saw the manhole and never felt running over the cover which I surely would have. I just heard a sound. Then I began to wonder why thieves, whose number one street item to steal is manhole covers, would take all the covers except that one?

I'm convinced I experienced a miracle that morning. I wasn't just lucky. It didn't just happen to be there. It wasn't just a coincidence. THANK YOU, LORD!

We found out last night, Trinity (our only grandchild) crawled for the first time a few days ago at my good friend's house. She happened to catch it on video. When they told me, I cried, just out of the blue, the tears came. I felt so foolish but was so grateful she got it on tape. How can I miss a baby we have only been around for such a short time!

Steve preaching with his French translator in Guinea, West Africa church with Sierra Leone refugees. The translator himself is a Sierra Leone refugee. 2008

2006

March 2006 - Kimberly, South Africa

The mossies (mosquitoes) are terrible at times. They are different than in the States. They are smaller and you don't realize they are biting until they start to fly away. They bite on the oddest places like the knuckle of your fingers or between your toes. This is supposed to be a malaria free state. None of the other missionaries take malaria pills so we aren't either. The threat of malaria doesn't bother me as much as all the blood that oozes from a mosquito when I kill one on me. I can't help but wonder if that is my blood or blood from an HIV infected person. They say you can't catch it like that but the mossies and I are still at war! Steve and I are getting so practiced in the art of "Dragon-Slaying" that we can actually catch mossies in mid-air. Now is that getting good or what?! The paper stated last week that in South Africa 3000 people per week die of AIDS or HIV related causes.

It's Saturday, so we took our mattress outside to sit in the sun after I washed both sides with the African version of "Power X." I might as well spit on them for all the good that stuff does, but at least it makes me feel like it helped. Our bedroom has been smelling like a gym locker room and we thought it was coming from the mattress. The sweat soaked mattress from all the bodies of all the people who have slept on that bed since 1995, which is the date we found on one of the mattress tags, would not give up the smell. I then sprayed the bottom box springs with Doom (bug spray) so no bugs would crawl up the legs (like millions of ants did in Zimbabwe that slept with me until I started moving and they started biting!) The room smells like Doom now, but we just put Vicks salve in our nostrils and sleep fine.

The nights are getting colder, but the days are still hot. I slept with my wool socks on last night but pulled them off before daybreak. We like it colder at night because we can sleep comfortably under the covers and not be "midnight snacks" for all the mossies.

May 2006 - Kimberly, South Africa

Tomorrow I am taking a cake to celebrate two of the South Africa Bible Institute students' birthdays. I thought the birthdays were last Tuesday and took a cake last week. They didn't tell us until the cake had been eaten that their birthdays were this week. I don't think they are expecting a cake tomorrow but are hoping for one.

The students are always so good to jump in and help with anything we do down there (manual labor) without our even asking them. Last week we put flat stones in the big mud holes in SABI's driveway and the fellas helped Steve dig dirt to cover them. Three days later, they helped him dig a little trench to drain water from the driveway. Steve was cleaning gutters and before we knew it, two of the students were on top of the roof helping, all in their good clothes and shoes. When we mowed and hacked down the waist-high weeds on their soccer-field one young man, Paul, came out to help us with two plastic sacks tied over his tekkies (tennis shoes) which he had just washed. Of course, the sacks didn't last any longer than it took him to put them on and by the time we finished five-hours later, his tekkies were filthy. I hand washed them for him the next morning.

Paul is from Zimbabwe, a very poor township a five-hour drive south of here. Paul buried his mother during term break. Last week driving to SABI we passed a small bazaar on the sidewalk or what we'd call a yard sale in the States. We stopped and I bought two pair of dress pants for R5 each ($1 US). They were too big, but Paul put one pair on and tightened his belt. You would have thought it was Christmas. He did look good in them.

It seems Africans hardly wear clothes that fit. They are always too big, but the fellas look so handsome when they dress for church. We took down some dress coats last week and the students snatched them up immediately. Paul didn't get one but wanted and needed one. We took a lady's coat down the next day. He wears it every day in class despite the good-natured teasing from the others. It was so cold one morning, I had to run hot water over my pen to get it to write!

The end of May 2006 found us wrapping up our teaching duties at the South African Bible Institute in Kimberley, South Africa. The day before final exams began we participated in our last chapel service with the students and staff of SABI. It was Janeece's turn to be the chapel speaker. Everyone participated in the emotional service which will long be remembered by all of us.

The day we left Kimberley for our next MRS assignment, we prepared one last homemade spaghetti dinner for the students. They told us we would be missed more than all the cakes and spaghetti we had made for them. One young man, speaking for the student body, said although we may never see them again, we should know that we now had children all over Africa.

How blessed we are! So many people have come into our lives and left their footprints on our hearts! Like the commercial says, there are some things MasterCard can't buy!

On May 30th we began our seventh MRS assignment. It was in Cape Town, South Africa for Jerry and Aleta Kennedy, former college class-mates. Jerry is a second-generation missionary. As with the other MRS assignments this one was similar and yet has its own distinct flavor. One aspect we appreciate in Cape Town is not having to check our drinking water for rat-tail maggots. They were in the water at Kimberley although we never found any in our drinking water.

The first night we drove ourselves to the Bible study, we turned right instead of left and ended up in Khayelitsha Township. We could DEFINITELY tell we were where we should not be! Of course, it was dark, and we had long left street lights behind. We had to drive another kilometer to find a wide place in the dirt road so we could turn in one swoop. This was to keep the criminal element from congregating around our car that stood out like a sore thumb amongst people who either walk or use pony carts or taxis. The kombie taxi in front of us realized we were lost and kept driving slower and slower until it stopped at a four-way stop sign and just sat there. It was then we heard his loud shrill whistle-call they use to get each other's attention. Thank goodness, Steve did not stop close to the kombie but several feet away, a trick we picked-up in Johannesburg to give one room to maneuver in case of an attempted car-jacking. It sure came in handy here as Steve had room to pull around the kombie and floor-board the gas pedal leaving our "hitch-hikers" behind.

A kilometer on down the road, we passed a gas station that was still open. We pulled in to the back, parking behind and among a line of bakkies (pick-up trucks) to hide until we could ascertain our position. Then we proceeded to the Bible study with no further trouble.

When we told the group we passed a street named Steven Biko, everyone's eyes got as big as silver dollars. After all the gasps and whispering amongst themselves, one African lady, looking at us, took her index finger across her throat from one ear to the other. Even in the daylight they don't go where we had just been. We know we are still under God's protection!

Psalms 139:9-11 "If I rise on the wings of the dawn, if I settle on the far side of the sea even there Your hand will hold me fast. If I say, 'Surely the darkness will hide me and the light become night around me,' Your right hand will hold me fast." (NIV)

We will be leaving January 12, 2007, for Masvingo, Zimbabwe to replace Ben and Karen Pennington. Ben has been asked to teach a semester at Ozark Christian College while on furlough. Once again, we will be sharing the gospel by preaching, teaching and helping in any way that we are able.

Zimbabwe is a nation facing 80 percent unemployment, 1,800 percent inflation rate and a shortage of almost everything. But there is no shortage of God's love and the church is actually growing stronger in spite of these difficult times.

Several have asked what they could send us during our stay in Zimbabwe. Our response is YOUR PRAYERS! We can use all of those we can get!

A friend in Zimbabwe shared her diary of one week:
"Monday began with electricity cut at 7:30 a.m. that lasted 11 hours. Tuesday another ten hours without electricity and water pressure dwindled to a fast drip. There were no street collections of garbage due to no fuel. Butchers were complaining their meat was smelling and spoiling in the heat.
Wednesday there was no water but there was electricity. We should not be too capitalistic and ask for both services even though we pay for them.
Thursday water came back on but now it smells of sewage. It is the color of urine and has oily bubbles on top."

We must all lean on God's promise to give us strength to walk through the waters.

June 2006 - Cape Town, South Africa

It has been over three years since we have been home long enough to have a garden. I miss the fresh picked beans and corn on the cob.

There is a colony of 3,000 penguins here which actually come up and walk among the people sun bathing on the beaches, taking sunglasses, toy sand shovels, and items of clothing. The penguins are nesting now, and one can get within inches of them. Their babies are just balls of fur. We sat on the sidewalk and watched them walk and swim. It was so funny watching them waddle up and down the rocks and hop over curbs. I'd love to pick them up and just hug them!

We attended a fete (like our garage sale/bake sale) at a Presbyterian church close by one weekend. The church conducted a "Glamorous Grannies" pageant which was so cute.

The grannies ranged from being so shy they did things to keep from being seen like carrying a large potted plant to hide behind. Another hid behind her 18-month-old grandson. Still another left the stage and did not return. Some grannies strutted around the hall mingling with the people before the pageant to show off their outfits and tiaras while others stood flat against the wall trying to hide in the cracks between the cylinder blocks.

The grannies took turns introducing themselves. Some of their "off the cuff" remarks brought tears to our eyes. The first granny had on an old apron and came wobbling out on a cane (play-acting). She said, "I have bags under my eyes, wrinkles on my face and bunions on my feet, but when I'm playing with my grandchildren they don't even notice!"

The second granny informed us, "It doesn't matter if I win today. My grandchildren already think I'm beautiful." The third granny stated she had "six and a bit" grandchildren. The fourth granny admitted, "I'm a very UN-glamorous grandmother jumping on trampolines, kicking soccer balls and playing cricket on the ground with my grandchildren." The fifth granny was dressed in a flowing, long purple skirt with a purple feather boa wrapped around her neck, purple shoes and purple dyed hair. No wonder her name was Emerald. The way she pranced around the stage one could tell she was really enjoying all the attention. In her introduction, she claimed, "I have a mixed bag of grandchildren Some have my DNA... some don't. Some live in South Africa... some don't. Some eat too much... some don't, but they all make me feel glamorous."

Each granny also had to answer one random question. The first question (corresponding to the number she chose) was, "The door is jammed and you are stuck all alone in the office with the best-looking male employee. What would you do?" Granny's maturity shined through in her answer, "I'd make small talk." Then she grinned great big and turned red.

The next questioned granny was asked what she wanted from her family for Christmas. "A B-I-G hug from each of my family members and a picture with all of them."

The next question was if you were a Survivor contestant and only allowed to take one item, what would it be and why? This granny answered in one word, "WATER!"

After a drum roll and several delays to increase the anticipation, Emerald was announced the "Glamorous Grannies" winner.

Although Emerald was the winning granny they were all rooting for each other.

For some of you who may need a fresh idea for your next Mother/ Daughter Banquet, Glamorous Grannies may just be what you're looking for!

October 2006 - Terre Haute, Indiana

We returned home to fight wasps, ants, and mice for possession of our car and truck. I guess they thought these were their new "homes." One mouse decided to expire in the truck. We think the ants were just hibernating as they re-appeared on warm days. Our spray can of ant killer kept those appearances short lived!

Our first task was getting the trailer aired out, utilities turned on, and vehicles running as we had speaking engagements scheduled the first three weekends in the States. Luckily, the suitcase that didn't make it home with us from the airport did arrive at three o'clock in the morning not long afterwards.

We adjusted to the American way of life again such as driving on the other side of the road. Having lived in Africa for three years makes driving on the right side of the road seem wrong. We also had to adjust to all the new designs on the US currency which made us think we were spending counterfeit money. It still seemed odd to us for store clerks to only put one or two items in a plastic bag. In South Africa and Zimbabwe, shopper have to furnish their own shopping bags or purchase them from the store. Therefore, shopping bags are always stuffed to overflowing! The price of gasoline seemed to be a daily topic in the US. As of August 2006 in Zimbabwe, gasoline was $16 US per gallon, IF you could find it! The US price of $2.40 per gallon seemed like a great bargain to us.

The day we arrived home, our daughter, Rebekah Joy and our granddaughter, Trinity Jade, came to see us. Trinity was not too sure about us at first and acted shy. It was only a short time before she realized her grandparents were more than just voices over the telephone.

Being 23-months-old, Trinity was very active and discovered new words daily. One Saturday Rebekah (her mom) had to work and Janeece was in Illinois with her mother, so Papaw got to baby-sit. At home that night Rebekah asked Trinity, "What did you and Papaw do?" Her reply was, "I WORK! I TIRED!" So Papaw forgot the nap, fed her hot dogs for meals, and had her outside with him as he worked in the yard. Their bond is now stronger, and Trinity will have a face to put to that voice on the phone.

Close to Kimberly, South Africa - Easter Sunday Praise and Worship - 2006

2007

January 2007 - Masvingo, Zimbabwe

Excerpt from e-mail from Rebekah Joy, (Janeece and Steve's daughter):
Trinity had a bad day yesterday. She stayed home with Mimi as daycare called the day before to say that there was no daycare on Friday due to so many kids going home with the flu, so they were closing to go in and clean.

Anyway, she was missing you guys pretty bad yesterday and she was mad! When I got home she said, "Mommy, wanna go bye-bye. Go Grandma - Papaw's house. Papaw at home." I told her no, remember Grandma and Papaw are in Africa. She thought for a second and said NO PAPAW - GRANDMA NOT AKIKA." I said, "Yes they are sweetie, they aren't at their house. They're in Africa." She sat there (on the toilet no less!) and was in deep thought for another minute and then looked at me and smiled that crafty little smile and said, "I go bye-bye, Go Akika. See my Papaw!" I couldn't help but laugh. With tears in my eyes I had to tell her no, we couldn't just drive to Africa like we could your house! She then got mad and started having an attitude about everything because I wouldn't take her to Akika. So, I told her that we would call Grandma and Papaw tomorrow when I got home from work.
Rebekah Joy & Trinity Jade

February 2007 - Masvingo, Zimbabwe, and Springfield, Illinois

The past few days have been a whirlwind and yet as I sit on the airplane, traveling over 400 mph, I wonder if we can go any faster... hoping to reach Mom quicker. The two of us had talked of this scenario long before Steve and I left for Zimbabwe and had decided

I wouldn't have to return from Africa. Regardless of what we had decided, after speaking with Mom's doctor, my dilemma was not whether to come but when.

We have felt God's presence every step of the way, from being able to call the States on phone lines that only allowed a few USA calls to be completed all of last year, to being able to secure tickets clear through to Indianapolis within two days of calling with NO LONG lay-overs, to not missing my flight. I was sitting five feet from the gate, completely oblivious to everyone boarding around me. The plane was loaded and ready to leave when they paged me one last time before off-loading my luggage.

Steve and I could hardly get through our prayers that morning. We had NO IDEA how we would get good-byes said at Harare airport just hours later. I had prayed for God to help me stay numb until I reached the plane. God went way beyond that. Just as my luggage went out of sight on the airport conveyor belt, I remembered I had not locked them yet. (Airport approved locks.) The next 30 minutes were spent trying to do this which kept both our minds occupied. Then an airline official suddenly appeared and said to follow him, he would take me back to lock them, but I could not come back out to where Steve was. We had ten seconds to say our good-byes. God also pre-arranged Steve's preaching schedule for the next two Sundays to be in churches to which Steve will have no trouble finding his way. This month's weekly responsibilities will also keep him in Masvingo. We were able to purchase 25 liters of diesel which has been as scarce as hen's teeth to obtain, to partially refill the fuel tank for Steve's safe solo journey back to Masvingo - Two more prayers answered.

Gale and Debbie Heiliger picked me up at the Indianapolis airport in our car which I then drove the three and one-half hour journey to Memorial hospital in Springfield, Illinois taking time only to stop by our trailer to grab my winter coat and gloves. Rebekah and Trinity

Jade followed in her car as she had to work the next evening. I went to the hospital in the same clothes I wore upon starting this journey 38 hours before in Africa. Another prayer was answered as we were able to be with Mom three and one-half hours before her struggle ended. She went very peacefully.

Thank you for your prayer support. We have felt them continually.

Return from Springfield, Illinois to Masvingo, Zimbabwe

My luggage arrived, almost a week late but all in one piece. They didn't ship it to us like last time. We had to drive to Harare to collect it, which is about a seven-hour round-trip drive, not counting the precious diesel which Steve had to source. Every time we fill up, the price has increased. It was running about $1 US per liter making it about $4 per gallon. If I remember correctly, the two tanks on the Mazda truck hold 110 liters.

It didn't even look like my luggage had been opened. After I signed for my checked luggage I turned to see the man in front of me, who had just collected his "lost" luggage as well, go through customs. Knowing what "fun" the custom officials could have with all the unused medical supplies of Mom's I was bringing in, I decided to walk past customs and not stop unless someone told me to. I walked out the airport door without even so much as a glance from custom officials.

Mom's medical supplies will be put to good use. The tubing for oxygen tanks cannot be obtained in Zimbabwe. A member of the church here is on oxygen 24/7, making it a constant battle for his family outside of Zimbabwe to source and get it to him. They were delighted to get the tubing which the hospital in Springfield was just going to throw away! The plasters (band-aides) were dispersed among many. One pensioner was using a small piece of cloth to wrap around the heel strap of her shoe to keep it from rubbing blisters. She was so thankful to get plasters to replace it. Even those who did not benefit directly from the supplies were so appreciative that the hospital in America would allow the supplies to be sent to their people in Zimbabwe.

Mom had several nearly new full tubes of skin cream and bottles of antibiotic mouth wash. Only a few drops leaked but were caught in the double layer of Ziplock bags in which I had packed all of them. The pages of Mom's paperback book of crossword puzzles and word finds will be torn out and divided among the residents of Pioneer Lodge next Sunday after our evening services with them. This will help keep their minds active, and they love working them. This is also where Mom's bedpan for broken hips and her small disposable breathing treatment kit were given. Though Mom didn't have a broken hip, that type bedpan is much easier for patients to use. Most of the gauze, rolls of medical tape, etc., will be given to the Mucheke Old People's Home just outside of Masvingo. The small bottles of powder, toothbrushes, paste, lotion, combs, etc., that Mom got every time she went into the hospital or was transferred to another, will also be distributed among the Africans here. I even had room in my luggage to take back some of Mom's cotton tops and a pair of flowered pillowcases which I thought could be used as material in the church's sewing group. However, the look in the eyes of some of the ladies who were almost Mom's size when they saw the almost new tops convinced me not to cut them up but give them away to be worn. I now see Mom's tops walking around Masvingo. I even had room to pack some of Mom's Tupperware and a thermos jug that we will use here to store drinking water to use when the water is shut off every night. Neither will return to the States with us but will be given away as well.

Mom, who was supportive of our mission work in life, is even now helping in our work.

April 2007 - Masvingo, Zimbabwe

We started our eighth MRS assignment on January 14th, 2007 in Masvingo, Zimbabwe. It has changed little since the last time we did an assignment here, except for the economic situation. This trip, Sunday worship finds us in many different locations preaching the Word the last Sunday of each month serving in the city church of Masvingo.

One of the churches on our rotation is Mandizvidza where the church meets under a tree in good weather. There were 53 people sitting on cow hides and sacks on the ground. They also had four wooden benches on which we got to sit. The chief of the village was even there. A herd of cows grazing wherever they wanted to (as there were no fences) meandered through on both sides of the "church." The bells around their necks made it hard to keep focused. However, it was a wonderful service. I don't think we have ever been in any grander "church."

Afterwards, we ate lunch with one of the families in their round, mud-brick hut complete with thatched roof. A thin coat of cement overlaid the mud-bricks on most of the huts in the village. It was much cooler inside them. Chickens were also in the hut with us and were quick to eat morsels that we dropped. Lunch was served with sugar cane sticks for us to chew on as the dessert. It was delicious!

The villagers insisted we take home maize (corn), pumpkins (squash), and sugar cane they picked from the scattered patches growing around their huts. We later learned it is the Shona's custom to do this with any visitor. We had expected to come straight home after the church meeting, so we had nothing to give them in return, although we were not expected to. We did share the only thing Neece had in her purse, an opened pack of cinnamon chewing gum from America. She tore off little hunks and gave some to several in that part of the village. It was a big hit. The oldest lady in the village even asked for more. We had enough to give the two young men who stayed and guarded our vehicle. It was parked a half mile from the village, which was w-a-y off the tar road. To get there, we drove four miles off the main road on nothing but a dirt path worn bare by the ox carts and people. The path was so narrow we had to stop to let a donkey cart coming towards us pass. The ruts and rocks were such that we expected to have a flat or hole in the pan before getting back to the main road even though we were driving slower than a person walking. At times there was not a path at all. We would NEVER have found it without the man we picked up going through Masvingo to show us the way. It was his home village. He works in town and travels back to the village about once a month.

Last week the US Embassy contacted us for the sixth time in a little over two weeks warning us of "instability and political violence in coming days..." We passed through five police road blocks as we traveled to Harare for graduation exercises at Zimbabwe Christian College and to make hospital calls on a church member who had surgery. So far, this has not interfered with Steve's preaching in the village churches, but we have been warned to travel with copies of our passports.

We appreciate your concerns for our safety. Things seem to be cooling down. There are still police road blocks everywhere, but we are usually waved through. If memory serves me correctly, as of today we personally have only been stopped three times and have only had to get out of the vehicle while they searched it once. Usually, cars, buses or trucks are stopped in front of us, which is why we have to stop, but are waved on after they look in the windows.

If I (Janeece) were given a choice of where I wanted to live, in Africa or America, I would choose Africa (Zimbabwe) in a heartbeat EXCEPT for our daughter and granddaughter being so far away. The people here in Zimbabwe do not put on airs. They are not defined or "owned" by their possessions. That is not true of the entire nation; however, or it would not be experiencing the economic meltdown that it is today. The Zimbabweans with whom we work are sincere and humble, whose only hope for the future is found in the Lord in whom they trust. My spirituality is but as filthy rags in comparison to theirs. We talk of religion. They live it. We recite the Lord's Prayer, "Give us this day our daily bread." They experience it literally.

We pray our grand prayers thinking the words we choose will make them more powerful. The most powerful prayer I have ever heard was prayed this past Sunrise Service. A Zimbabwean whose entire prayer to God was to forgive his sins. I've never heard such a humble, heartfelt prayer. It was as if God was sitting right there beside him and I was eavesdropping on their conversation. His prayer took us into the very presence of God. I can't remember the last time that happened in the States. Of course, we've been in and out of Africa since 2002 living most of the time in Africa, so perhaps that is an unfair statement.

The Christians here are so deep spiritually speaking! I am the one who benefits from being over here. They are as common as an old shoe but sure do know their Bibles and it is not just lip service. When we go into the village churches, they not only share what little they have with us to eat, but send pumpkins, ground-nuts, maize (corn), sugar cane stalks, tomatoes, etc., home with us and everyone riding with us. I feel so blessed for our paths to have crossed. Because of God's sustaining power, we have found that wherever God has placed us to do His work, we have found people just as dedicated. Perhaps it is because this is where we are working now that our hearts are here. We have been so blessed by God through these people over and over again. Oh, how I love God's people in Zimbabwe! And how I LOVE being here despite the physical hardships.

Again, thank you for your concern, but the safest place for us to be is in the center of God's will, and that's where we are.

August 2007 - Masvingo, Zimbabwe

Almost every Sunday finds Steve behind the pulpit in the village churches. That pulpit has been located under a tree, in school classrooms, in rundown church buildings, and even in the modern town-church of Masvingo Christian. In the churches we have sat on grass mats, dried cow hides, pieces of cloth, short wooden benches, chairs with and without backs, and concrete blocks.

We have eaten everything from Cape Buffalo to Maponi Worms, to chicken feet, to sudza, to goat intestines fed to us after morning worship services. We have been given mealie meal, sweet potatoes, gourds, African pumpkins, sugar cane, ground nuts, round nuts, sugar beans, tomatoes, rape (like our spinach), grass mats, and live chickens. But most importantly they gave us their hearts.

We have driven over tar roads, dirt roads, stone roads, no roads, and some "paths" that were questionable as to whether they even qualified as roads. Some roads had grass along the sides and in between the two tire paths in the middle, taller than the grass along the sides, grass taller than the truck itself, and with ruts that seemed almost as deep. We have forded bodies of water across paths with a person wading barefoot in front of the truck to scout out the holes and water depth.

We have been stared at by humans and animals alike and sometimes wondered if this is how the first American settlers felt being stared at by Indians who had rarely seen a white man. But, whatever road we traveled, it always led to a warm reception of ladies singing and dancing accompanied by the beat of drums made from animal skins, the blowing of the kudu's horn, and the giggles of young children trying to watch us from behind the safety of their mother's skirts.

No president of any nation, no visiting head of state, no touring movie star or statesman has ever had as warm, as honorable, or as sincere a welcome as we have received from our brothers and sisters in Zimbabwe! Most important, the people have blessed us by letting us in to their hearts to share in their lives.

The African village church's attire varies from suit jackets and ties for men to threadbare, holey T-shirts for children. It seems to give the men a sense of wearing new clothing if the designer label (that Americans remove after purchasing suit jackets) is left on the sleeve. The older married women, called the "MaMa's," are dressed in the traditional, hand-sewn, red and white Christian Church/Church of Christ church uniform. Some uniforms have been used and washed so many times they are almost faded to pink.

In the village church of Nyamawenga, while Steve was taking pictures of the children, a 76-year-old "MaMa" grabbed Janeece's hands, pulling her into the big circle of women. Dressed in their church uniforms, they danced and sang to the beat of an empty plastic container (used to carry water) in lieu of a drum. They wanted to teach her how to worship God the African way by doing a type of "shuffle" they use while singing in church. Before it was over, Janeece was shuffling with the best of them and stomping her feet in a rhythmic pattern on the ground. Dust from the parched earth rolled up in thick clouds settling on everything in sight... mainly their shoes and legs. Janeece was filthy and church hadn't even begun!

It seems the longer they sing and dance, the closer to God and farther from their situation they are drawn. For that brief time reality seems to be forgotten as they take hope in a better life that awaits them. It's a promise they cling to! Their God is not just a religion, but a way of life, a way of hope, a way of coping one more day, one more hour.

This week Steve and I almost ended up in the middle of a supposedly peaceful women's march in the streets of Harare, Zimbabwe. It was to commemorate the International Day of Peace. While marching the women also handed out flowers and leaflets while singing songs about national healing.

The women marchers were intercepted by an estimated 50 riot police who beat the unarmed marchers with baton sticks. There were a number of injuries with many being taken to the hospital. Twelve of the women were arrested. Steve and I thanked God for the side street we found after realizing what was coming our way. I quickly hid the flower that one of the ladies had given me.

Later there were reports of politically motivated youth in Harare commandeering car parks, markets, council properties, bus and taxi ranks where they were extorting bribes, intimidating people and using violence against people who reported them to the police. The Minister of Home Affairs who is over the police department told reporters, "There is nothing I can do to stop their invasions." (I wonder where the fifty riot police are?)

The closer we get to elections in Zimbabwe the more frequent these incidents become.

A recent occurrence reported in the government newspaper best illustrates the slant with which stories are written. First was the story of police in Harare who apprehended four men but forgot to handcuff them before leaving the men unattended in their police car, whose motor was still running, to chase another suspect. The four apprehended men put the car in gear and drove away. Police in a second car chased the four men until running out of fuel before the four men could be overtaken. The government newspaper reported the escape as "the conclusion of an otherwise highly successful police operation."

The second newspaper story declared Air Zimbabwe's two-month long strike as having ended after the aging airline was given yet another bail out. This time it was for 28 million US dollars. One of the first resuming flights from Victory Falls to Harare only had one passenger on board. The airplane seats 60 passengers. I wonder how long this government bailout will last?

November 2007 - Morogoro, Tanzania

"Where are you now?" A question that we are often asked. Presently, we are in Morogoro, Tanzania, working in partnership with Pioneer Bible Translators starting our ninth MRS assignment. We finished our eighth assignment in September where we ministered in Zimbabwe since January 2007.

It was in Zimbabwe the Scripture **Isaiah 65:24** became more than just words.

"Before they call, I will answer..."
These words came to life over and over in Zimbabwe when: ZESA (electric company) did unannounced load sheds (turning off power for up to 22 hours at a time), often just as Janeece was finishing tasks that required electricity.

"Before they call, I will answer..."
Being home when our neighbor decided to burn down his GIANT bougainvillea. The flames, which shot 25 to 30 feet into the air, caused burning branches to fall into our yard, sitting the dry grass on fire with embers blowing over onto the roof of our house. Our

water, which the company shut off almost every night, had just been turned back on. The garden hose was already connected and lay just yards from where it was needed to help fight the fire.

"Before they call, I will answer..."
When our back truck window was broken by a thief <u>with us in the vehicle</u> in a "smash and grab" attempt at a stoplight. He got nothing; however, it helped us find a source to exchange our Rands for Zimbabwe dollars when we didn't have enough Zimbabwe currency to pay for the repair. It usually takes months to get replacements for vehicle windows. Ours was also tinted and curved, but the store had it <u>in stock</u> and replaced it the next morning!

"Before they call, I will answer..."
Parking in front of a store just as fresh baked bread was coming out of the oven and smelling the aroma as it drifted into the street allowed Janeece to be among the first in queue to get a loaf, our first in two weeks. She was so excited to have bread that she left the rest of her errands to drive straight home to share it with the African family living behind us so we could all have bread while it was still warm.

"Before they call, I will answer..."
With directions such as "Turn right at the anthill," it was the "angels unaware" sent to help that got us to the village churches located on communal lands not even accessible by road.

"Before they call, I will answer..."
When meat was no longer available in the stores, we found small tins of ham in Harare, which we have NEVER seen in all of Zimbabwe, just as our meat supply ran out.

"Before they call, I will answer..."
Never going to bed hungry.

"Before they call, I will answer..."

After publicly announcing Zimbabwe would no longer allow foreign fuel coupons to be used in Zimbabwe as it had the past two years, the government recanted and honored them. We had just purchased $1000 (USD) worth of those coupons.

"Before they call, I will answer..."

Having enough pencils sent by South Union Church in Illinois to give one to all the school-aged youth at a church in the bush.

"Before they call, I will answer..."

Being able to cut two watermelons in enough pieces so 150 church attendees could each have one.

"Before they call, I will answer..."

Being told by a prominent business woman that the government was going to change currencies the next day so spend all your old currency, as it would become worthless. We spent more in two days than we did for the next three months, but the government didn't change currency. (Still hasn't a year later!). We thought we had really messed up but the sugar, flour, steri-milk, margarine, cooking oil, tins of vegetables, etc., that were readily available then is what we survived on the last month living in Zimbabwe when nothing could be bought in the stores. The shelves were empty. Not only was there enough for a month, we still had food supplies to give to others. It was almost like the widow's container of oil that just kept pouring out more and more oil. We even found ten chicken feet in our freezer instead of the five that we remembered putting there. This allowed us to double the number of Africans we fed, including ourselves, with sadza, relish, cabbage, and those chicken feet.

"Before they call, I will answer..."

God smoothed our way before we even knew it was bumpy.

November 2007 - Morogoro, Tanzania

Three days after Thanksgiving we left for Morogoro, Tanzania, to begin our ninth MRS assignment. Morogoro lies 120 miles west of Dar es Salaam, which is the capital located on the Indian Ocean.

Working with Pioneer Bible Translators we laid groundwork for distributing Scriptures translated by Word for the World. There are 17 Bible translators working with seven different language groups that have translated New Testament books several of which are being field tested now. This means that limited paperback copies are made of the newly translated book of the Bible. They are given out and taken to the villages where seminars are held to help elders, pastors, and others work together on it. They go verse by verse to make sure of the spelling, sentence structure, exegesis are accurate, and that it is in the vernacular of that particular language group. In this way it will be usable and accepted by the people as reliable.

On one of our first evenings in Tanzania there was a 5.7 magnitude earthquake. The guards were so frightened they started shouting in Swahili, but we knew it was not a thief. The shaking stopped, so we went to bed. Some Tanzanians were so frightened they slept in their yards the rest of the night.

This MRS assignment of ministry has included Steve preaching in local Swahili congregations with the assistance of a translator. Janeece took on volunteer duties of forty to fifty hours a week writing checks, paying bills, balancing two bank accounts, preparing salary payments for 16 employees, (mostly security guards at the two compounds with shifts 24/7), checking receipts, and helping prepare reports for the US government which is required of non-profit organizations such as PBT.

Our duties here in Morogoro, Tanzania will end on March 24, 2008 at which time we board a plane and fly straight to Cape Town, South

Africa to begin our tenth MRS assignment. Only God knows the course of our lives beyond Cape Town. By this time, we will have lived in Africa for almost four and one-half years of the past six years, relieving career missionaries and helping with their ministries.

Excerpt from 2007 e-mail:
Dear Steve & Janeece,

Thank you so much for the time we were together. You have been extremely helpful to us as a family and also as a congregation. You have been our pillar of strength. You were always there to help when we needed help. You encouraged us when we needed encouragement. Without your help, life was going to be difficult.

God took care of us and showed His love to us through you. We are so thankful because we have a loving Heavenly Father who cares about us, who loves us, who blesses us, who encourages us. We are so privileged.

I think with God's help I can preach now. I was your interpreter when you go out to preach, and I think that helped me to be confident.

I don't think I will be able to write everything you have done for us all the time. May what you do to others, be done to you also. Thank you for your love and your time you have set aside to come to Zimbabwe, no matter the situation or the circumstances here. You chose to come and be with us. May God bless you and always be with you wherever you go. May He always guide you, protect you, provide for you and give you wisdom to do the work He has for you.

Thank you once more for your love, help, and everything you did for us. We will always love and miss you.

God's peace be with you.
Joseph, Rhoda, Prince

(Joseph was Steve's Shona translator. Joseph now has three children, is an elder of the largest church in Masvingo, and takes turns preaching for a rural church outside of Masvingo, Zimbabwe.)

Church under the trees. Joseph translating for Steve. 2007

Elephant charging the truck. Steve put the truck in reverse throwing sand, as we tried to get distance between us and the elephant. The noise of the sand being thrown against the bottom of the truck caused the elephant to stop for a moment which aided our escape. 2007

2008

January 2008 - Morogoro, Tanzania, East Africa

Our New Year was ushered in with lots of firecrackers (or gunshots) around us. The dogs and monkeys were scared to death. This morning the monkeys won't even come out of the trees to forage for food on their daily trek to the mountains via our yard.

We are in Morogoro, Tanzania, East Africa where life economically, politically, socially, and everything else "ically," has improved. We were without electricity for two days over Christmas, which kept us from contacting Joy and Trinity until last night (12/31). They have frequent power interruptions here but these do not last nearly as long or nearly as frequently as in Zimbabwe. Thank you, God!

The American washing machine we have access to is "very tired," as one African put it. I am afraid to use it for fear it will konk out while I am washing in it, making us feel responsible for replacing it. Therefore, I did our laundry by hand last week. Steve has been warned to within an inch of his life if I see him walking around in his sock feet! Ha-ha!

We do a lot of walking here, so much so, Steve has already broken down his "Wal-Mart special" tennis shoes in less than four weeks. New ones or even used ones that are in worse shape than his run around 25,000 Tanzanian shillings which is approximately $23-24 USD. They are also Chinese knock-offs of poor quality. We went to the "market" (outdoor stalls, side by side) to get a pair for him. The ones he had were better than the ones we found. All the shops had a big, deep ditch in front. Periodically, there were pieces of rickety boards with nails sticking out or teetering slabs of stone which act as bridges on which customers were to cross to gain access to the shops. This gives shopping a whole new dimension. Of course, this makes Steve just love shopping that much more! Add to that trying on shoes while balancing on one foot while positioned at the ditch's edge. I mean, how much better can Steve hope it to get?! One cannot even hold on to the stall's walls that are made of tree limbs tied together with anything they can find. The walls are draped with empty maize sacks or discarded pieces of cardboard. They have to be re-built after each rain.

We did pass a couple stalls where the old Maasai tribe ladies were selling a few hand-strung, beaded necklaces with matching bracelets and earrings. I'm sure the "canker-crud" coating on the earring "wires'" would have been very compatible with pierced ears. They also had pieces of porcupine skin, turtle shells, ocean coral, seashells, etc., which would be confiscated from us at the airports. I am hoping to develop a relationship with the Maasai ladies. They are already very friendly. They smile so big and jabber up a storm. We both laugh as they talk "at" me. I held out my hand to shake hands with the first old Maasai woman seated on the ground, who was sewing/stringing colorful beads. Small curly grey hair was beginning to grow back on her otherwise shaved head. It wasn't until she raised her hand to shake my hand that I noticed her thumb and some of her fingers were missing. While shaking her hand, I also saw she was missing some toes, but the scars weren't clean like they had been cut off. Then I remembered where I had once before seen scars like this... in India in the leprosy hospital. I was thankful that none of the sores were runny, which made me feel a bit better. I marveled at how she was able to work on her craft without the use of a thumb.

We had no way of communicating except by sign and body language. I pulled out some Tanzanian shillings to see what it would buy, but she either didn't understand or it was not enough money to buy anything.

In town, we occasionally see the Maasai, who are a warrior tribe. The men, dressed in short colorful cotton material wrapped around them, always have a thick stick with a natural wooden knot at the end, a big knife strapped to their waist and carry a short spear. The women, walking behind them, likewise wear colorful material but theirs goes all the way to the ground. Both men and women have their heads shaved. We will have to come back to these stalls on a Sunday afternoon when many more make-shift stalls are open, so we have been told. Steve can hardly wait!

March 2008 - Morogoro, Tanzania, East Africa

Our last newsletter ended with us in the mountain village of Tawa where Steve preached at the beginning of a seminar led by Tanzanian, Edson. That evening, to help build relationships with the Muslim villagers, we were to show a recently translated film in their Lughuru language about the life of Christ. The brand-new sound equipment was borrowed from Tim, who volunteered to run it. They arrived in Tawa the day the seminars ended. Tawa is about a four-hour drive from Morogoro (where we lived from November through March 2008). The trip was made going 15 to 20 mph most of the way because of the rough roads.

It took us 30 minutes to set up the equipment as sweat poured off all of us in the 90-degree weather. The last 15 minutes it began to sprinkle. Villagers would look at us, point to the clouds and ask, without saying a word but using hand gestures, when was it to start? Everything was finally connected. We had a sheet tied to two outside house pillars for a screen. The two oversized speakers were in place. Tim started the generator and then turned to Edson to ask, "Where's your DVD?" Our hearts melted as Edson just looked at Tim in bewilderment saying, "I thought you had everything we needed?!" By then, the light sprinkle had turned to rain. People were already beginning to disappear. Many children had gathered to see the Lughuru film that had been announced all day on a rented megaphone. Everyone was told we would come back to show it. Perhaps this was God's way of being sure the village would look forward to the team's return. It wouldn't be the first time He has used rain for His purpose!

The 25 or so children remaining were gathered together as one of the translators told a Bible story to them in Swahili. They stood on a porch as he spoke from under an umbrella in the pouring down rain. Grown-ups were milling around acting disinterested, but we could tell they were listening from under their umbrellas as well.

The rain had caused a swiftly running small stream to overflow the short concrete bridge that Steve had to drive across to get to the place where we would all be staying that night. We could see the edge of the bridge had been broken, but because of the water we could not ascertain if it was sturdy enough to drive across or how deep the water was. Of course, all the African passengers we had accumulated by then assured us of its strength.

Was the bridge indeed strong enough to support a 4x4 over-stuffed with passengers, luggage, food, and water or were they saying this so we all wouldn't have to walk the rest of the way on foot in the downpour? Whether it was sturdy or whether it was God's hand we drove across, we made it!

The room where we stayed that night was clean, as were the restrooms, or should I say, restroom. The only restroom/shower room was the men's. Neece was the only lady. The rooms were clean but had thousands of mosquitoes in them. We learned to tiptoe into those rooms so as not to disturb the mosquitoes that covered the walls. Of course, the "toilet" was not the Western style porcelain stool but the hole-in-the-floor-have-to-be-a-good-shot type African squatty-potty.

The shower room was big enough for a pan bath, only we didn't have a pan and didn't know where to get water as the tap in there didn't work. We watched others using the rain from the previous night that had been caught in a type of rain barrel. We used that water also, putting it in a large plastic cup we had been given for tea. With no fan or a/c in the 90-plus-degree heat, we definitely needed a bath. We felt like new people after our "teacup baths!"

We found out last week that regulations have changed since we flew to Africa last year. They now require a yellow fever shot for anyone from Tanzania entering into South Africa where we will be flying in less than three weeks to start our tenth MRS assignment.

Neither the private clinic nor the government hospital here in Morogoro had the serum to give the yellow fever "injections," as they call them. They do not know what we are talking about if we call them "shots." Of course, we had to go to the government hospital here to get that information. The government hospital has no phone to call to ask and does not take appointments. Sick people just show up at the hospital and wait their turn to be seen. Sometimes it is hours before a doctor arrives. Sometimes there are no doctors and people wait for a day or more. Babu went with us to the government hospital here in Morogoro. We were directed to three different places in three different buildings all over their compound before finally arriving at the correct office for vaccinations. It was there we were told the injections are given in the government hospital in Dar es Salaam only on Friday mornings. This was Thursday, so we went the next morning on the bus that the ticket sellers were promoting as "The Express Bus!" I'm sure it was only to get our business as we did not arrive any earlier than the other Dar buses we have taken.

We left our house before 5:30 a.m. to catch the 6 a.m. African bus into Dar. We again asked Babu (which means Grandfather in Swahili) to go with us as we would be going to the government hospital. Government hospitals in any country are not usually run as efficiently as the private clinics. Perhaps, one of the coolest parts of the day is 5:30 a.m., so our two to three-hour journey to Dar was enjoyable.

Oh, the things we saw that we would have LOVED to have taken pictures of to share later. Men on bicycles carried everything from beds, to 12 to 15 feet long boards that were one foot by ten feet, to large trays containing 30 eggs each tray stacked four feet high, to four old-fashioned three-foot-tall metal milk containers tied to handlebars and balanced on both sides of the back tire.

Women seldom ride a bicycle except as a passenger and then they sit side-saddle behind the seat, unable to straddle the bike because of their kanga. A kanga is a very colorful, long piece of cloth wrapped around the waist and worn like a skirt. It goes all the way to the ground and restricts leg movement when tied tightly. Steve got me one for Christmas. It is very comfortable and is used like our aprons back in the States to protect the clothing under it from getting dirty.

We saw one man's bike with FIVE people on it! Two were seated behind the seat. One was balanced on the bar in front of the seat which connected the seat to the handlebars. The fifth person was seated on the bicycle's handlebars facing the driver with his arms wrapped around the person sitting on the bar between the seat and the handlebars. The driver had to peddle with his legs going to the outside to keep from "kneeing'" the person in front of him.

Bicycles are the poor villagers' truck and are used as such. Many are so loaded with firewood, beds, vegetables, etc. the person cannot even get on the bike but must push the bike along by walking beside it. A typical stalk of bananas is usually three to four feet tall and could easily weigh 70-100 pounds. One bicycle had six stalks of bananas balanced from poles tied to it. The man had great difficulty even pushing his giant load along the road towards town.

We could tell we were getting close to Dar es Salaam, Tanzania's capital. Traffic is so congested on the four lanes of tar road that the pace was reduced to a crawl. One is tempted to get out and walk. When President Bush and Laura visited last week, traffic was even worse as streets were closed for hours at a time, totally trapping some vehicles within the barricades. The road to Arusha was closed the entire day. It connects to the Kilimanjaro airport into which Bush flew. Although people were told of the closings in the newspapers, villagers don't get daily papers. They were the ones trapped, all day! We heard three safari trucks with their clients were also trapped.

The Saturday the Bushes were in Tanzania we went to the local outside market in Morogoro where we often go to get everything from vegetables, rice, flour, coconuts, and spices, to fresh slaughtered meat hanging from hooks. The meat has a very good flavor. Perhaps it is all the flies that "season" it! The "butcher" chops, or should I say, "hacks," the meat until the bones splinter. One mustn't stand to close because of the flying splatters of blood. We found this out the hard way! Usually "Europeans" send their guards or African helpers to the open-air market, so we stick out like a sore thumb! This day, the vendors were unusually polite and helpful, full of smiles. We were not followed by beggars nor hounded by merchants trying to push their wares on us. The next morning in church one of the members told us the people thought we were President Bush and Laura who had come to inspect their market!

We got off the bus in Dar and hopped into a taxi driven by Juma, a "friend" of Babu. Here, a friend can be classified as anyone you have met at least once before. The first stop was a petrol station as all taxis are rented so the drivers keep very little fuel in the tank, so as not to lose it when the taxi is returned. Juma didn't have any money, so we had to pay part of our fare so he could buy petrol. He only put in

71

three liters worth, which is about one gallon. The fuel indicator didn't even move off the "E" in empty. It wasn't long until the car kept dying. It was out of gas. We coasted into another petrol station that God saw fit to place by us at that particular moment!

We made it to the government hospital and after inquiring of three people, arrived at the correct building and room. There were ten people in front of us. After speaking with some of them, Babu informed us they were waiting for the serum to arrive. As we sat on the well-worn wooden bench, we leaned against the concrete wall that helped to cool us down. We were as hot as red firecrackers after creeping along in the now 80-plus-degree heat in the taxi whose windows could not all be rolled down,.

On the door of the clinic was a sign written in English and Swahili that said, "Yellow fever injections are only given on Tuesday and Friday mornings starting at 9 a.m." It was now 9:15 a.m. Being a government hospital, it would be very conceivable for the serum NEVER to arrive. My mind wandered to scenarios of dirty, re-used, unsterilized needles like I myself had seen used in India where they were sharpened with a whetstone between injections. Would we refuse the injections if such were the case here? Without it, South Africa would not let us enter from Tanzania. The missionary we are replacing in South Africa will be leaving within hours of our planned arrival. We could NOT afford to be quarantined for six days at the border. Within ten minutes the serum was carried in by the nurse who would later administer our injections. In 15 minutes, it was our turn.

The room we entered was small, containing three desks. The first desk is where we paid for the injection and an additional amount for the yellow fever certificate. The nurse at the second desk entered our names onto the certificate as a third nurse gave the injection. She opened a sterilizer that had long ceased to function. The door didn't even stay latched. She brought out a handful of syringes that were individually wrapped in what looked like "straight-from-the-manufacture's" packing. Our fears were gone. I hardly felt the injection, but later wondered if dirt from our skin could have been pushed inside as no alcohol was used to clean the site, the top of the bottle of serum, or the needle. Guess not, as it has been several days now, and our arms didn't even get sore. We were very impressed with the organization and efficiency of this one-day clinic. **"Before they call, I will answer" Isaiah 65:24.** If one Scripture were to define our MRS mission trips, it would most definitely be this one.

July 2008 - Conakry, Guinea, West Africa

We started our eleventh MRS assignment on July 8, 2008 in Conakry, Guinea, West Africa, after finishing our last two assignments in two separate African countries, one in East Africa, the other in South Africa.

Following our November 2007 through March 2008 Morogoro, Tanzania assignment, we flew straight to Cape Town, South Africa arriving at Jerry and Aleta Kennedy's house around 11 p.m. There was little overlap as we drove them to the airport at seven the next morning.

We had "relieved" them two years ago, which made this transition much easier. While there, we served at the Cape Town Christian Fellowship Church with Steve helping with the preaching, communion meditations and Tuesday night Bible studies. Janeece taught at the women's Sister Meetings.

We were also at Macassar Township Church where Steve would preach, lead a Thursday night Bible Study and teach a three-hour college course on Revelation every Saturday. While Steve preached, Janeece taught the youth Sunday School class. She also taught their bi-weekly youth group.

Just weeks before we left, the xenophobic (fear of strangers) atmosphere hit its peak in Cape Town. Thousands of illegal refugees, escaping their plight in Zimbabwe and other countries, flocked to Cape Town. They were accused of taking jobs and homes from the poor of Cape Town. In the informal sectors, Captonians (native residents of Cape Town) were chasing those foreigners out of their homes, beating, raping, and even setting them on fire. While we were there, forty people were killed in May alone. A family from Malawi with which we had contact had us write a letter for them to carry around for us to be contacted in case he got into trouble. He was VERY fearful. He worked as a gardener for various people and his wife did domestic work. They had no option but to continue being out and taking public transport. It got so bad the police could not handle it by themselves and the army was called in to help.

In May, our assignment ended amid this atmosphere. There was more security at the airport. We took two of the water bottles they give you on planes to drink and filled them three-fourths full of coke and froze them in the Kennedy's freezer to take with us so we wouldn't have to buy any at the airport. We checked in and Janeece sat down with the carry-ons while Steve went to the loo. Neece dug the frozen pop out of her purse and rolled the bottle in her hand to try and get the ice broken up a bit before opening it. As soon as the lid was twisted, it exploded, shooting the top and frozen pop everywhere! It was so loud, it sounded like gunfire! EVERYBODY STOPPED and looked her way. You could have heard a pin drop in the airport. Nobody moved. Nobody talked. Nobody did anything! Neece pretended like nothing was wrong and continued to try drinking frozen pop that wasn't giving her even a drop of coke as it had all been "shot" out.

After what seemed an eternity, Steve returned and traded places with her. Neece hadn't been gone a couple minutes when two police officers dressed in full body protection, except helmets and shields, came rushing in to respond to the "gunshot" with guns of their own! Steve didn't even know what actually happened and thought he was going to be arrested for sure! Steve wasn't arrested and Neece wasn't thrown in jail. Guess we have another chapter to put in the book everyone keeps trying to get us to write.

We are now in Guinea. The airport here at Conakry is definitely third world as there were many people wanting to help inside the baggage area. This would not be allowed in most airports. Not only did we have to watch for our luggage on the conveyer belt, but also the suitcases we had already put on our carts to be sure they didn't "grow legs and walk off" by themselves.

The customs tables were rickety wooden benches barely sturdy enough to hold luggage. Even though we did not speak French, which is the country's main language, the customs agent was clear in her English as she asked if we had anything for her! Janeece shook her hand. Again, she asked if we had anything for her, to which we told her, "Jesus loves you." She waved us through without opening our luggage.

For the first day or two at the missionary's flat where we are staying we felt like we were in the middle of the ghettos in America. Of course, being the only "Europeans" here also draws more attention than with which we are comfortable. Our flat is on the third floor. The street below is very lively with daily life and the continual honking of horns. We are across from the nightclub area, so we get free entertainment every night... all night!

We almost ran over two people who would not move from the driveway of sorts when we got here. We looked for the guard on duty who is paid to watch the flats to introduce ourselves to him but were unable to find him. No one even knew where he was. That didn't help our feelings of security. We have been told the missionaries have not had any break-ins here. Being on the third floor would make it more difficult for thieves. (Our legs should be in good shape by October. Ha!). Two of the inside doors do not lock. We keep telling ourselves, if the missionary can live here (and have for years), we can surely do the same. We have felt much safer in many other places, but we know the safest place for us to be is in the center of God's will. That is why we are here, in Conakry, Guinea.

Having settled in now and getting to know the many people who seem to be living on the street in front of the flat, we feel more comfortable. The political unrest and exchange of gunfire between the police and the army that the country experienced in May has subsided. The strikes all seem to be over and the airport is open again and back on its regular flight schedules. The U.S. Embassy here did issue a travel advisory this week, but at this point we do not feel like we are in any danger. Of course, we always take all necessary safety precautions.

Our first Sunday at the church we walked with the minister who lives just two doors down from us. He always arrives at the church an hour ahead of time to help set up. They didn't need our assistance, so we walked on down to the ocean. It was FILTHY! We would have had to walk through ten feet of garbage just to get to the coastline. The sand was black from all the sewage that drains into it from the city. At least, we THOUGHT it was sand. The water itself was a terrible brown color. Even the caps of the waves, which are usually white, were a dirty tan. We have been warned not to eat certain fish that live close to the shoreline for fear of contamination. The day before we had walked to the coastline straight out from our flat. Although the color of the sand and water were the same, the great amount of garbage was not visible.

Two ladies were in the ocean up to their necks, fishing with a net connected to a branch tied into a circle like a hula hoop. They kept their "catch" in a large, round plastic tub balanced on their heads. Although we couldn't actually speak to them in words, we did get to see their catch of eight tiny shrimp, three and five respectively. If one could get past all the human contamination, the view of the primitive two and three-man fishing boats floating way out was much more picturesque. The usual sound of waves lapping up on the shore is not heard here, perhaps because homes have been built so close to the water's edge that many stone breakers have been installed by the Guianese government. The contamination is so bad the ocean does not even smell like an ocean! The entire town of Conakry seems to be in the same condition as the ocean.

Steve is helping with preaching duties at the Conakry International Christian Fellowship that meets on Sunday evenings. This is composed of expatriates, embassy personnel, and missionaries living close by or that come into Conakry for supplies. Janeece shares song leading duties there, although her main responsibilities this assignment are the daily bookkeeping tasks in the Pioneer Bible Translators' mission office. It is located in their compound 15 kilometers (nine to ten miles) from our flat.

We are getting to know the people around us better, as they are us. Children who used to run from us crying now run to shake our hand. Every evening when it is not raining, we take "safari walks" around the neighborhood to introduce ourselves to people and invite the ones who speak English to the English-speaking Sierra Leone church on Sundays. We never do this on Fridays which is the Muslim "beggar day." They are out in full force then. Guess we should have known there would be more beggars here when the second thing the customs official at the airport asked was, "What do you have for me?" We shouldn't complain though, because how many times have we asked exactly the same of God, maybe not in word but in action or attitude?

We do our work here in Africa continually being refreshed by the words of David, **"You hem me in behind and before. You lay Your hand upon me. If I rise on the wings of the dawn, if I settle**

on the far side of the sea, even there Your hand will guide me, Your right hand will hold me fast." Psalm 139:5, 9&10 (NIV)

September 2008 - Guinea, West Africa

We can hardly believe the difference Ramadan, a major Muslim religious holiday, makes in the daily lives of the people in Guinea. Their normal way of life is totally topsy-turvy. Devout Muslims fast from sunrise to sunset and do not even swallow their own saliva. People spit everywhere, sometimes hitting pedestrians, motorcycle riders, etc. We had to be careful of taxi drivers spitting out their front window and the spit flying back into the back window onto our faces. The last day of Ramadan all Muslims met in the streets of Guinea to observe their mourning prayer time. Chalk lines were drawn on the dirt for people to sit/kneel in rows. Following this was their fete (feast) where meat from cows slaughtered the day before was prepared and eaten. People walk the streets wearing new clothes, new shoes, and new hats. If children speak the traditional greeting to grownups before the adults do, they are supposed to give the children candy or small gifts. It reminded us of some of the "secular Easter traditions" in America.

Every evening during Ramadan, which lasted the entire month of September, there is a special feast to celebrate the end of that day's fast. Expensive foods and beverages are consumed that are not eaten any other time because of their cost. Most Muslims spend more money during Ramadan than the other eleven months combined. It was during this time a taxi in which we were riding was stopped and surrounded by soldiers some of whom were armed with automatic weapons! We were later told they were trying to exhort money from the taxi driver to help with their Ramadan expenses. The Lord opened a window of opportunity for us to be able to slip out of the back seat and hop into another taxi as the irate soldier threw open the taxi door and grabbed our taxi driver by the neck to pull him out of the vehicle. It seemed like God made us invisible with the soldiers' attention being so focused on the driver.

December 2008 - Terre Haute, Indiana

Our assignment in Guinea ended in time for us to be home to vote. What a blessing that was for us, coming from a continent where force, intimidation, rape, murder, starvation, the burning of homes, stealing of voter registration cards, beating, coercion, etc., are used to win elections or stay in power. Hearing the USA losing presidential candidate concede that very night saying the voice of the people had been heard, reminded us of Zimbabwe, where the will of the people is still being ignored ten months after their elections. How blessed we Americans are! Please keep Zimbabwe in your prayers as living conditions continue to deteriorate and the country seems to be on the verge of imploding.

As of today, our next assignment is not until June 2009. Of course that could change the next time we read our e-mails. It is the first time in years all our luggage has been unpacked and the suitcases put in the garage. It will also be the first time since 2004 that we have been home for both Christmas and Resurrection Sundays, our daughter's and granddaughter's birthdays, etc.

This year, 2008, has been the busiest since MRS started. We finished three assignments this year, one in Morogoro, Tanzania, East Africa, one in Cape Town, South Africa, and one in Conakry, Guinea, West Africa. Until next year's assignment, Steve has been hired by Ivy Tech Community College of Terre Haute, Indiana to assist in teaching offenders at the Wabash Valley Correctional Facility in Carlisle, Indiana. Janeece is substitute teaching.

Over the past six years we have learned that one of the good things which comes of scarcity is appreciation. Loss of hot water, electricity, phone service, internet, free elections, good sanitation, health care, rule of law, and other taken-for-granted things, then become appreciated. This Christmas we pray the distress created by the current recession will have the same positive effects for us. We have personally seen prosperity become a greater enemy than want, so perhaps having less will create appreciation for what we do have. If surplus tempts us to be soft and careless perhaps times of challenge will bring out the best in us. This year our prayer is that less will become more for all of us and that you have a Christ-centered Christmas and a blessed New Year.

Excerpt of a response from a letter of inquiry about the MRS ministry:
MRS consists of just my wife and me with much help from Saltair Church of Christ and Bob, their minister of twenty-five years, who serves as our forwarding agent.

We started by using our retirement funds with very little support, going when missionaries asked for help. Between assignments, we raised funds which were usually just enough for the next MRS trip. We now have enough support for MRS trips without using retirement funds but have been unable to replace used funds or add to them for the past six years. We live very frugally and leave our future in God's hands. Most of the time we do not know where we will be next, days before the current assignment is completed.

Most of our assignments have had eight to ten weeks between them. Some are back to back. Presently, we have eight months until our next one in Cape Town, South Africa. It is the longest break between trips we have ever had. As a result, we are getting temporary jobs until then.

It is not an easy ministry.

We live in the missionary's house while filling the ministry needs. That housing has proven to be very "interesting". We have slept with Vick's salve in our noses because of the smell of the mattress. We had close to fifty bites (that was just on one leg in one night!) before getting rid of the dust mites or whatever was causing it. We've had backaches from the condition of the mattresses, had our toothbrushes mildew during rainy seasons, wear clothes that always felt wet, etc. We never complain because this is how the missionary lives ALL THE TIME! We can surely put up with it for a few months. We have lived in areas that were physically unsafe but did not know it until we were already on the field. On our last assignment, we had no hot water except what we boiled and only had electricity six hours every other night from midnight to 6 a.m. Our hot showers in the States, were the first we had taken in four months. In Zimbabwe, we never knew when we would have water, electricity, or telephone (internet depends on that as well) for our entire nine months there, but it was the assignment from which we received the greatest blessings.

The people we work with and minister to, make all the difference! They live like this ALWAYS, not just for a few months like us. God's help and watch-care over us and them is evident almost every day. It has given us so much greater appreciation for the little things in life. We NEVER take anything for granted, especially washing machines and dryers!

2009

Excerpt from an e-mail June 2009:
Subject: Guinea news update: I am passing along the following article without further comment:

Burn armed robbers, says Guinea Crime Chief.

Guinean citizens should burn any armed robbers they catch to avoid filling the country's prisons, the military government's anti-crime chief said Tuesday. Lawlessness in the capital city Conakry has risen in recent months, with soldiers accused of being among the main culprits of robberies and rapes. "I'm asking you to burn all armed bandits who are caught red-handed committing an armed robbery," said Captain Moussa Tiegboro Camara, appointed by the military junta to oversee the fight against drugs and serious crime. "The prisons are full and cannot take more people, and the situation cannot continue like that," he told a meeting of city officials, adding that residents should form self-defense committees to protect themselves against crime. The National Council for Democracy and Development (CNDD) seized power in the world's biggest bauxite exporter last December after long-serving President Lansana Conte died.

Excerpt from an e-mail June 2009:
HOWDY! The above forward was just received. Conakry, Guinea, West Africa is one of the three countries in which we worked last year. That was the city where our flat and the man's flat living across from us was broken into while we were working at the mission compound. Don't think for a second these people will not follow this mandate! We saw it happen in Cape Town, South Africa last time we were there and that was when it was AGAINST the law! Pictures of it were on the front of their newspapers. It was awful!

A man from Malawi trying to get refugee status from South Africa for his wife, two children and himself came to the missionary's home once a week trying to earn Rands to feed his family. The missionary and then we, while the missionary was gone, would pay Collin to do any little job we could think of to help him. One morning he became very scared. Their papers, identifying them, had been stolen the previous month. This would allow any policeman to arrest them and start the deportation process. That morning on the train a group started talking to him in Afrikaans, one of the official South African languages, which he could not understand. This was how the "locals" identified foreigners whom they thought were taking jobs and cheap housing from them. These were the ones targeted for receiving an "African necklace." They would throw an old car tire over the person, douse him in petrol, and light him. Collin truly had reason to fear! We typed him a letter with our contact information on it so if he were arrested perhaps they would let us vouch for him and release him.

We just do not know how blessed we are in America!

I (Janeece) think I'll take a copy of this to read to my classes at Wabash Valley Correctional Facility where Steve and I are working until our next assignment.

July 2009 - Cape Town, South Africa

Greetings from Cape Town, South Africa where we are on our twelfth missionary relief assignment. We arrived here 40 hours after leaving home, on a Sunday morning during their worship time. We quickly took showers at the missionary's home where we will be living and returned to the church service at Cape Town Christian Fellowship. The congregation had a "bring and share" (like our pitch-in dinners) to say good-bye to Jerry and Aleta Kennedy, and to welcome us.

Having relieved the Kennedy's previously, we pretty well knew their routine and our ministerial duties. So, with only one-day overlap, we took them to the airport to return to the States on furlough. After three days in the same clothes, we were tickled to see our luggage finally catch up with us. In all the years of travelling, we have always packed extra clothes in our carry-ons for just such an occurrence, but this time decided not to so they would be lighter to handle.

We jumped into the work the very next day with Cape Town Christian Fellowship's home Bible study that Steve will continue to lead every Tuesday night. He was also to start teaching an extension college Bible class. The first week we were here, an Afrikaans house-church leader from Bishop Lavis came by and asked if we could also help with their flock. There were 26 Afrikaners in the small house-church the first time Steve preached. Janeece taught their ladies a couple Saturdays later. She used the same lesson taught the previous Saturday for the ladies at Cape Town Fellowship. Her 55-minute lesson only covered one-fourth of the material she had prepared. The ladies at both Bible studies ended up sharing and discussing the lesson questions almost as much as Janeece taught!

We received an e-mail from the Brian Alford's, farmers in Chiredzi, Zimbabwe, whose farm was "allocated" (taken with NO remuneration given) by the Zimbabwean government. They were not allowed to take their furniture, tractors, farming equipment, cows, horses, livestock, etc., nor pick the mangos and oranges that were ready to harvest. It was their entire livelihood. The missionary we relieved there a few years ago had a friend that invited Brian and family to move to North Carolina and work on his farm. They applied to our U.S. government for green cards two years ago. Their funds are running out even though both work in Chiredzi at other menial jobs while living in borrowed housing with their three young children. They were notified by the U.S. Embassy to come for an interview, which is the last stage before being given the proper paperwork for green cards. They have been in constant touch with the North Carolina man during these two years. It just so happens the owner of the North Carolina farm supports the mission work in Chiredzi and is coming to visit this week. He will be able to meet the entire Alford family. Mrs. Alford e-mailed us and said, "God's timing is perfect and life is always good with Him, wherever we are."

September 2009 - Cape Town, South Africa

Excerpt from e-mail:
Just thought y'all would like to read the following e-mail from Chidimoyo, Zimbabwe. Steve and I were there on our second missionary relief trip to Zimbabwe to hold a minister and minister's wives' week-end conference. We had the opportunity to visit Kathy McCarty. Kathy is a single lady who has been at the mission hospital for 30 some years, starting with internships in Zimbabwe during summer breaks while still a nursing student in the States.

The mission hospital is in the middle of nowhere, accessible only by a single dirt road that is so rutted and pothole filled we could only drive 10-15 miles per hour. People come from miles and miles and miles away as it is the only hospital that has medicine, a doctor, an x-ray machine that works, and an operational theatre where surgeries are still being performed. They have a storage room full of peanuts, etc., which the patients trade for the hospital services as many have no money. The hospital charges one chicken for x-rays, eggs, cabbages or such for medicine, etc. In turn, the hospital uses this produce, eggs, chickens, etc., to feed the patients in their hospital. Kathy says the system is working great. Every patient is made to pay something, even if it is just berries they pick in the bush or roots they dig up, which helps everyone keep their dignity.

When we were there, an ox cart and wheelbarrows were used to bring patients to them. Ox carts were also used to take their dead back to the villages to bury. On laundry day, the blue-colored hospital sheets are boiled in giant black pots over outdoor fires, stirred with big wooden spoons and washed by hand. They use so much soap (in two-foot square bars, rubbed on by hand) it is impossible to rinse it all out. The sheets dry on rope clotheslines tied among the trees and are ironed with heavy cast-iron irons heated over wood coals.

We saw several children wearing hand-knitted wooly caps in the middle of summer. We were told, that the mothers believed this would help keep the evil spirits from others standing in line with them at the hospital, from entering their children. They believed the evil spirits could enter small children through the soft spot at the top of their heads. If they were too poor to have wooly caps, the mothers would coat the top of their baby's head with cow dung! After the dung dries, one can't even smell it, and the flies cease to be a bother as well.

The hospital is a bush hospital with few doors and there are no screens over the open windows, but it is considered one of the best in Zimbabwe. This is because of the medical services it is still able to provide, PLUS the patients do not have to bring their own bedding or furnish their own meals. Tea is served twice a day, and a meal! This usually consists of sudza and relish, a staple for most Africans. In a land where the unemployment rate is now 95 percent and international aid feeds over three-million people, a hospital serving food is almost unheard of. Every morning they have devotions with hospital personal leading them. They speak loudly enough that patients unable to come to their open doorways are able to hear from their beds. Every Sunday night there is a church service in the chapel for those who can walk there. They are joined by the many who sleep on the ground outside waiting for the hospital clinic to open the next day. Some walk for hours or travel by bus to arrive at the hospital at all hours of the night and day. Steve preached for the chapel service while we were there.

When the hospital is between doctors, which is quite often due to the exiting of thousands of professionals for better living conditions and better pay in other countries, Kathy does most of the emergency surgery procedures herself. If there are special spots in Heaven, we're sure Kathy's name will be on one of them.

October 2009 - Cape Town, South Africa

We had to renew our visas last month, which is just a little stamp in our passports that allows us to be in South Africa for another three months. Our current visas didn't expire for another month, but we were officially required to have them renewed a month early to avoid being in trouble with the government. It is always an "anxious" time for us during this process because they may or may not renew the visas.

We usually have some type of adventure in the process of obtaining visas or getting them renewed. Once in Zimbabwe they only extended our visas seven days when we had expected two months. We ended up having to return to the States four weeks before our assignment was concluded. Of course, this was during the time of their presidential election and we were told all foreign visitors had to leave the day before the election. That was when we had to drive a beer truck the five to six-hour trip to the airport.

Last year, we had to get yellow fever jabs (shots) to obtain visas to enter South Africa from Tanzania. This necessitated a four to five-hour African bus trip to Dar es Salaam. I had to use the bathroom TERRIBLY - BADLY and had to have the bus stop in the middle of nowhere. Almost the entire bus unloaded to find bushes, shrubs, trees, big weeds, rocks, ANYTHING and NOTHING AT ALL to hide behind. Modesty was to the wind, but all sixty to seventy of us were back on the bus on our way in less than four minutes! Ahh-ahh the memories...

Today's visa renewals were no exception. Whatever trepidation we had was countered with the expectation of finding out what new adventure God had in store for us. We weren't disappointed. We brought out passports, proof of medical insurance and repatriation coverage, in case we got sick and died while in South Africa. The South African government requires medical insurance and repatria-tion coverage so they will not have to foot the bill to treat us or return our bodies to the U.S. We also had a letter from the missionary we were relieving stating why our visas needed to be extended, and we had a local bank ATM balance slip showing the US funds available to us. We blacked out the last four numbers of the balance sheet that showed that the funds were sufficient to provide for our extended stay in South Africa. Big mistake! They wanted to see the four digits to be sure it was our account and our funds. We NEVER carry credit or debit cards with us, as Americans are sure targets for robbery in most African countries.

We had to come back the next day, which was the last day for us to renew our visas to be in compliance with regulations. Lanius, the government official who was helping us, told us they did not really enforce the deadline requirement. We asked Lanius for the govern-ment paper she was using as a checklist to obtain the proper information from us and asked her to sign it. We told her it was so we would be sure to get her the next day, but it was also for proof we had come to the Home Affairs Office within the official time allotted. This was in case another "unexpected government holiday/strike, violence, etc.," kept us from returning and Home Affairs suddenly decided to start enforcing ALL their official policies concerning extending visas. We learned not all government officials act within government guide lines. We returned to the

Home Affairs office the next day with the ATM printout showing the four digits as instructed. Only through God's urging did we also bring the ATM card. Good thing, as they also wanted it. Lanius took it back to an office out of our sight, where she was going to make a copy of the ATM card. We knew this would probably happen as this was the procedure used in 2003 when renewing our visa in Johannesburg, South Africa.

Lanius ASSURED us the information was safe. Just the same, we are going to be monitoring that account very carefully! In two African countries we have been able to use a USA debit card intermittently, meaning one month the ATM will take our debit card, the next it won't, or it takes the funds out of our account in the USA but does not give us the cash in Africa. Everything is always such a challenge in Africa! Makes living in the USA, with everything at our fingertips, almost dull in comparison. Sometimes, we crave that "dull" lifestyle. Things like flipping a switch and having electricity or turning on the faucet and getting water whenever you want it are things we used to take for granted!

We got our visas renewed and were able to pick up our passports, in which they stamped our renewals the very same day! Usually, the Cape Town, South Africa office makes one return in ten to thirty days to collect them. Returning home, just blocks from the Home Affairs office, we drove through of a mob of angry Afrikaners throwing stones at security guards running down the middle of the street. A security guard ran by my side of the car. He picked up a rock the size of a soccer ball and threw it back at the mob. We were driving in the direction the rock was thrown. The rock landed ten feet from our car but did not hit anyone. Luckily, (and we know luck had nothing to do with it!) there were no cars driving next to ours. This allowed Steve to put distance between us and the stone-throwing mob.

Like we said, it is ALWAYS an adventure renewing our visas and ALWAYS a blessing seeing God work us through it.

One night, returning home from the Macassar Bible study that Steve taught, we found the security gate wide open. Our hearts went into our throats! The outside security lights, which we always switch on before leaving even though it is still daylight, revealed no one on the premises. The inside lamps, which we also leave on, showed no shadows moving inside the house. The door was still locked, there were no signs of break-in, and the dog was acting normally, so we carefully entered the house. It ended up being a family of geckos living in the electric box that controls the gate which made it open at will. After relocating the gecko family and replacing them with mothballs to prevent their unwelcomed return, the gate has not since malfunctioned.

We are here in Cape Town filling in for career missionaries, Jerry and Aleta Kennedy. Steve preaches in four different churches and teaches two different home Bible studies. Janeece teaches two different groups of ladies and helps with a Sunday School class. Their faith in God to take care of everything sometimes puts our faith to shame. God has blessed us over and over through these African people. Last month one of the young boys who was in our township youth class a few years back was up front preaching! Just to see their maturity in Christ gives such satisfaction.

Recently, we received a phone call from a lady in one of the congregations we assist. She said that when we came their family was experiencing much domestic strain. They were having trouble coping with life. She thanked us for "weaving our magic through our prayers and lessons." Their family had turned around and now had life worth living again. Only God can cause change like that.

Pony tonga (school bus). Notice the bookbags hanging from the cart's shafts on the side of the pony. Kulpahar, India 2010

Janeece singing with Kulpahar brothers and sisters in Christ. 2010

2010

January 2010 - Kulpahar, India

We're finally here in Kulpahar, India. We left our house at 9 a.m. EST, Tuesday, Jan. 12th and arrived at Kulpahar, India on Thursday, Jan. 14th at 9:30 p.m. EST. (It was 3 p.m. Friday, Jan. 15th here as India is 11-1/2 hours ahead of Indiana.)

We had a scheduled seven-hour lay-over in Frankfurt, Germany whose airport had been shut down the previous two days due to snow. We arrived at dawn in Germany. That sunrise was the most beautiful we can ever remember seeing during a landing. The ground was pure white being covered by snow with the yellow twinkling of houses and street lights bursting through. The bright red hue of the sunrise on the other side of the plane bouncing off the bottom of the wing's jet engine added to the picture-card perfect view below. It's hard to believe Heaven will be any more beautiful, but the same Hand created both.

The missionaries had warned us of heavy fog in Delhi, so we were not surprised when the pilot announced over the P.A. his horizontal visibility was 100 meters (300 feet) but were shocked to hear his vertical visibility was ZERO. He stated he might be forced to abort the landing **and be** diverted to Hyderabad (located close to Madras). This would be the equivalent of a pilot in the States saying he could not land at Indianapolis, Indiana but would be landing in Atlanta, Georgia instead. We wondered how we would contact the missionaries who, by this time, were already at the airport to pick us up. What of the booked train tickets already purchased for the five-hour ride to where a car was to be waiting to drive us the last three hours to Kulpahar Christian Mission?

The fog was so thick we could not see the tip of the plane's wing even with the blinking light on the end of it. The pilot added that 100 meters was the very minimum allowed for a landing at the Delhi airport, but he would ATTEMPT it. (Emphasis mine.) The cabin became dead silent at that point, even the two babies, who had been crying most of the journey, were quiet. We quickly re-familiarized ourselves with the closest exits and contemplated moving our passports from the purse to each of our pockets as well as our list of emergency numbers, accounts, and e-mails. We wondered how many prayers of different religions God was hearing at that moment. All eyes were glued to the one monitor suspended from the ceiling at the front of the cabin watching the altitude figures decreasing since there was no other way to determine how close to the ground we were. We flew by the airport the first time. No one knew if we were now headed to Hyderbab or not. There was almost an audible sigh as we saw the monitor show the map of India with a tiny plane on it slowly turning back around towards Delhi. The suspense was broken when we saw masses of muted lights flashing past the plane's windows and realized they were the runway lights. We gave our seat belts an extra tug.

We had not had this feeling since flying to India in 1975 on Air India which we were advised NOT to fly this time by Indian Nationals themselves. Seconds after touchdown, the entire cabin broke out in applause and the babies began crying again. This time, it was sweet music to our ears.

The plane stopped where it landed, not moving off the actual runway for over an hour. We were praying no other planes would be using this runway. All the gates were full, and no plane was even attempting to take off. When we finally arrived at the terminal, we could not even see the building! The next day we read in an Indian newspaper that the flight control center had lost its automated system for over an hour. As we have said on so-o-o many occasions, we not only felt your prayers, but we SAW them in action!

With so few planes landing, no one could understand why it took so long unloading the luggage. I finally asked the customs official for permission to leave the terminal to notify the missionaries, Sharon Cunningham and Leah Moshier, whom we hoped we would recognize, that we were here just two hours late!

The guardrails were lined with people crowding to catch the first glimpse of returning loved ones. There were also MANY taxi drivers holding signs with people's names. Our name was on one such sign. Leah, who had helped establish Kulpahar Christian Mission 54 years ago and who had worked at the mission throughout those 54 years, was now 91-years-old and was in the hospital there in Delhi. We were told it was not serious, but she would be there for a couple days to receive antibiotics by I.V. for an infection. They sent a taxi for us. The taxi driver also had a note and cell phone from them.

Even in the taxi, visibility was barely two car lengths. We noticed on the road tiny twinkling lights, like the ones we had just taken off our Christmas tree. They lined the edge of the road over the bridges. Not only was the driver but WE were also VERY thankful for them! We arrived at the YMCA in Delhi at 4:30 a.m. Before we left the next day at 5 a.m. for our train, we had time to visit Leah in the hospital. (How exciting it is to think we will be working with a missionary about whom we had studied in Missions class at Kentucky Christian University! We feel like we already know them thanks to our GREAT Mission's professor, Mr. G!) We were impressed by how modern the hospital was. It even had a Subway kiosk in the lobby. (That was the best sub sandwich!)

We took time to exchange dollars (USD) into rupees (Rs). The first bank we entered was being refurbished. Broken chairs, blocks, pieces of concrete, trash and huge mounds of dirt were piled in corners. Had we not been with a trusted friend of the missionaries, we would have refused to even go into the derelict building.

It was a short taxi ride to the train station the next morning. We had forgotten how the face of one who is not an Indian National could instantly double and triple normal prices. We were painfully reminded soon enough. There must be an invisible union between coolies for once a coolie engages in trying to fix a price to assist you with your luggage, no other coolie will step in to offer a lower price. We managed to get the four coolies Rs800 fee (800 rupees, India's currency) down to Rs400, still a far cry from the Rs150 usually paid by residents. Fearing the train would leave without us being aboard, we had to agree.

Our disappointment was soon forgotten as minutes before the train pulled out, a couple of backpackers seated across from us noticed their camera case was missing. In it were their train tickets, money, and passports! We all began looking under our seats, trying to help in their search. The young man told the young woman he had to go back to the platform to search. Five times she made him promise to get back on the train before it left. He returned empty handed. Within inches of bursting into tears, he stated he remembered carrying it onto the train. At that instant, we both looked at each other and had the terrible feeling our coolies may have had something to do with the disappearance of their camera. As the train began to move, the two backpackers grabbed their belongings and darted out the train door. Our hearts ached to see their desperation. We thought how much more God's heart must ache to see us in our desperation of trying to find Him but always looking in the wrong places.

The rocking of the train as it left the station reminded us of an exhausted mother trying unsuccessfully to force-rock her baby to sleep. We needed no spoon to stir the sugar in the hot tea that was served, as the train was jostling fiercely enough to do the job for us. The trick was to try and drink the tea between jostles! Mothballs decorated the ledge separating the double window panes, keeping rodents from running through or building nests, we supposed. Their smell just added to the scents that make up India.

As the train moved along we saw through the window many concrete train trestles still lying where they had been unloaded so long ago that their once-ridged forms had now taken on the shape of the rough ground upon which they lay. At many railroad crossings, tractors, that are common rural transportation, sat in lines like cars do in the States waiting for the train to pass. Our train traveled through Agra, a famous tourist town where the Taj Mahal is located, yet within 50-feet of the tracks were ten people relieving themselves on the trash dumped next to the tracks. One boy carried a bucket of new refuse to add in the city's dump to which three chickens came running! The terrain at one place we passed looked like the Badlands of South Dakota with mountain-size piles of dirt. We discovered later that this was the best dirt from which to made bricks so the "mountains of dirt" were actually valleys made from years of digging and carting away dirt for bricks.

In the fields, home-made scarecrows were dressed in saris (Indian dress). We saw the carcasses of three oxen whose bones were picked so clean they looked like props in the dry desert of an old TV western show in the States. However, the item that amazed us most was the women's artistic displays of cow pies which they call dung cakes! With trees not readily available for firewood, Indians also use dried cow dung for their fires. It's the ideal firewood as it is light-weight, easily stored, bug/rodent/rot proof, doesn't smell when burned and an abundant supply is always at hand. The women mix the dung with straw/weeds to help hold it together and then pat the cakes out much like Americans pat out hamburger patties. After being dried in the sun, the patties, which are the size of a super-

super-duper-quarter-quarter-pounder, are stored in various shapes: rectangles, circular domes, etc. We felt as privileged as if looking through a display window at Macy's due to all the time and effort that was put into their design, form and artistic presentation. If you want to really "go green" and leave no carbon print, take a lesson from these women!

After a five-hour ride, we got off the train at Jhansi, where three men, raised in Kulpahar Kids Home, were waiting for us. Again, we found each other by a sign they were holding with our name on it. Two men were actually sent in the mission's vehicle to collect us, but neither spoke very much English. They were afraid of not understanding us, so stopped to get the third man, Gabriel, a former Kulpahar kid who now teaches at a school in Jhansi. It is so cold here the government has closed all school classes through grade eight. It has been a month since these children have been to school. With no school, Gabriel was able to assist the other two "Kulpahar kids." They enlisted the assistance of only two coolies to carry our four suitcases, weighing 50-pounds each, for a total of Rs150! (just under $4 USD). Each coolie carried one suitcase on his head and pulled the other by its handle. (All four bags have wheels.) We had paid Rs400 to coolies in Delhi to carry the same suitcases.

Gabriel was dropped off three kilometers later and we spent the rest of our three-hour car ride to Kulpahar Christian Mission trying to converse and take in the sights of rural India. We felt like we had been transported back to Biblical times as we shared the tar roads with small, two wooden-wheeled carts pulled by a team of oxen tied to the carts with wooden yokes. At one point, we had to wait for an ox to be re-tied to the cart as the wooden peg had fallen out and allowed the ox his freedom. He didn't get very far since the rope that was used for reins that ran through both oxen's noses still kept him connected to the other ox. On several of the hill/mountain tops, we could see the small temples where Hindus go to worship and sacrifice to their idols. We remembered God's warning to the Israelites in the Old Testament NOT to worship on the mountain tops like the pagans who worshiped their idols there.

We thought that during our conversation back and forth with Sanjay, the driver and Uttam, his assistant we were able to understand each other reasonably well until we asked how long they had to wait for us to arrive. Uttam looked puzzled, like he was trying to search for the correct word. I tried to help by saying, "Was it a long time?" His puzzled look left as he proudly answered in a thick Indian accent, "Yes. Ten years!"

February 2010 - Kulpahar, India

The mission is spread over three adjacent compounds containing a total of 35 acres in all three compounds. The main buildings on our compound are the mission house/office, girl's hostel, and kitchen, where all meals are cooked over an open fire in a large stone fireplace for all the children in all the hostels and almost 100 workers and family members. The second compound is about 200 yards down the road and is made up of the mission hospital, medical lab, doctor's quarters, cricket field and mission personnel housing. Directly across the road is the third compound, which is the largest of the three. It contains the Kulpahar Christian School, mission chapel, boys' hostels, cemetery, a field for planting food staples used in the mission's kitchen, and a building for the team of oxen used to work the field. All three compounds are completely enclosed by eight-foot-high brick walls and are supplied with water from open wells located on each compound. There are a total of 32 Christian families living in mission provided housing which is part of their salary. The mission is the largest employer in this vicinity.

As a private Christian school recognized by the government, Kulpahar is unparalleled in the region. Their 28 teachers, comprised of 22 Christians, five Hindus and one Muslim, teach close to 400 students from kindergarten through grade 12. The children receive instruction that exceeds the standards of education offered by their Hindu counter parts. Last week, the homework of grade one (six-year-olds) consisted of multiplication with TWO numbers on top and one on bottom. There were also division problems that had remainders for this first grader! By grade two, they know their multiplication tables through 20. Sixth graders are exposed to three different languages! For this reason, many prominent Hindu families send their children to Kulpahar Christian School rather than the local schools in the community. This seems to be one of the mission's greatest influences in the community as they have chapel to start every school day, but it is called Opening Exercises.

Daily Bible studies are also offered but not compulsory. Parents must sign permission slips to allow their children to participate in the Bible studies to help protect the mission against false accusations that have been brought against the school in the past of children being forced to participate and become Christians. (These charges were brought against the school by a disgruntled worker who was terminated several months previously.) Of all the Hindus who attend the mission school, 95 percent participate in these Bible studies. One Hindu father was asked why he allowed his child to participate in the Bible studies to which he responded, "Everything that is taught there is good. There is nothing bad so what is wrong with that?"

The mission school was started years ago to educate the orphans that were being left on their doorstep. It is VERY IMPORTANT for Christians to have an education, since illiterate Christians have no way to earn a living. They must compete for jobs with non-Christians who will ALWAYS be given preference.

Several adult families, of which one or both parents were raised in the Kulpahar Kids Home as orphans, do not have incomes to support the college training for their own children. Leah Moshier, who is 91-years-old and helped start the Kulpahar Kids Home over 60 years ago, uses her personal funds to pay part or all of this second generation's college education as she considers them her grandchildren. Her love is not lost on the 800 plus children she helped raise since 1946. Although the mission is no longer taking orphans, most of the 800 would not be here today were it not for her and the late Dolly Chitwood putting into practice Christ's words, **"...as you have done it unto the least of these, you have done it unto Me..."** The Hindu religion teaches that orphans and widows are being punished for sin in their past life, so Hindus don't/won't help an orphaned child. This ministry is a testimony to God's love!

In Hindi, the word travel means "to suffer." That describes most forms of travel in India perfectly, and yet Leah's "children and grandchildren" travel hours and hours just to be with her for a short time. For many, she is the only Mother they ever knew. After they finish college or technical training, the "orphan children turned adults" are not obliged to return to the mission, but many do, using their skills to help out.

At present, the mission hospital is not operating at full capacity due to the lack of a resident doctor. A few weeks after we arrived, two doctors, who were husband and wife, made a seven-hour round trip drive to Kulpahar to inquire about the position which the missionaries are praying can be filled by a Christian doctor. At present, trained nurses, many of whom are Kulpahar alumni, provide medical assistance to both residents of the mission and the villagers. A lab technician is also on duty at the hospital. He is a Kulpahar alumni, too.

Helping care for abandoned, poor and orphaned children and bringing them to Christ has been one of the ministries of Kulpahar Christian Mission since its inception over 60 years ago. There are former Kulpahar kids everywhere, working in almost every profession. You can't guess what Peter, one of these former Kulpahar kids helped us do! Peter is a self-taught computer whiz.

By buying a cell phone for the equivalent of $125 USD, he got our wireless laptop to connect with the internet with the cell phone acting as the modem! We hoped it would be fast enough for us to use SKYPE which meant we could call the States through our computer for a fraction of the cost, but the server is too slow. We think it is AMAZING to have such sophisticated technology in such a remote part of India. We hardly ever used a cell phone until now. The cell phone we had to buy in Tanzania that was stolen in Guinea when our flat was broken into was never replaced. Peter said this phone could be used in Africa and the USA, as well. Just to think a cell phone is our umbilical cord from India to you is amazing! What will they think up next?!

We tried to down-load a forward we received of a two-minute video off YouTube. It took us 26 minutes to get it downloaded. The second one we tried was a two and a half-minute video which downloaded for almost four hours before the internet went down, which it does several times a day. Even then, only one second of the clip had been downloaded,

With Peter's technology, the mission was able to install a small satellite dish which not only allows the missionaries access to internet but allows a VCR video to be played in the mission house and shown in the children's hostel located several hundred feet away. Every Sunday evening (for the girls) and Saturday afternoon (for the boys) a video is played. Of course, the electricity goes out several times before the video ends and the system has to be re-started by hand each time, but they're not complaining. In fact, the children have learned how to work this flaw to their advantage. One evening we were at the house and in charge of re-starting the system each time the electricity went out. Usually one of the children runs to the house to be sure the system is re-started promptly. Since we were busy working on other things when the power was cut, we re-set the system where the child said. We later learned this allowed the children to see one hour of the video over again! Children are children no matter where we are!

We went to the hostel last night to attend the little girls' nightly devotions. They were held in their dining hall just before supper which starts at 7 p.m. We use the term "dining hall" very loosely as the little girls' (first through grade four) dining hall is a small room with seven picnic-bench-type tables crammed into it. Believe it or not, they could get a couple more tables in the room the way they have it arranged. The little girls numbered close to twenty. Many had their coal black hair, which was cut just below their ears, held back by hair bands or odd shaped bobby pins. Some were already in their flannel nightgowns made by tailors that work and live on mission property and in mission houses. (This is part of their "pay package.") Others were still in their play clothes having changed out of their green school uniforms earlier. Play clothes are dresses with slacks worn under them. Most of the slacks look like sweat pants. We imagine when warm weather comes, they won't wear the slacks. All the children's clothes in the hostels are provided (or made), washed and mended by the mission. That in itself is a monumental task which employs many Indian workers as it is all done by hand! There are no washing machines, but they do have two VERY TIRED (old) dryers which are only used when weather does not permit clothes to be hung out on the clotheslines. Steve has to be careful walking around the compound at night not to decapitate himself on the many wires strung from the metal, not wooden, poles which need to be used because of the termites. Even train track tresses and electric poles are made of concrete to keep from being destroyed by termites. The mission has a special generator con-nected to the dryers because the government's electricity always goes off at 7 a.m. and then is sporadic during the day.

The little girls' eyes, which are such a dark brown color they sometimes look black, twinkled as they sang their songs. Many songs had motions, and they sang louder than we have heard some church choirs sing! In the middle of one such song the electricity went off again for the umpteenth time that day. It instantly became so dark that we could not see our hands in front of our faces. The girls didn't skip a beat. In fact, had we NOT had our eyes opened at that moment, we would not have even known anything had happened. From the sounds we continued to hear, the girls were still doing the motions with their singing. Eventually the light, which seemed to be missed by no one but us, came back on. One little girl stood and began to pray, at least we thought she was praying since everyone had their heads bowed, so we did, too. She prayed so l-o-n-g and s-o-o fast, we began peeking to make sure everyone else still had their heads bowed. When she was no longer talking, we raised our heads thinking the prayer was over. We saw most of the girls' heads still bowed and eyes shut but their lips were moving. They were having their own silent prayers. The matron, a single woman in her thirties who watches after the girls and lives with them in the hostel, spoke to them in Hindi and they all got up to leave. Devotions were over.

Janeece hugged the little girl closest to her and told her "goodnight," then all the little girls came over to be hugged. We hugged most of them way more than once and finally stopped as they were just rotating back around to be hugged again and again. They kept saying, "Goodnight, Auntie. Goodnight, Auntie." How we would have LOVED to have tucked each one of them in bed since most were orphans and had probably never experienced being "tucked in" every night. They are all so eager to be loved.

You'll never guess what we saw walking down the road tonight on our way to the church compound!

A BIG, FAT, INDIAN ELEPHANT! Today and tomorrow are Hindu festival days, so we assume he was headed into Kulpahar to join in the celebrations. He must have walked from a distant village because there are no elephants around here. I can't remember when I've seen such a BIG, TALL Indian elephant. He didn't have the lighter pinkish color around his ears and eyes like most Indian elephants that make them look anemic in comparison to African elephants.

There was a big lump on his back right hip about the size of a basketball which was probably all that remained of an old injury, along with the limp in his walk. The mahout, who stays with an elephant his entire life, was on his back, while another man walked beside them. When they got to us, the mahout spoke to the elephant and he stopped. Then the man on the ground made motions all too common in India of people asking for money. Luckily, the road was wide enough they could not stop our walking past them until we had given them something as has been done to us before when in a vehicle on a small crowded street. In South India in 1995, at that time, the elephant actually put his trunk into the car window to take the money out of your hand which he then passed up to the mahout on his back. You don't argue with an elephant that is inches away!

Some Hindus consider elephants sacred. Giving money to them is supposed to bring you blessings, we were told. The Indians were just as excited to see the elephant as we were. Many were riding their bicycles in front of and behind him.

May 2010 - Kotagiri, India

We were invited to attend a Hindu wedding of the son of the mission's milk man. He lived just 600 yards down the road from the mission compound and owned water buffalo. He milked them every day and sold most of the milk to the mission. Buffalo milk is VERY rich and made us sick to our stomachs if we drank it without diluting it with water.

The bride-to-be lived far from here, which is quite common. The "baraht" (all the wedding party from the groom's side) travel together to the wedding and the bride's family has to put them up and feed them from two to four days. After the wedding, there is a farewell ceremony in which the bride's spokesman speaks to the bride's new in-laws asking them to take care of her, love her, etc.

The groom's spokesman responds by telling the bride's family how they will take care of her and thanking them for their hospitality. The bride is then escorted by her father from her family's side to the groom's side. There is a lot of crying which shows the bride loves her family and how much she will miss them. Usually the bride and groom live with the groom's parents and the bride has to cook for everyone. These days many of the educated brides have jobs that the grooms want the brides to keep so the duty of cooking is lessened if the mother-in-law is kind. Some mothers-in-laws are not kind. Two off-spring of grown Kulpahar children from the children's home here married each other and moved away to live. Whenever they return to visit, the mother-in-law (who is a Christian) does not allow her daughter-in-law to go visit her mother who lives on the same compound just five houses away! The bride's mother has to come visit her at the mother-in-law's house with everyone around, so she has no time alone with her own daughter. Even then, the mother-in-law says when the mother can come visit, because the mother-in-law has the last word!

There are several parts to the Hindu weddings that we have attended: the hulda, the wedding itself, the cake cutting., the dinner, and the farewell ceremony. The hulda is a ceremony for the bride which only ladies attend. It is held the evening before the wedding and is intended to help beautify the bride's skin. The bride, wearing old clothes, sits on a small stool placed in the middle of a beautifully hand-drawn picture of flowers done in chalk dust on the ground. There is a thick, almost clay-like paste made with several local spices that is spread by the bride's friends onto the bride's arms, legs, face, neck, and ears. We were only familiar with the turmeric spice in it which badly stains skin and clothes. No one wears good clothes to the hulda as they sometimes get the paste spread on their clothes as well. Many of the ladies took some paste and spread it on their own bodies to improve their skin. Whether it helps or not, we don't know. We do know it changes the color of their skin just enough to make it appear to glow. Afterwards the bride washes it off and has mehandi applied. Mehandi is beautifully intricate designs, hand-drawn upon her arms, feet, and hands with ink that will wear off after a few weeks. Many people are invited to the wedding, and it can be a very costly event for which the bride pays.

India, where we served the first six months of this year, is an extremely Hindu area (80.5 percent), and the mission was continually under scrutiny. We were asked to keep a low profile but even then twice our names appeared in a local paper stating places where we were supposed to have traveled. We had never even heard of the cities, let alone traveled to them! The paper named a school where Neece was to have spoken to the students. That didn't happen either. The paper also quoted us as making certain statements about the country and its people, statements that we NEVER made! Thankfully, the comments were of a positive nature. The article was written by a man to whom we were introduced in the village and spoke with for only a few minutes but who had big political ambitions. We also had an officer from the Central Intelligence Department of India (like the CIA in America) waiting at the mission gate to question Steve's interpreter, Mr. Lal, about the Good Friday services at which Steve preached. They interrogated Mr. Lal for an hour, asking such questions as, "Did we have permission to conduct the service? What was done in the service? What was said?" Mr. Lal used it as a time to present the entire plan of salvation to the officer and nothing negative came of it. Only God can take such a situation and turn it around to His advantage!

We have served in many places where Christianity was not the major religion and sometimes not even readily accepted. We have served in a country with anti-conversion laws. This means, it is against the law to preach, teach, or even talk to someone about letting Jesus Christ become Savior and Lord of their life. This is enforced with visa denials or cancellations, expulsion from the country, or even jail time. It can also be dangerous for people in those countries to work with us, as newly converted Christians have been beaten, been ignored by friends, and have had their families refuse to recognize them as part of their family any longer unless they denounce their newly-found faith and return to their former beliefs. For this reason, we ask you to not put any of our correspondences, our e-mails, or newsletters on Facebook, My Space, websites, or any other site that has unrestricted access. This does not mean you cannot forward our e-mails or newsletters to others you know. We welcome you to share our ministry with your acquaintances, but uncontrolled access could leave us or those with whom we work open to ones who do not worship Jehovah God and who wish to do harm to missionary individuals. Nowadays, all a person has to do is Google a name to find information that could be harmless in America but have dire consequences in a foreign country when twisted out of context.

This past month seven adult Hindus from a nearby village who had been worshiping with us accepted Christ and were immersed at their village. They are being questioned by the villagers as to why they converted but are standing strong. Many villages cast out Hindus who become Christians. Friends ignore them and some families who cannot change the new Christian's mind beat them into renouncing their newly-found faith and refuse to recognize them as part of their family any longer. But as the apostles, who had been beaten for preaching Christ in the temple and commanded to no longer do so by the Sanhedrin, said, **"We cannot help speaking about what we have seen and heard."** Already, the former Hindus plan to build a room on their property for Bible Study to which they can invite others. On Sundays, they have to leave their homes before dawn to bicycle to Kulpahar to worship with us. With our temperatures now reaching 115-120 degrees in the afternoons, you can imagine how hot that return trip gets! Please keep them in your prayers. One was from the Brahaman caste, the highest caste.

Although, officially, India is no longer practicing the caste system, even here in Kulpahar, such is not the case. At one of our weekly Ladies Bible studies, Neece picked up a waste can to collect trash from the ladies. Their collective gasp and look of disbelief instantly told her this was a task THEY thought she should NOT be doing. She was asked to let someone else do it. Although they are Christians and believe all are equal in Christ, the culture in which they have been raised makes practicing this very difficult at times.

God is continuing to keep His children safe, especially the past couple weeks. Just minutes before the mission's outside Sunday School classes were to begin a venomous Russell viper was killed within feet of the blanket upon which one of the girls' classes met. Last night, a cobra that was almost three feet long was killed outside the boys' hostel. "Just a baby," we were told!!!

A Hindu father whose wife passed away two years ago had been keeping his son at a Catholic hostel where the nuns took care of him. The father had no desire nor was he financially or physically able to raise the child himself. Living in a rented room, he said he could not keep the boy. Since the Catholic hostel was for girls, it was just temporary, but the father kept putting off finding somewhere else for his son to go. After two years, the nuns finally said, "Enough!

For the sake of our girls, you must come and get him TODAY!" The father called Kulpahar Christian Mission and asked for them to take his son, Ashish.

After prayer and consideration, the mission agreed they would accept Ashish at the beginning of the next school term. Two days later, the father was at the mission's gate to drop off his son, two months early! Ashish is only four-years-old and won't turn five until September. The father signed papers which would allow his son to attend a daily Bible class so the mission would not get into trouble with the government for "forcing" Christianity on him. It would also allow the mission to rear Ashish as a Christian. At that point, Ashish knew his father was leaving him, and he began to cry. Our hearts were about to break, too. The mission put them in a guest room to rest, have some lunch, and give the father privacy to tell his son good-bye. The boys who play volleyball with us said Ashish cried all night in the small boys' hostel where he will live from now on. The next youngest hostel boy is 11-years-old. The following day, they put Ashish in school which he left and walked back to the hostel.

Ashish is now adjusting well, and it is so encouraging to see the older boys take him under their wing and care for him. Don't be fooled. He can be a rascal and has caused a couple of the older boys to cry as well. We have heard he is full of mischief in the classroom although he is very smart. He has come a long way from being forced to shake our hands to now throwing kisses to us when we leave the compound. Who knows where he learned that?! He can be very well behaved, too.

Can you imagine giving up your four-year-old child for strangers to raise? Many of the hostel children have stories similar to Ashish. Some of the fathers sat at the mission gate and mourned for hours after giving their children over to the mission. One such single father had three pre-school children who were living in a two-wheeled, horse-drawn tonga (wagon). The children were on their own during the day while he worked using the horse and tonga to make a living. He could hardly feed the children, let alone clothe them or pay school fees. He knew it was not safe to leave them alone during the day. They had nowhere to even get out of the weather. They ended up spending their entire lives at Kulpahar and loved it. The father eventually stopped coming to see them because of the expense and great distance he had to travel. I guess he saw how well they were being cared for by the mission and knew he would never be able to do the same. Mothers seldom bring the children to the mission due to the culture or being deceased. These Kulpahar lady missionaries are the only mothers many of the hostel children have ever known. The families can take their children during school breaks, but many never come back because they know they cannot feed them for that short time. Some actually don't want them, especially if they are girls.

The first baby left at the mission was a three-month-old girl. Due to the mother's death and the family being so poor, the infant was fed mostly opium for months to keep her from crying before being left at the mission. She still suffers the physical effects from that opium diet. Although the mission is no longer accepting babies, more than 800 children have grown up in this compound and still consider the missionaries a mother.

Being the only parent some of these children have ever known, it falls to these missionary ladies to arrange marriages for many of them, as is the cultural practice in India. They allow the final consent, however, to be given by the Kulpahar bride or groom-to-be after talking a couple of hours with the prospective spouse. That is sometimes their only contact until the wedding, but these marriages seem to last better than the "pick and choose a spouse" method used in America. Last month things were abuzz on our compound in preparation for the arranged marriage of one of the grown Kulpahar girls. Since she did not have a father, one of the missionary ladies walked her down the aisle. They do this quite frequently.

June 2010 - Kulpahar, India

Early one morning while it was still dark outside, I walked barefoot to the bathroom. I considered not turning on the light, but something told me I'd better. When the light came on, not more than ten-inches from my foot, was a l-o-n-g multi-legged creature almost as long as my foot! Few crawly things give me goose-bumps, but this one sure did. He would have been perfect for any horror film! It had to have been a male because no female could ever look that terrible! Afraid HE would get away to crawl into one of our shoes some night, I ran to the bedroom and grabbed a shoe. Of course, it was Steve's as his was longer than my shoe and would allow my hand to be farther away from the crawling monster when I hit him. The first two blows didn't even faze him! He continued crawling at the same speed.

I increased the intensity of the third blow, and he didn't even curl up! By then, I wanted to have enough left of him for someone to identify, so the next two blows were directed at the end that I thought was his head. I couldn't even see any eyes on the "thing." By now, his tail was beginning to wag back and forth for something to sting. It reminded me of a scorpion, but he looked more like a millipede. His tail was forked with both "prongs" of his stinger being almost a half inch long. I finally took the edge of Steve's tennis shoe and grated it on his head, back and forth against the concrete floor. After repeating this last course of action several times, he stopped moving. One could not tell I had even tried to "saw" his head off. He was still fully intact!

Counting his legs, which at this point were not all fully intact, he had from 36-40. When I touched his back, his outer coating, which was pinkish in color, was not hard like that of a roach or cricket. He

111

was segmented like an earthworm but not as soft and wet as one. He was half and half.

I didn't want to pick him up, so I put Steve's shoe beside it to keep Steve from stepping on it should he come to the bathroom before morning. The next morning, the "pink millipede" was STILL ALIVE and wiggling! Steve used the rest of our bottle of insect spray on him. (Now, why didn't I think of that?!) This time he curled up and we KNEW he was dead.

Steve tossed him outside for the birds but three days later, he was still there. Even the birds thought he was too ugly to eat!

Excerpt from e-mail to Janeece concerning her night-time visitor: Is this your friend? (It's a small picture, so hopefully it won't cause you problems.) According to the internet there are over 600 varieties of this crawly monster, called the Scolopendrid or giant centipede. I had one of those "barefoot at night, wait, better turn on the light" experiences a few years ago and my light also revealed a centipede, but mine was much smaller and easier to kill. The internet says, "... is toxic to humans and causes severe swelling, chills, fever, and weakness. However, although bites are painful, they are unlikely to be fatal." You be careful!

Following the India Christian Convention, we accepted the invitation of Emyrs and Usha Rees to visit their mission work in Yerpedu, which is a couple of hours drive from Chennai (formerly Madras). The mission was originally started in 1973 by Emyrs' parents, David and Lois Rees, as a leprosy hospital. They also worked for the eradication of T.B. Both Lois and David are buried on the mission compound.

Steve was busy working on the devotion he was to have for hospital personal the next morning, so Emyrs and Usha's seven-year-old "adopted" son, Santosh, wanted to take me back to see the new "Christmas house." We stopped to skip rocks on two of the water holes in the middle of the mission's field which were dug to catch rain water to help with irrigation. Cyclone Lila had hit India's coastline the day before, so both holes were full.

Santosh pointed out the Christmas house located in the back corner of the field. It was a small ten feet by twelve feet rectangular building with no walls, just a high corrugated roof held up by a steel post in each of the four corners. The floor was a smooth four-feet-high slab of concrete accessed by four steps which stretched the entire length of the smaller side of the structure. The simple framed structure looked new. In fact, it was still surrounded by small piles of left-over sand, broken rocks and three blackened spots on the ground where fires had burned.

I was taking a picture when Santosh picked up a bone the size of my hand and stated he was going to take it back for the mission's guard dog. He had picked it up from one of the three blackened burn spots. Upon closer examination of the debris in the burn spots, I saw many sun-bleached bones, ribs, pieces of leg bones, ball joints, sections of a back bone, part of a broken jaw, and pieces of a skull... a human skull! It wasn't a Christmas house but the mission's crematory! Santosh had misunderstood the word!

I immediately told Santosh I thought the dog would like our left-overs from lunch better than that bone. He dropped it without me even having to ask him to leave the bone. "Thank you, Lord, for children who listen the first time!"

When the mission admits a patient to the hospital, they are required to be accompanied by someone who will help with their care. Sometimes, however, unaccompanied people are admitted. When no one claims the body of a deceased patient, a man is sent to his village to find any relative or friend. Like most rural villages, electricity is very sporadic in Yerpedu. This renders the mission's mortuary ineffective, so if no family member or friend is forth coming, the mission's "Christmas House" must be used.

Cremation is commonly used by the Hindus, who make up 80.5 percent of India's population. If a family is too poor to afford cremating, they wrap their loved one in cloth and put the body in one of the three sacred rivers in India, preferably the Ganges. The sacred Ganges River is also used to wash their bodies, their animals, dump trash, and drink from. Needless to say, there is much sickness in India that could be prevented.

Not far from us, Hindus moved into a shabby, two room, mud-brick dwelling that had no roof and looked like it hadn't been lived in for years. Scraggly shrubs, weeds and piles of rocks surrounded the place. In front was a large open well that also served as a Hindu shrine and had six or seven red cloth flags stuck in the ground around the well to show it was a Hindu temple.

Before they moved in, Steve and I peeked over the edge into the well. About ten feet down and dug into the side of the well is a shelf on which there is about a four-foot stone idol of their "monkey-god." There is room in front of the idol for a person to stand and place offerings. Behind the idol is a large hole that looks like it goes into a cave which we were told tunnels back under the house and was hand-dug.

Every evening walking to the church compound, Steve and I would wave to the Hindu man who was the only one "cleaning up the place." He slept on a wooden frame crisscrossed with rope for his mattress. Several times Steve and I were busy talking to each other when walking past and we would hear someone yelling, "Salaam." It was our Hindu neighbor making sure we greeted him. Even when I walk past without Steve, he often acknowledges me first by waving. I guess I'm old enough and my hair white enough for that to be allowed.

Little by little, they are acquiring more and more possessions, including two oxen, three dogs, a clothesline tied between trees, a tile roof on the house and just last week, a metal front door that can be locked. They've come a long way from when they first used the house in which to store harvested wheat stalks!

July 2010 - Terre Haute, Indiana

In July, with our assignment fulfilled, we left India. Our visas only allowed us to stay six months and the missionary's schedule was such that we could not fly directly from India to Africa. We, however, enjoyed our 22 weeks at home and were able to attend the North American Christian Convention in Indianapolis.

September 2010 - Cape Town, South Africa

We were able to get from and to the Indianapolis airport and soon found ourselves in Cape Town, South Africa to relieve Jerry and Aleta Kennedy. Compared to our work in India, where, according to their website, "Visitors to India are prohibited from preaching at a called gathering or be subject to a fine and possible expulsion from the country," our ministry here in South Africa is very open. We feel more like keepers of the aquarium than fishers of men. But after living for six months continually looking over our shoulders, a little unguarded time is more than welcomed.

2011

April 2011 - Terre Haute, Indiana

After having served in India and South Africa for all but 14 weeks last year, we are finally back in the States. We were to have returned to India in January this year for a four to six-month assignment where we would be today, but the missionaries notified us in December that their furlough had to be delayed. It has now been rescheduled for next year.

A missionary from Hong Kong had been e-mailing, asking of our doctrinal beliefs, but we had no other requests for relief work in 2011. We settled in to finding jobs upon our arrival back in the States. This helps us support ourselves so as not to use mission funds while in the States. Each time, however, it gets more difficult to put together a decent resume after holding jobs for such a short period of time between assignments. But God always provides, as He has again this time. If it weren't His leading, we know we wouldn't be hired.

God is blessing us by slowing us down to have more time with family and friends in the States. He is also teaching us a lesson in patience by bringing us to trust and lean upon Him more as we wait for our next assignment.

Our next assignment was a matter of much prayer and contemplation. We figured God is the One who started this ministry over nine years ago so we would continue to let Him lead us when and where He wanted us to be.

The very next day, Ken Smyth e-mailed to ask us to relieve them in Hong Kong during their furlough to the States starting in August

2011. Ken and his wife, Linda, have been ministering in Asia for over 30 years and in 1980 helped cofound Chinese Christian Seminary, an undergrad Bible College.

Hong Kong, a Special Administrative Region of the People's Republic of China, has grown from what was a simple fishing village into the world's eighth largest trading economy. It is situated in the southeast corner of China. Hong Kong is home to more than 6,970,000 people. Buddhism and Christianity are the most common religions. Most of the people in the area where we will be working are Chinese who speak Cantonese and English.

A missionary with Pioneer Bible Translators (we worked with PBT on two different assignments), recently e-mailed us the following description of an incident which we wanted to share with you.

Excerpt from missionary friend's e-mail:
"Recently, we had an interesting conversation about gold with some friends here in North Africa who came over for tea. One of the men was describing his recent work in a gold mining town some distance from here. Knowing nothing about gold mining, we made small talk about the process and how it's located, extracted, and purified. Our friend gave a short narrative of the process that ended with an interesting detail: "When you finally find a good piece, you must take your knife, cut your finger, and spread your blood on it." We asked our friend why this was done. He answered, "So the owner will not harm you."

We asked, "The owner? Who owns it?"

Their response made us pause, "The demons."

"The demons?"

"Yes. But if your blood is on it, then it belongs to you. If it is covered in blood, the demons will flee."

This cultural insight delivered so casually over tea has such a thought-provoking idea behind it.

We don't know much about the gold industry, but we do know something about the power of blood. We know the mark that makes evil flee and are ever grateful to belong to the One whose blood is upon us! There is POWER IN HIS BLOOD!"

July 2011 - Terre Haute, Indiana

Suddenly and without warning, on June 13th, my soulmate of almost 40 years "...finished his course..." and went home to receive his eternal reward. The death certificate reads "myocardial infarction as a consequence of diabetes mellitus." During our entire married life together, Steve had never been treated or had trouble with his heart. So shocked was Steve's doctor that before signing the death certificate, he had them double check to be sure they were talking about the same Steve England.

A celebration of Steve's life was held in Terre Haute, Indiana, with burial of his earthly remains in the Mound Cemetery in Illinois, where years before we had secured plots.

 People immediately began asking whether or not I would continue in this ministry.

Steve and I were to leave the next month on our fifteenth overseas assignment. It was to Hong Kong. We had never had an assignment in Hong Kong to relieve any missionaries. I know no one there, nor am I familiar with how to get around in the city. Without praying about it, I immediately answered that I definitely would not be going to Hong Kong but was waiting on God to know what my future held.

I continued praying for God's direction and even did my own "Gideon's fleece prayer" (Judges 6:36-40) to help me recognize God's answer. Within days of Steve beginning his new life, I contacted the four missionaries we had assignments to relieve that were scheduled through 2013. Only in the e-mail to Hong Kong did I apologize for putting them in a bind, implying I would not be coming to Hong Kong. The other e-mails were just five or six sentences telling of Steve's new residence.

To know whether I was to continue with MRS, my Gideon's fleece-prayer was for one of the missionaries to contact me (not me contact them), asking me if I would still come to relieve them. Just one hour earlier, our, I mean, *my* forwarding agent, Bob and I spoke of my Gideon's fleece prayer, and I had prayed with Bob and Sharon, the church's secretary, waiting for God to somehow show me what He wanted me to do.

Not more than an hour later, I opened an e-mail from Ken Smyth, the missionary in Hong Kong, requesting I still come to relieve them if able to do so.

I know it must be God's leading because I had already totally dismissed the Hong Kong assignment, thinking I would be of little help and probably more of a worry to those at the mission, since our ministry is to give the furloughing missionaries peace of mind about the work, their home, etc. It seemed my coming would just cause more stress. It appears that just the opposite was true.

Another missionary couple, Jim and Betsy Mollette, work with the Smyth's in Hong Kong. Betsy fell and broke her hip. They are in the States and will most likely not be returning to the field except to close bank accounts, etc., making the need for my help in Hong Kong even greater.

Excerpt from Ken's e-mail:

"I am writing this as a special e-mail to you. I don't know how you see things and what your direction is at this time, but I will just get to the point of the letter. If you feel led of the Lord and able to do so, we would still like to have you come during our furlough for the period of time as previously planned. There is still a vital role that you can play in the work at this time.

1. Help with the children's ministry during the sermon times. With Linda not being here and Scott having to preach at least part of the time, that means two significant regular children's ministry personnel are not available.

2. Lead the Sunday afternoon Bible study with the Philippine sisters. Those who are here and able to teach already have considerable responsibility. Thus your presence would help to relieve some of the pressure on them and give them the opportunity to learn new perspectives on the Word of God and Bible study from you.

3. Be a personal worker and encourager with the Filipinas there at the church house. Betsy has played a major role in being "mommy" to those sisters. Of course, Jim is part of that, but Betsy is the key person of the two of them in helping the Filipinas. With me being gone also, they don't have anyone readily available during the times they are there and could talk personally with someone for advice, encouragement, prayer, etc.

4. Help out in other miscellaneous ways as the need and opportunity arise.

Under the current arrangements, we would plan to have you stay at the church building, where you would be readily available to meet with others even during the week. Without Jim and Betsy being here, you would be living by yourself there, unless any of the Filipinas needed a special place for short times. That happens now and then, but not often. Furthermore, it is only a five-minute walk to the grocery store and other basic services. Fairview Park is very safe, and we would have no concerns about you being out and around there. In fact we could basically say that about Hong Kong as a whole. Transportation is modern, efficient, clean, and air-conditioned, though very crowded especially at certain times of the day.

I would still consider it an honor to have you come and the church would certainly be blessed by your presence. I just felt led of the Lord the other day to write to you."

I felt like a burden had been lifted after reading Ken's e-mail.

Looking back, it seems that every time I remember saying NO to something, that is exactly where God puts me!

In South Africa, when Steve and I filled in as instructors for the South Africa Bible Institute, they sent us a list of classes needing to be taught and asked which ones we would be willing to teach. My reply was any class except Old Testament History. Which class did I end up teaching? Old Testament History! I ended up loving it and learned so much! Sending me to Hong Kong... That's just like God, stretching us to the point we HAVE TO DEPEND ON HIM!

My Gideon's fleece prayer was answered.

Unfortunately, I had already cancelled our plane tickets but knew if it was God's will for me to fulfill our assignment in Hong Kong, it would pose no problem. God would work it out, and He did. They let me use our ticket refund to purchase my ticket, which was not only cheaper, but also a direct route to Chicago to Hong Kong with no layovers or plane changes. Thank you, Lord! Isn't it awesome how God confirms His will in our lives in such unexpected and clear ways?

After talking with my daughter and praying about it a few more days, we (God and I) have decided. I will be leaving for Hong Kong as originally planned, August 15, 2011.

GOD'S GOT THIS!

Most couples, after having dated a while, choose a song that they then consider their song. From then on, every time they hear the song played, they instantly think of each other. "Savior Like A Shepherd Lead Us" was our song.

Every year on the Sunday closest to our anniversary, my husband would be sure "Savior Like A Shepherd Lead Us" was included in the morning worship songs. As the pianist would play the introduction and I would recognize the song, I would look up at him seated behind the pulpit. When our eyes met, the corners of his mouth would barely turn upward, but he never completed the smile in case anyone else was watching.

My husband and I were married almost 40 years when, without warning, he suddenly stepped into eternity. It happened so fast he did not even have time to close his eyes. I closed them for him.

The next day, while making arrangements for his Celebration of Life, I realized I would be going home to an empty house after dark. It left me cold and uneasy. I thought to myself, "You are just making your own monsters in your head!"

How many times has Steve been in a meeting or worked late at the church and you have come home to a dark, empty house? This is no different. You are making monsters for yourself!"

The day proceeded pretty much as planned. That evening as I pulled into the driveway, my mind again reminded me, it was dark, and the house was empty.

Realizing this would just be the first of many, MANY "monsters" that I would have to conquer, I took a deep breath and reached down to shut the radio off.

Guess what song was playing? - "Savior Like A Shepherd Lead Us"

In that instant, I KNEW - God's got this!!!

As I walked into the dark, empty house, it was with a boldness I had never before experienced. I knew from that day forward I did not have to fear what the future held for me. God had it under control. There would be <u>nothing</u> He would not protect me from or help me through.

He is still right there with me. His arms are so tightly wrapped around me, it's like a protective cocoon that keeps me close to Him.

I am still living in the peace and boldness I found that night in my driveway when I KNEW - God's got this!

How am I doing now?

I'm doing okay. Not much appetite, but sleeping is no problem. I just work till I drop. Besides my full-time job, I have cut 14 trees down around our trailer that Steve had always wanted down for fear they'd fall on our trailer during a storm. I had always talked him out of it. Halfway through the 14th tree, the chain flew off the chainsaw which probably saved the rest of the woods. Later, I managed to get it back on and finished.

I find myself praying more and more about the little things that before I always thought were too trivial to bother God, like the mower starting, the chain not flying off the chainsaw again, remembering how to change the line in the weed-eater, or getting the checkbook balanced. God even helped me find a slow water leak in two pipes under our trailer that, with a little help, we had fixed in just over an hour. **"Before they call, I will answer." Isaiah 65:24** (NIV)

I dreamed about Steve... I can control my waking thoughts but how does one control their dreams? Guess I just have to pray a little harder and be a little more tired when my head hits the pillow.

Excerpt from e-mail July 2011:
(Received shortly after Steve stepped into eternity from one of the boys from the mission with whom we played volleyball. We had visited with Kaushal and several other "volleyball boys" in Agra where they attended college.)

hiii,,

how are you ?hope you are good by grace of God..i m OK here

...rainy weather start here...i praying for you... god is love you

because he is great in all time in every situation ..and i also love

you... byeeee,. take cae..   your child.. kaushal

Love in any form of language helps soothe the soul.

November 2011 - Hong Kong

Someone once said to not ask the Lord to guide your footsteps if you are not willing to move your feet. I guess I didn't move my feet fast enough because I found myself way past my eyeballs with things to do, and only a week left in the States to do them. I have never had such a difficult time trying to prepare to leave on an assignment. It seemed the more I did, the more there was to do. I continued working at the secular job I had until just before leaving for Hong Kong. I thought I had allowed enough time to finish writing my ladies Bible studies, lessons, pack, and do all the last-minute items. I forgot to take into account I would also be doing what Steve normally did in preparing to leave for several months. Things like wax cars, spray weeds, get the yard in good shape, back up all the files on the computer, sort through flash-drives/CDs to take, and lots of assorted other tasks. This was the first time EVER I went to the field with lessons unprepared even though I worked all night several different times trying to finish everything in a timely manner.

My plane ride was uneventful. I met up with Ken and Linda Smyth, the missionaries I am relieving, at the Hong Kong airport where they were holding a sign with my name on it. Having never met, this was one sure way of finding each other. Upon walking into Fairview Park Christian Church house, where I am to live upstairs for the duration of my assignment, I found a whiteboard filled with welcomes and greetings from many of Fairview Park Christian Church's members. They are just as warm and loving in person. I find this almost everywhere we have ministered. Cards from a couple of supporting churches and individuals were also waiting when I arrived. I surely felt supported, uplifted and remembered.

I can see the tall buildings in China from the church yard that is approximately thirty feet by eighty feet. This is the lot space, not the house, which is even smaller. Of that, there are only two spots of grass about twenty feet by eight feet. It takes me longer to put extension cords on the electric weed eater than it does to actually cut the grass.

My first Sunday we had two who wanted Jesus as their Savior and Lord of their lives. Both are among those I teach in my Sunday afternoon Bible study, although their decisions were made before my arrival. They were baptized before Sunday worship services began. It is done this way so the new believer can join their church family in partaking of communion on the same day. I thought that was a very good idea. Having no baptistry, the baptisms were done in a child's large wading pool with the candidate seated in the middle and then being helped to lie down flat for the immersion. Someone in the church takes various pictures on their digital camera of the entire proceedings, their confession before the entire congregation, being greeted and welcomed, the actual baptism, being presented a rose by the one who helped lead them to Christ and receiving a new Bible from the church. Later, those pictures serve as a border for their baptismal certificate. It is not only colorful and impressive but is laced with so many good memories of such an important day in their life.

The church (referring to the body) is unique in that nationalities from several countries are involved in our weekly services: Columbia, South America, China, Hong Kong, the United States, Philippines, and Australia. Although the electric keyboard is used most often, I've been told they also sing to the guitar. I've not experienced that yet.

Leftovers from lunch are eaten by the Filipinas who reluctantly leave around 8:30 p.m. to return to their employer's home. They usually occupy one tiny room or share a bedroom with the children. What a life. Even though I am worn out by day's end, I am so blessed! Thank you, Lord!

My meal today was interesting. I was treated to Snake Soup and Pig's Ears. I was told the soup had five different kinds of snakes in it. Yes, the snake tasted like and looked like stringy chicken breast. There were other spices in the soup so I really could not tell you what it actually tasted like. Even taking just a piece of snake, which was cut into very small pieces, did not help. The pig's ear was cut into very thin strips like noodles that had cartilage in every piece. That made them very crunchy in spots and soft elsewhere. The ears I ate were bar-b-q and tasted good, but I had to focus my mind elsewhere when chewing the cartilage.

The church celebrated Hong Kong's independence, another national holiday, with 45 members/attendees sharing expenses to rent a boat which took us to an island in the South China Sea. We shared a pitch-in meal with no "exotic" items on this menu. Since coming to Hong Kong, I have eaten snake soup, chicken feet, tree bark, seaweed, fungus, jellyfish, squid, turkey gizzard gristle, sea cucumbers, octopus, pigeon, pig belly, duck feet, and a milk tea containing giant tapioca and noodles that are like gummy worms except they have no taste. The milk tea is delicious!

My assignment here in Hong Kong ends the day before Thanksgiving. I will fly back into Cincinnati, Ohio, where I will be met at the airport by Kim Wilkerson.

When I left Fairview Park church, my luggage was 16 pounds overweight. I debated over and over whether to take the extra out and give it to people in the church or take it, hoping the scales that I was using were off. I decided to say a little prayer and take the extra.

I made lots of small talk with the check-in agent at the United counter while he checked on my seating and reservations. I asked him if I needed to put a United baggage tag on my checked luggage. He said I should in case it got lost. I jokingly said, "Oh, YOU aren't going to do that, are you?" We kept talking and he got two priority luggage tags out and proceeded to put them on my two checked bags. It was one of the few times my checked bags arrived at the same airport at the same time as I did! AND I didn't have to pay for the extra 16 pounds!

The United agent asked if I had relatives in Hong Kong which opened up the way for me to talk about God. He asked if I was a Christian. After answering, I asked him if he was a Christian and HE WAS! I shook his hand warmly and we talked another five to ten minutes as no one else was in line.

A few hours later, I was in line at the gate to board. Of course, I was way to the back of the line talking to another lady in front of me, when this same Christian ticket check-in agent came up to me, took my bag, and in a stern voice said, "Follow me." The crowd grew quiet as all eyes were on us. I knew I wasn't in any trouble but everyone looking at me thought otherwise. The agent went right up the middle of the line. I felt like I was following Moses through the Red Sea as the people started parting left and right to let us through like the waters must have parted for the Israelites.

The ticket agent turned around and got my ticket when we got to the gate. He took my ticket up himself to be validated, then had me follow him through the gate door and down the aisle to where the men were who pat you down. My ticket agent spoke Chinese to the men, they glanced at my carry-on and waved me on without putting one finger on me! The agent continued to walk me to the doorway of the plane, and I was the very first person to board the plane! Talk about preferential treatment! I felt like the biggest VIP ever!

God had taken my biggest fear of luggage being overweight and turned it into my biggest blessing!

I'll probably never meet that ticket agent again and yet, I will most certainly never forget him, a fellow Christian God placed on my path.

December 2011 - Terre Haute, Indiana

This is my first Christmas since Steve stepped into eternity. I am missing him.

Did you ever think that maybe...? Just maybe... That very first Christmas was a sad one?

God's only Son left the righteousness of Heaven to come to earth where He would put on the filthy rags of human form. Leaving behind His robe of purity, He traded living in a place whose streets were of pure gold and the gate of pearls, to nestle in a bed of animal fodder covered by the smell and sounds common in barnyard surroundings. He left a dwelling where there was never suffering, hunger, tears, darkness, or sin to become everyone's sin.

I wonder how happy God was that first Christmas, to NOT be sharing Heaven with His Son? ...knowing He had sent Him to a world that would not receive Him, but instead would taunt Him and ridicule Him His entire life and in the end, would even torture Him to death. I wonder how "merry" God was that very first Christmas Day?

This season was my hardest time yet, but God was faithful. It seems the song service is the hardest part for me, and it wasn't until Christmas Eve services that "it hit." I would have been fine but at the first service I attended at Staunton at 8 p.m. a lady came up and went on and on about how hard it must be and how I must miss Steve. It was then I realized the wisdom of God sending me, just weeks after Steve stepped into eternity, to a country Steve and I had never been to (Hong Kong) and to people who didn't know Steve.

I then attended the 10 p.m. Christmas Eve service at Union Christian Church, where Steve's celebration of life was held in Terre Haute. God sent people to me just at the right times. Before the service, when slow melancholy music was playing, one lady came over, hugged me, and asked if I wanted to sit with their family since I was in a pew by myself. Later, another God-sent lady gave me a hug before the service and invited me to their family breakfast the next morning. That was all the encouragement I needed to make it through that day.

Christmas Day was Sunday. Joy and Trinity have always come to our trailer after church to eat lunch with Steve and me. That didn't change. I was stirring the baked corn that morning when tears just started rolling down my cheeks. My thoughts weren't even dwelling on Steve. Still stirring the mixture and with my eyes open, I just said a one sentence prayer asking God to help me through this.

I dreaded going to church knowing I would be blubbering like a baby. The baked corn dish took ten minutes longer to cook than I planned, throwing me behind time-wise. I hurriedly put the ham and baked corn back in the oven and shut the oven door for them to stay warm while we were at church. I grabbed two of Steve's handkerchiefs, which I knew I'd need during the song service, rushed out the door, jumped in the car, and headed to church.

I was making good time and was going to arrive just as the first song would usually begin when a thought raced across my mind. "Did I shut off the oven?" I couldn't remember turning the oven knob. Surely I did. The farther I drove, the more unsure I became. I was more than half-way to church when I gave in, turned around and headed back home. Just before arriving home, I also wondered if I had unplugged the lights on the Christmas tree. Since the tree was a cut "live" tree, I never leave the lights on, especially now with it being so dry.

When I got home, I found the oven off and the lights unplugged. Coming back out the front door, I thought to myself that God had a reason for putting those thoughts in my head which would make me very, very late for morning worship and on Christmas Day, to boot! I thought perhaps He kept me from being involved in an accident.

My drive back to the church was slower and way more peaceful, emotionally speaking.

Entering the church's front door, I met the pianist, who plays for both services, walking down the hallway. I had missed the entire song service! I LOVE the Christmas hymns and really hated not getting to sing them one last time before they are forgotten for another entire year. The pianist gave me a big hug and I continued into the service, slipping in beside my daughter and granddaughter who had saved me a seat. The sermon was wonderful and over much too soon. We were going out the church door when I realized I hadn't shed one tear, something I would NOT have been able to manage had I been in the song service. God had answered my hastily whispered prayer yet again - His additional Christmas gift to me this year.

I KNOW it is because of the prayers that continue to be offered to God on my behalf that I actually half-way enjoyed this Christmas season and made it through today. What would have been the beginning of the 40th year of marriage for Steve and I was celebrated by drinking the McDonald's mocha beverage Steve brought home to me 30 minutes before he began his "new" life. I had put it in the freezer on June 13th, planning to drink it when we returned from Steve getting his blood-sugar tested at the hospital.

I returned. Steve didn't. For months, I have planned to use our anniversary as the day I would finally allow myself to "wisp." (As one dear senior saint calls it - Wallow In Self-Pity.) Today, that day finally came and I didn't need to "wisp," thanks to your prayers AND God's faithfulness!

131

Our anniversary is over. It is now 4:30 a.m. December 31st. I'm glad 2011 is almost over, but I look forward to seeing what God has in store for me in 2012 and how He will use me.

Janeece eating with chopsticks. Hong Kong 2011

Helping prepare lunch by cleaning chicken feet in a rural church in Zimbabwe. 2017

2012

March 2012 - Terre Haute, Indiana

Two days before I was to leave for India, I tried a new recipe that was to be cooked in the microwave. It was called a 3, 2, 1, Cake. The recipe calls for combining an angel food cake mix with any other flavored cake mix. The egg whites in the angel food cake allow the regular mix to bake properly. This is stored in a zip lock bag on the shelf. Three tablespoons of this mixture are combined with two tablespoons of water and cooked on high in the microwave for one minute. (Hence 3, 2, 1 Cake) At 10:30 p.m. that night, I was desperate for a bite of cake, so I tried to remember the recipe without turning on the computer and double checking the e-mailed recipe. I remembered all the ingredients but in the wrong order and quantities. I used one CUP of mixture, (instead of three tablespoons) two tablespoons of water, (which was correct) but cooked it for two minutes in the microwave, not one minute. (1, 2, 3, not 3, 2, 1)

I have never baked a cake in the microwave, so I stayed in the kitchen and watched through the glass window. I moved five feet away for just a few seconds to wash my glass in the sink. By the time I turned around, smoke was bellowing out every vent the microwave had! I quickly opened the microwave door, which automatically shuts it off. Big mistake!

Smoke rolled in giant clouds out the opened door. I slammed it shut, unplugged it, and began unwinding the cord from around all the other appliances on the cabinet... toaster, blender, crock pots, etc. only to realize I also needed to remove the pens, ceramic pot holders, and other items decorating the top of the microwave.

It had been snowing most of the evening, and I had just swept one and a half inches of snow off the top step out the back door. I ran to open the back door, which is only eight feet from the microwave. Returning to the microwave, I picked it up to take outside. The microwave was heavy enough I had to hold it against my body to carry it. Of course, that put my face directly over the smoke still pouring from the vents. I began coughing. My eyes were watering. I seemed to be stepping on the one pair of Steve's shoes I kept at the backdoor, over and over. I used the microwave to push the back door open, but it only opens 90 degrees. A chain connected at the top by the factory keeps the door from swinging open clear back to touch the side of the trailer. The handrail on the other side of the steps left little room to maneuver. I set the microwave down on the top step.

Steve's mom had just given me a pair of blue, furry, house slippers that were very warm. I didn't want to ruin them by walking on down the stairs in the snow. I had to turn the microwave around so its door would be facing away from the trailer. Just as I opened the microwave's door to let all the smoke out, a BIG gust of wind blew all the escaping smoke back into the trailer. I stood half-way up to move the microwave so I could shut the door, tipping the microwave forward. The cup with the charred cake came tumbling out and fell down the stairs and over the stone steps. The mixture inside was so burnt, it kept the cup from even cracking. It was at this particular moment the neighbor's cat decided she wanted to take refuge from the snow inside our trailer.

For six years this cat has continued to "adopt" us when we return from an assignment. She stays at our place so often our granddaughter has named her Rose. As I maneuvered to stop Rose, I again tipped the microwave and out slid the glass microwave plate. It didn't fare as well as the cup.

The Lord blessed us with warmer, sunny weather, so for the next several days I had windows and doors open to air out the trailer while dressed in three layers of clothing. I moved the smoke-smelling microwave to the garage to air out while I'm gone.

Before I left, Rebekah, Trinity, and I tried one more time to cook the cake in the microwave. With the correct instructions, the 3, 2, 1 Cake recipe worked great! You should try it.

March 2012 - Delhi, Kulpahar, India

My plane trip to India was so much smoother and better weather than when Steve and I came in 2010. I was blessed to travel through two beautiful sunsets. You know how gorgeous a sunset can be looking at it from the ground up. It is even more spectacular seeing it from the sky down! As the plane traveled through the first layer of white clouds, it was as if someone was steadily pouring a bucket of white sand over the wing.

Before leaving, I considered taking a can of mace with me, mainly for Delhi, India. This is the first time I have even THOUGHT about such a thing. After praying about it, I decided if I got in a situation where I would even consider using it, fear would probably be showing in my eyes that could be like waving a red flag in front of a bull. I think it is better to help control a situation by controlling my reaction to it. I may be shaking like a leaf on the inside but showing confidence outwardly. After ten years of doing this through customs, airport security, and numerous third-world situations, I'm getting pretty good at it.

Late that week, my Bible reading told how Gideon and 300 Israelites were able to defeat the Midianites and Amalekites who were **"thick as locusts. Their camels could no more be counted than the sand on the seashore." Judges 7:12** (NIV)

"Grasping the torches in their left hands and holding in their right hands the trumpets they were to blow, they shouted, 'A sword for the Lord and for Gideon!' The Lord caused the men

(enemy) throughout the camp to turn on each other with their swords. The army (enemy) fled". **Judges 7:20** (NIV) These 300 Israelite soldiers facing so many enemy soldiers that they could not be counted did it WITHOUT EVEN HAVING A WEAPON IN THEIR HAND! I decided it would be better to rely on God and do my part by being extra careful, being aware of who and what all is going on around me, not going out after dark, staying where many people are, and not flashing money around, etc. God's power has not lessened. He protected the Israelites who were doing his bidding. He will protect me also.

That didn't keep me from feeling every ounce of my singleness as I walked the short dirt road from where I was staying to a gas station ATM in Delhi. I needed to withdraw several months' worth of support in rupees to take to the remote village of Kulpahar where I would be working. There are no ATMs in that part of India. The two machines both had signs written in Hindi attached to their screens. One sign had the word "Sorry" at the bottom. Assuming they were both broken, I retraced my steps. I could feel the eyes of every man there, looking at me, the only woman. I felt like produce on display in a store window, being inspected by all I passed. It took three days for me to secure even part of the rupees needed as most of the ATMs would only let me withdraw the equivalent of $83 USD. After four such transactions, the ATMs refused to recognize my debit card, but this is why I always take currency to exchange as well. Simple little tasks, such as withdrawing money from an ATM or adding time to your cell phone card, which could be done in minutes in the USA, can take days to achieve in a third world country.

I took a train to the mission station hundreds of miles away for the second leg of my journey. To get to many of my Delhi destinations, I could either take a taxi and pay "an arm and a leg," or ride the metro for the one and one-half hour round trip. Trouble is, I had never ridden the metro in India and had no idea how to do so. I didn't even know how to find one! Tasks like this keep me leaning on God to find strength and courage, for "All things are possible with God."

By following incorrect directions, I walked almost a mile to find a metro station that was only three blocks from where I was staying in Delhi. It was then that God started sending angels in every shape, size, and gender to get me to the places I needed to be, accomplish the things that need to be done, and have impromptu translators at just the right moments. His first angels that I met were at the metro window where I discovered I had to switch trains in order to get to where most of the businesses, banks, stalls, etc., were located. They helped me buy the correct tokens and explained at what station I would switch trains.

Watching the people in front, I found my way through security. Here was God's second angel, just a young lady doing the searches and sweeping the wand over our bodies. She had such a sweet face and innocent smile, it immediately put me at ease. One would have thought I was her Granny from the way she treated me.

I could no longer follow the masses as trains were going in all directions. God's third angel I recognized as one of the ladies in line behind me at the metro token window. She told me, "Come." I didn't even ask any questions but just followed her. We both boarded the same train where she disappeared into the crowd. I never saw her again.

Shortly after arriving at the mission here in Kulpahar, India, I was called to appear before the Foreign Registration Officer (FRO) at the district office of the Local Investigation Unit. I was asked, no, ordered, to bring my passport and a photo of myself. Every visitor to Kulpahar from outside of the state of Uttar Pradesh, where

Kulpahar is located, must submit an official form, a copy of their passport and visa within 24 hours of arriving here. I already did this and have had to do so since my first visit to Kulpahar seven years ago. They received my photo and the copy of my passport just days before, so what do they want with me personally?

The Kulpahar school principal, who only accompanies the Aunties to Delhi when handling important legal matters, was sent with me. It was then I felt the need to kick my prayer life up a couple notches.

The principal and I arrived at the office of the Superintendent of Police within the time specified. The lower level was full of uniformed police with me being the only female in sight. As we passed, the officers stopped talking mid-sentence. I felt the piercing eyes of everyone directly on me. What do they know that I have yet to find out? Was I dressed inappropriately? Thoughts bombarded my mind.

I was glad I had forgotten to change into my normal glasses. My sunglasses allowed my eyes to roam without being detected at who I was looking. I could not read anything from anyone's face. They were all stern and "all business" and all staring at me!

We were directed into an office the size of a small bedroom. Ten people already occupied the room. At first, I could not tell the employees from civilians. There were four lights on the walls, one on each side, but only one was working. A worker was trying to get a fan to run, only to have it stop when it finally went just two revolutions that sounded like metal scraping on metal. The only other woman in the room, an Indian, got up and gave me her seat. The thatched chair on which she was sitting had a hole right in the center. I sat as lightly as possible wondering if the remaining strands of plastic thatching would hold my weight. That's all I needed, to get my bottom stuck in a chair and not be able to get out on my own. I didn't laugh at the thought.

The principal was directed to a chair close to the employee working at three tables pulled together in a U-shape. The employee was entering data long-hand with a pencil into a notebook from other passports that looked exactly like mine. I strained to see the word KENYA on the front of one of the four passports he had.

Although there were many piles of files that made the office look cluttered, they were in neat stacks. There were several files sewn closed in white cotton material with Hindi writing on the outside.

We sat quietly while the employee entering the data, asked questions in Hindi of the Indian who submitted the Kenyan pass-ports. He produced an envelope filled with duplicate passport photos following one such question and gave four pictures out of it to the employee. As this was all that was happening in the office, everyone was watching and listening. I knew when my time came to answer questions it would be the same way, no privacy what-so-ever. My business would be everyone's business, but I've found that's the way it is in most third world government offices. One never gets used to it though.

Much information was copied from the Kenyan passports and visas onto the book with corresponding photos being pasted at the side.

In the hot, stuffy office I was so relaxed I began to get sleepy but knew better than to fall asleep! After 45 minutes, another man arrived. All the employees in the office stood, which was my only indication of his superior rank. I finally figured out the LIU (Local Investigation Unit) officer had arrived - 45 minutes late! When he smiled, if you could call it a smile, everything seemed fine. Amazing how the downward curve of one's mouth can change our perception of someone's personality in an instant.

In a gruff and authoritative voice, the LIU officer immediately asked if we had the photos for another Kulpahar visitor who had just left a few days earlier. His papers were submitted the same time as mine. He had also attached the required photo, copies of his passport and visa which had a photo of him on it, as did mine.

The principal looked at me across the room. By the look in his eye, I could tell this was the first time either of us knew of any such request. The principal said something in Hindi to the officer. Then the officer gruffly asked me in English if I had my two photos. I answered I had only been told to bring one, which I did. He asked two more questions, which were garbled, and I could not understand. The principal repeated them to me. One was the date I arrived.

The officer was holding the official required forms I had filled out and sent in a few days ago. All that information was included, so why was he asking when he already had the answer in his hands?

I thought perhaps he was trying to see if my answers matched what I had written on the form in front of him. The form asked for two dates, my actual arrival in India as well as the date of my arrival in the village of Kulpahar. I hesitated wondering which date he wanted. I couldn't remember when I arrived in Kulpahar as I had lost a day flying over, had arrived at one in the morning and the train to Kulpahar left in the evening and arrived at 5:30 a.m. the next day. It was a week before I even knew for sure what day of the week it was.

I didn't think I should ask for a calendar. I wondered if my hesitation would cause him to think I was trying to hide something. He finally specified Kulpahar, which I wasn't sure about, so I told him the date I arrived in Delhi. That gave me a couple more minutes to try calculating my arrival date in Kulpahar.

I'm sure my final answer was wrong. If he continued to ask questions from the form, I knew I was in for a long afternoon. The thought went through my mind, this must be how a criminal feels during an interrogation, trying to get his story straight but not remembering what he told the officers the first time.

The officer asked for my passport. I passed it to him through two employees as he was on one side of the room and I on the other. He asked where my visa was. I then passed my old passport to him. After looking at both, he gruffly asked why two passports. I explained the first passport with the visa had expired.

Would they tell me I was supposed to have my ten-year visa in my current passport? He checked the dates then shook his head in agreement and said nothing more. Thank you, Lord!

We sat for another 45 minutes. The employee was finishing up the four Kenyan passports when the LIU officer started barking out orders in Hindi. I understood enough words to know he was telling one worker to bring "chai" (tea). He pointed to people as he counted, I was not included. In this office, I had not expected to be.

The chai came in the typical small, clear, plastic bag, tied closed at the top. After untying the plastic corners, the worker poured the chai into small paper cups the size of the hard-plastic medicine cups on top of liquid cold medicine in the States. The first cup was given to the officer, then the employees and one to the principal. The principal asked if I wanted a cup to which I said if there was enough. A cup had already been put on a table for me which I thought was for the employee seated there. When I picked the cup up, it was so hot I did not understand why the tea had not melted the paper-thin plastic bag in which it came. The bags are like our pint-size Ziplock bags but much thinner and with no Ziplock. The tea was delicious, but of course I love Indian chai.

Later, the principal said he was hoping I would refuse because of not knowing how it was prepared. His body was used to their water, but he was afraid mine would not be. I told him I thought the chai would be hot enough to kill any germs and God would take care of the rest, and He did. Besides, I thought it better I did not turn down any acts of hospitality on their part.

The officer then apologized to me for any inconvenience this may have caused. At the time, I had no idea why he said that. We sat for another hour during which several of the employees were on three different personal cell phones, making calls, then taking turns handing their phone to the main officer. At one point the main officer read into one of the cell phones what was written on my stamped visa. By now the first employee had completed entering all the information from my passport and visa into his book and had pasted the photo I brought beside his hand-written entry.

Out of the blue, the principal got up, came over to me and said we could go! The LIU officer handed my passports to the principal, who handed them to me. He instructed me to check inside to be sure they were mine.

I had a thousand questions, but this was not the time or place to ask them. I walked over to the officer, shook his hand and in very crude Hindi thanked him for the chai, it was good. Actually it was only three Hindi words, tea, good, thank-you, but he got the message and smiled. Finally, he smiled! Thank you, Lord!

Once again, as we walked down the stairs and out to the mission car, all eyes were upon us. We passed the four Kenyan young men. I later learned from the principal overhearing their business in the LIU's office, the four Kenyans were coming with a circus to Mahoba. I hope I get to go see it even though the principal said it "was not good."

The principal then explained they could not find the reason for ordering me to come to the office. They called the officers who were not "in station" (at work) that day to see if it was one of them who made the order. No one would admit requesting that I appear. The main officer apologized two more times, which rarely happens, even admitting a mistake was made. Usually they will look until another error can be found or made up.

So many were the blessings God lavished upon us that day. From the smallest of the few strands of plastic strips in the seat of the chair not breaking for two and one-half hours, to the officer in charge actually admitting they made a mistake!

All that hype for nothing! I'm sure it was due to God's hand on the Hindu officer that he was in a frame of mind not to cover their mistake and also thanks to your prayers.

Resurrection weekend was extra special this year as I witnessed the births of my new brother and sister in Christ, who came forward at the close of our Good Friday service. The next afternoon, the boys from both boys' hostels walked over to our compound for the baptismal service. They used a portable baptistery which the missionary got from the States many years ago. The lady had been sprinkled as a child but wanted to follow Christ's example and be immersed. Besides all of us, her family, husband, and two-year-old daughter witnessed her rebirth.

The other candidate was Sulamen, a boy living in the mission hostel. He is very smart and the top student in Class Five. Sulamen plays volleyball every night with us. What a joy to not only have him on our team but in our family!

The hostel boys let me help cut palm tree-like branches from bushes to be used in church on Palm Sunday. The tip of every leaf on each branch has a point that is needle sharp, so we had to cut the undeveloped baby branches for the little boys and the girls from both mission hostels to use as they entered church singing and waving them the next morning. The mature branches were used by the Royal Hostel boys to decorate the church along with wild flowers and colorful bougainvillea blossoms. The church was beautiful! There were 30 some children singing and none of them were shy in their singing, even without any keyboard accompaniment. God must surely have been pleased with the extra efforts taken in remembering His Son's sacrifice and teaching innocent children to join in raising their voices to praise Him.

The fifty ties of Steve's that I brought to give to mission personnel and Royal Hostel young men were not enough. I had requests for "Uncle Steve's tie... very good" long after they had all been distributed. Resurrection morning, since so many men were wearing Steve's ties in church, made it seem like Steve was everywhere... saying the opening prayer, playing the keyboard, leading song service, singing the special (Imagine that!), serving as elder at the communion table, a deacon taking up the offering, preaching, and a church member sitting on the floor on the men's side of the church, as is their custom here in Kulpahar, India. It is hard to believe that it has been a year since Steve stepped into eternity!

One of the Hindu chawkidars (guards) on duty at the gate of the church compound on Resurrection Sunday had to bring both of his primary-aged children to work with him that weekend. His wife was brutally murdered last year while he was on duty and his children in school. Now he has no one to watch his children when they are home while he is working, so he brings them with him. The mission sends over food for his children on those days. I had one left-over package of jacks, one small rubber ball, and one girl's hair band I found hiding among my clothes. No coincidence, I'm sure! I gave those to the chawkidar's son and daughter. I played a game of jacks with them, even their father played. Since I don't speak Hindi and they don't speak English, this was the best way I knew to show the children how to use the jacks. At least it would help them pass their time. Another Indian chawkidar helps tutor the children using their school books on those days, but instead of tutoring, they call it tuition. I try to bring the children a pencil, a small notebook, crayons, or sweets whenever I see them with their father so they will not dread coming to the mission with him. Again, I can see God's hand working, even in this dreadful situation. I may not be able to witness verbally to this family, but I pray they can see my God through me. Not a god of stone like theirs, but the true, living Jehovah God. This is what I try to accomplish during my safari walks when I go out to visit neighbors and Indians I pass along the road. This is helping to build rapport, as Indians are beginning to walk out to the road to see me, bringing their children for me to meet. Even though we cannot understand each other's verbal language, there is no mistaking the smiles on their faces and the look in their eyes as we take turns jabbering at each other. No translator is needed for understanding these actions.

One evening at the boys' hostel, Uttma, who speaks broken English, asked if I wanted to see his two baby parrots and three fish. Parrots are as numerous here as wrens are in the States. His baby parrots have big, colorful beaks compared to the rest of their bodies that still have no feathers. They don't seem to be afraid of us. It is hard to believe something this ugly now will look so beautiful when full grown. Just the opposite of sin, which is so attractive in the beginning, but so ugly in the end.

God's watch-care over me becomes more and more evident every day, in the most unexpected ways, at the most unexpected times and through the most unexpected people. The first time I came to Kulpahar, the three single missionary ladies told Steve that the boys needed a man to build a rapport with them and be a type of advocate to, perhaps, help the Aunties see things from their perspective instead of a woman's all the time. This is when we started going down to play volleyball with them each evening.

Two years later when just I returned, the boys asked me to again play volleyball with them, which I gladly did. Our evening volleyball games usually end at dusk after which many of the players escort me back to the girl's compound about three blocks away. Almost all of them have been brought up in the mission hostels. Tonight as we left, one of the young men said something in Hindi as he took hold of my hand while we walked. Another boy translated and said Uncle Steve used to hold my hand as we walked. He didn't know why Uncle Steve held my hand, but they would hold my hand now. Talk about feeling God's love and protection through these fellas! I let him hold my hand for a while and then started talking while pulling my hand away to gesture with it. As soon as my hand went back down to my side, a different volleyball player took hold of it. I guess Steve succeeded in building a rapport with them! And I am so blessed by it, even though this only lasted a day. Thank you, Lord! Thank you, Steve! Praise be to God who works through the unexpected!

Two weeks ago the people who are helping to keep an eye on my mobile home and car, e-mailed to say someone had tried to start a fire in two different locations on the property. One fire was down by the pond which is almost dried up. The second fire went up the side of a large tulip tree and burned the grass up to the gravel I put down around the outside of the garage. The fire marshal said with it as dry as everything was, he had no idea why the fires went out and did not spread! (We know why!)

Tonight I was told someone had tried to break into my mobile home. The sheriff said they were probably casing the place and would return later. He recommended things of value or anything I did not want to lose be removed immediately.

My heart is in my throat...

Where would they even begin to sort through all the things gathered during almost 40 years of marriage and ministry?

- Perhaps the television set that was given to us years and years ago during minister appreciation week. Being only connected to an outside antenna, it only gets three channels, but it is worth much more than any amount a thief might get by reselling it.
- Or perhaps remove the grandfather clock given as a going-away gift from the church for almost 13 years of ministry there. It's so big and heavy it would take two to three people to move since it has to remain in an upright position at all times and not be laid down.
- What about all of the Asian and African knick-knacks covering the walls and on shelves, collected and received as gifts over ten years of fifteen foreign mission assignments? What price would a thief be able to collect for all the memories they hold?
- Or all the family and ministry photos?
- How much would a sound system that plays cassettes, 33's, 45's and 78 rpm-size records be worth?

"Remove anything of value," I'm told. That would be everything the trailer holds, including the eye screw put in the top ceiling joint, the only place tall enough to hold our daughter's freshly pressed wedding gown the day before her marriage.

All this is not worth much in the eyes of the world but means the world to me.

Do I have it **all** moved out?

During the last ten years, I've lived longer outside the United States than within the USA. I didn't have all these "valuables" with me there. What difference would it be to live within the USA without them as I now live outside of the USA without them?

Maybe God is trying to tell me something. "Where your treasure is, there will your heart be also."

Perhaps that is why God gave us memories, to store all our "valuables," all our Kodak moments within us to take wherever we go, wherever we are, where no man can break in and steal them from us. It won't matter where we live then, because we'll have all our "valuables of home" within us.

The grandfather clock will stay put, as will the TV, and the stereo. I'm living without them now. I can live without them when I return, if that is in God's plan for me.

"It was by faith Abraham obeyed God's call to go to another place God promised to give him. He left his own country, not knowing where he was to go. It was by faith that he lived like a foreigner in the country God promised to give him. He lived in tents with Isaac and Jacob, who had received that same promise from God. Abraham was waiting for the city that has real foundations-the city planned and built by God." Hebrews 11: 8-10 (NCV)

As Abraham waited, so I wait.

May 2012 - Kulpahar, India and Cape Town, South Africa

One week before my assignment in India ended, I found myself with a fractured right arm having been accidentally knocked down on a sun-dried mud brick. Being in the remote village of Kulpahar, there were no hospitals close. I went in the mission car on a 20-minute drive to the village of Mahoba, where an older doctor had his practice in his home. He took an x-ray with a machine that I am sure I saw in a museum in the States. It was connected to a generator, so even when the electricity is off, it works. He waved the x-ray in the wind until it dried and then held it up to the bare light bulb to read.

Deciding the one bone in my arm was fractured, the doctor went across the road to an open-air roadside stall and brought back two of its customers for his assistants. The one man held my elbow and the other my fingers as they began pulling against each other while the doctor applied a soft cast. Plaster was only applied over the fractured area, with gauze and cotton covering the rest. This allowed room for my arm to swell and would be replaced with a permanent hard plaster cast the next week, which was two days before I flew to South Africa to begin my next assignment.

I asked Auntie Sharon, who speaks Hindi, to tell the doctor not to make the cast thick under my fingers so I could use the computer. I was within days of getting every book written in English in the mission school's library entered on an Excel sheet by title, author, publisher, place published, number of pages, price, Dewey decimal number, edition, volume, and book number. The mission school will be having an inspection at any time which is required to keep its accreditation with the government of India. The listing of every book in their library is just one of the requirements to pass that inspection. Although the doctor just smiled when I said it (I think he understood some English), he must have complied because four hours later I was trying to type again. I couldn't type nearly as fast, but God blessed me with almost pain-free mobility of my fingers at that point.

The next morning I was back in the Kulpahar Christian Mission school office in India, typing library book entries onto the Excel spreadsheet. The fingers on my fractured arm kept going numb, which kept me from feeling the computer keys, and I began typing Chinese! I would then stop and either massage my numb fingers or hold my fractured arm over my head until the feeling came back. Then I would type some more. After three hours of this, the throbbing finally won out and I called it a day. Each day after that I was able to type a little longer. Six days later I was to return to the doctor in Mahoba to have my soft cast replaced by a permanent hard-plaster cast. By then I was within two to three hours of completing my Kulpahar, India assignment by having entered every book in the school's library onto the Excel spreadsheet. All 3864 of them! That is until the electricity went off. The back-up didn't work, and I lost an entire day's worth of typing!

Traveling back to the doctor in Mahoba, I never gave a second thought to how he would remove my soft cast. I'm glad I didn't know! The doctor pounded the plaster cast until it broke the plaster and then took a razor blade and cut the entire cast off. By the time we got to the razor blade step, the pain was secondary to thoughts of wondering if an open cut under a hard plaster cast for five weeks would heal properly. My prayer life was suddenly in high gear. I thought to myself that this was surely an effective way to keep one's mind off the pain. When the soft cast finally came off, there was a huge black and blue spot under my arm from my elbow to my wrist.

The doctor left me sitting in the small room while I watched him walk across the street to the same open-air roadside stall as last time to bring a customer back with him to assist in setting my arm again. This time Sanjay, the driver of the Kulpahar mission car, was at my elbow, and the "customer assistant" was holding my fingers. Both were pulling against each other again while the doctor applied the hard plaster cast. Before leaving the mission to come to Mahoba I asked the Aunties to please tell Sanjay, who is a Christian, to ask the doctor not to make the cast so long it covered my knuckles making it impossible to use my fingers. I still had a day's work of "retyping" to finish entering the books onto the Excel sheet. Also, please not make it heavy and fat so it would not fit into my winter clothes that I would be wearing in South Africa, without having to cut the sleeves. This time the "make-shift assistants" did not twist as they pulled. Thank you, Lord!

As soon as I got back to the mission, Auntie Linda (a former nurse) and I got the scissors and "custom-fit" my cast. She did an excellent job! We only put a couple little slits at the bottom of the cast next to my elbow so the cast could expand, as it was pinching. Although my fingers did not have as much mobility as with the soft cast, I was able to return to the mission school office and finish entering all 3864 books onto the school's computer, one day before I left Kulpahar, India for my next assignment in South Africa!

Walking back to the girls' compound, I shook hands with the chawkidar (guard) to say good-bye. As I felt wetness on my arm I thought his hands had been wet from getting a drink at the road-side well. I then realized it was sweat running down my arm from under my cast and dripping off my elbow! Why wouldn't it in India's 116-degree heat?!

What is it about a new white plaster cast that people can't resist writing on it? In Delhi, storekeepers I had never seen before came up with their ink pens and asked if they could write on my cast. Naturally, some of the girls in the Kulpahar mission hostel signed my cast, as did the volleyball boys. Some drew pictures of themselves. One of the chawkidars took several minutes signing his name in English. The way he held the pen, printing so slow and concentrating on making each letter, he reminded me of the kindergarten children I taught in the States who had just learned to print their names. When finished, he hollered in Hindu at the other chawkidar to look at it. At least from their reactions I think that is what was said. He was so proud of his work. The Aunties told me later he had misspelled his name, which he had just learned to write

151

"NARADA". I had names written in Hindi, in English, in Afrikaans, and later in South Africa, one man signed using his African name. Even my Hindu neighbors signed my cast. After studying the other signatures the grandfather carefully put "his mark" that looked like an "S". He handed the pen to his son who also drew an "S", but it was backwards. The grandson then stared at their scribbles and just made a small mark that looked like a snake. Three generations, in one household, that could neither read nor write.

June, July, and August were very trying months for me physically having my right arm in a cast, then in a splint. It was during that time I received a snail-mailed letter which ended with the Scripture found in **Isaiah 41:13** *"For I am the Lord your God who takes hold of your right hand, and says to you, Do not fear; I will help you."* (NIV) The letter was written 5/21/12, I fractured my right arm 5/22/12. Once again God's perfect timing. Those words gave me strength right when I needed it most. THANK YOU, LORD!

My Bible lessons are not only difficult to write but they are even more difficult to read after having hand-written them! My hand stiffened to the point I was unable to type. It became more painful, with swelling in the fingers. An x-ray taken here in Cape Town showed I had not just fractured one bone, as the doctor in India thought, but had broken both bones in my arm, one in my hand, and torn ligaments to the fingers. Comparing it to India's x-ray which the doctor gave me, showed the one bone was pulling apart instead of healing properly. After removing the cast my arm was put in a splint and I was told to be careful with it until the hand specialist saw me three weeks later. I took very good care of my arm, babying it, protecting it, and not using it for anything which is when Reflex Sympathetic Dystrophy (RSD) set in from lack of use and shock of the injury to the arm.

The hand specialist said surgery would be counter-productive at this point, however, I could still regain 70 percent mobility in my wrist.

My fingers became swollen to the point of not being able to close them. My right shoulder and elbow started freezing up. A shot of cortisone in the shoulder only helped a little with the pain for just two weeks. I was told these are all symptoms of RSD. Because I was in the early stages of RSD, it was caught soon enough that I shouldn't have any other symptoms, but it will probably take a year to recuperate. I continue with weekly physiotherapy treatments here in Cape Town, as well as the daily two-hour therapy I do on my own. I have an appointment with a hand specialist in Indiana the second day after I return to the States just to be sure it is continuing to heal properly.

At present my fingers are always swollen, but I can still see wrinkles in the knuckles which my physiotherapist, Fazlien, says are "beautiful wrinkles" because that means the swelling isn't as bad as it could be. So I've got b-e-a-u-t-i-f-u-l winkles! Aren't you jealous!

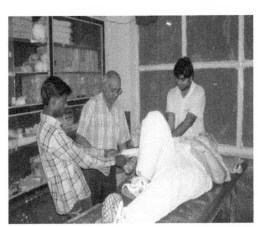

Doctor in Mahoba, India

The doctor's "assistants" were randomly found at the open-air market across the road. 2012

2013

March 2013 - Delhi and Kulpahar, India

As my train was pulling into the station in Delhi, India and slowing down, the coolies had already jumped aboard. I followed. We were the first ones on so we had plenty of room to store the luggage above my seat. I always love becoming re-acquainted with India as it passes by the giant train windows. In a land of ox carts and pony tongas, it's as if this is a place time has forgotten. Some harvesting by hand has begun of the mustard that was sown in among the wheat. It is taller and ripens first. Looking like two-feet tall yellow weeds with bushy tops, the mustard reminds me of the weeds we used to call "tickle grass" growing up. When the bushy part got into your socks or down your shirts, it would make you itch terrible!

I couldn't keep my eyes open. Whether it was because my seat was positioned so I could only see where we had been, not where we were going or that I only had five hours of sleep in the past 72 hours, I don't know, but the five-hour train ride passed quickly.

Tej, one of the railroad employees kept waking me up to see if this was my stop, if I wanted water, if I needed help with my luggage.... Thirty minutes before my stop Tej helped get my luggage to the boogie's exit door. I watched as this skinny, young looking "boy" single handedly pulled my 50-pound bags off the shelf above both our heads hardly breaking a sweat. I squeezed his upper arm and told him he was strong. He just beamed.

One of the two exits from the train had been blocked by a mound of suitcases stacked from the floor to the ceiling. Now my luggage was blocking the other exit. Tej, I and the other two railway employees were all crammed with this luggage into what space was left. We were in a narrow passage between railway cars with the only access to the outside by doors on either side of the ten to twelve-foot wide car. As the train rounded a bend the stacked suitcases blocking the one exit started to tip over, threatening to crush us for sure. We all lounged at the stack, pushing it back up while Tej rearranged some suitcases on the bottom to keep them balanced there. I thought the new arrangement wouldn't last long, but long enough for me to get off safely.

Tej looked at my hair and said, "Your hair is white. It good." as he felt it on the top. Most Indian women AND men dye their hair black. It is rare to see one with a full head of naturally whitened hair but looks so-o-o beautiful against their dark skin when you do.

One of the other railway employees was peeling an orange while sitting on top of one of the suitcases. He shared part of it with the rest of us. Seeing it peeled in front of me, I knew it was safe to eat. I started to take one segment as it was passed to me but Tej said, "I put it in," as he gently placed the orange to my mouth. I remembered the partial bag of sunflower seeds I brought from the States after cleaning out my cabinets before leaving. Retrieving the seeds from my carry-on, I poured some into one hand of each of the three railway employees. For the next ten minutes, we shared sunflower seeds in quiet. I was the only one to use the dust bin attached to the wall for my empty shells. The others spit theirs on the floor. From the looks of the boogie, I was the only one to have used the dust bin in some time.

Those few moments were so peaceful, so enjoyable, I usually only feel this content around God's children.

I wondered if these three railway employees were angels unaware?

I examined them closely to see what an angel unaware could possibly look like. There was no glow coming from their eyes, no feathers growing among their jet-black hair or out the back of their neck.

If they were angels unaware and I recognized them as such, would they really be angels unaware?

We arrived at the Jhansi station. Sanjay, the mission's driver, was one of the first smiling faces I saw in the crowd. By the time the train stopped, he was at the door. Tej unloaded my luggage. Sanjay took them from there. I could be at ease now. Turning to Tej, I wanted to hug him but knew better. As I gave him the traditional tip I squeezed his arm and thanked him. He was busy counting his tip, as he re-entered the train.

I wondered if I would see Tej on my return train trip to Delhi?

No doubt, the Lord already has it all figured out.

I just continue being blessed over and over - "Beyond what I can receive..." just for following God's will. How blessed can one be!

Ladies are not to touch men in the regular Hindu village culture, but that didn't stop me from grabbing each of the hostel boys up for a good hug and a grandma kiss on the cheek. Needless to say, they were waiting in line for them before I finished!

When the boarders leave the mission hostel to go home between terms for four weeks, it is the uncles or fathers that fetch the children. Little affection is shown in most cases. With my own eyes, I have seen daughters, who have not seen their families for months, go up and only shake hands with their fathers! And fathers who don't expect more, or want more, maybe? Many of the smaller five to seven-year-old children will stand stiff as a poker when I hug them, but before long, they loosen up. One evening last year after devotions I was taking turns hugging each child goodnight, but never seemed to get to the end. It was then I saw the child I had just hugged go to the back of the line to receive another hug. I should have remembered from it happening before, but I was enjoying it as much as the children.

April 2013 - Kulpahar, India

Jai Masih Ki! (pronounced "jah-moo-see-key") means PRAISE THE LORD in Hindi. I do not think there is a better way to describe the last seven months than these three little words we say to each other every Sunday here in Kulpahar, India. Jai Masih Ki! - Jai Masih Ki!

I am writing this from India where I have been since March 2013 assisting the Kulpahar Christian Mission. Leah Moshier, one of the three permanent resident missionaries with the mission, is now enjoying her eternal residency with her Maker. All the responsibilities of the mission are now being shouldered by the remaining two, Linda Stanton and Sharon Cunningham, who asked my help, not just this year but next, as well. You may remember, it was here I broke my arm in May 2012, just two weeks before traveling to South Africa for back to back assignments.

In South Africa they thought I would be able to regain 70 percent mobility of my hand through therapy, and I began a rigorous course of action. Somehow, one of the bones in my wrist/arm moved in the healing process and positioned itself so that it is longer than the other bone in the wrist. With the longer bone partially blocking my wrist joint, it prevents my wrist from moving as it should. From South Africa, I made an appointment with a hand specialist in Indiana for the second day after returning to the States, which wasn't until four months after breaking my arm. It was then I learned my arm had been "mismanaged," leaving me with a permanently deformed hand. Two therapists in the States, Ashim and Nathalie, continued trying to help me achieve 70 percent mobility, which is considered functional, through aggressive therapy, but my hand didn't respond. After seven months of continuous therapy in three different countries, outpatient surgery was finally done four days before Christmas 2012.

I didn't see that much difference after the surgery, but the therapist said there was. Therapy continued for two more months. I was released two weeks before leaving on my next mission assignment here in India where I am presently working in the Kulpahar mission school library to assist in satisfying government requirements for the school to maintain its national certification.

Measurements of my hand during that last therapy session showed I had achieved 50 percent mobility. I was told I still had a "window of opportunity" until mid-June 2013 to possibly improve my mobility; therefore, I continue doing therapy exercises daily. I also have a splint I try using twice a day which forces the palm of my right hand into an upright position like to receive change from a cashier. This upward position is achieved immediately after removing the splint, but within an hour the hand is back to its former neutral position. I force my bum hand to try and do everything I ask of the other hand, but it sometimes gets in the way more than it helps and has trouble holding anything. Guess the reality of what that deformity means in actual functioning (or dis-functioning) has been made ever so clear. It puts a kink in and limits me in everything I do. I'll never play volleyball again, or softball, or basketball like before. My fingers won't straighten. I can't throw a softball over-handed from second base to even make a play at first. With my curved fingers the ball just falls ten feet on the ground in front of my feet. I especially notice the deformity when trying to type on the laptop. Because of it the fingers on my bum hand can't position themselves or stay on the proper keys. After typing or writing a long time, my crooked fingers get stiff, hurt, and I continually hit the wrong keys, but at least I can type. I am trying to adapt.

Overnight I became an old woman. They say you are only as old as you think you are. Guess that makes me 102. I think I know how Hannah must have felt when her heart's desire of having a child kept her from seeing the blessings God already had surrounding her. I just have to keep reminding myself, God did not rescue Shadrach, Meshack, and Abednego from the fiery furnace, God saved them IN the fiery furnace.

I am thankful I can do more now with my hand than when I arrived back in the States. I can pop ice cubes out of their tray, open a can of soup without spilling most of the broth, twist fresh pepper out of a pepper-grinder, and balance silverware between my fingers to eat without embarrassing myself. I am grateful for every little improvement.

Although I'd rather not have had this broken arm, I have been blessed in so many ways through it:

1. Getting to witness to my Muslim therapist in South Africa, as well as the entire room of patients/therapists who were continually listening to our conversations about the Quran, Mohammad, Holy Scriptures, and Christ, all during Ramadan!

2. Being introduced to Ashim, my Hindu therapist in Indiana, whom I think God led me to in order to plant seeds, or water, or witness, or build on the foundation coworkers already had laid.

3. Getting to really "know" my other Indiana therapist, Nathalie and her family (previously just an acquaintance), who made my recovery her personal mission.

159

4. Continually being ministered to by the saints at Union Christian, Saltair and First Christian.

5. Continually being uplifted in prayer by fellow sisters and brothers in Christ when I could barely keep my head above water both physically and spiritually.

6. Teaching me so many better ways to do things, look at people, and handle situations.

7. Strengthening my faith by learning to walk without sight and getting to know the depth of God's heart.

8. Feeling His presence.

9. Letting the trials shape my heart to be more like His.

10. Learning to trust just by knowing He was there.

11. Learning it is only by becoming completely empty that God can work through me in a more powerful way.

12. Seeing the little miracles He continually sends to keep me encouraged.

13. Finding His grace is sufficient.

I traded a little deformity in my right hand for all these blessings for the rest of my life. I think I came out on top with this deal.

I've decided to sanctify/dedicate my right hand to God. Is there such a thing? To sanctify something is to set it apart for God's use. Maybe I should sanctify my entire being. But I feel I did that when I accepted Him as Lord of my life and was baptized. ANYWAY, from now on I'm calling my bum right hand, my "God-hand". When I think of it in this way, I focus on watching all the ways the Lord uses my "God-hand" in spite of its limitations. As Nathalie pointed out, I HAVE MY HAND AND IT WORKS! I AM BLESSED!

Today was an absolutely wonderful day! It didn't begin that way. Yesterday, four Hindu day workers, disgruntled for not receiving a full day's pay for half a day's work, gathered a group of men to cause trouble on our mission compound. Some were carrying sticks. The walled compound, gated entrance, and chawkidar (unarmed guard) kept the group from entering. The police were called, and the four men were taken to the police station for questioning. Other mission personnel were also questioned. Two of the four workers were jailed.

This morning started with them lying on the road, with their pillows, to block the compound entrance. As this is the only way in or out of our compound, I always pass through this gate in the morning, walking to work at the school compound. It is approximately three to four blocks away. I did not realize they were still at the gate when I started walking to work. Just before I reached the gate, Uttam, who "just happened" to be driving the jeep from our compound to the school compound, stopped by my side.

Uttam, in his 30's, was raised in the mission hostel. I first met him in 2010 when he rode shotgun for the mission driver who picked Steve and me up at the train station in Jhansi, a four-hour drive from the mission compound in Kulpahar. We were later told that Uttam was reluctant to come because he could not speak/understand English well. We have become very good friends, doing lots of our talking, not only with words but hand gestures. Uttam speaks and understands English better so I can now tease him a bit, which he dishes right back.

Uttam was wearing his devilish grin when he stopped by my side. Without saying a word, I knew he was offering me a ride. I so enjoy Uttam's company that I couldn't get in the jeep fast enough. As soon as I shut the door, we began teasing, while he continued driving to the compound wall. When the chawkidar opened the gate, there was the group of men! Immediately, we both stopped talking.

One of the men was lying on the road, looking at us defiantly. As Uttam drove closer, the man did not budge. Uttam was able to squeeze between the gate, the group, and the man lying on the road without touching any of them. The calmness with which he maneuvered the jeep helped me keep a nonchalant look on my face. As we passed within inches of the men, I tried not to make direct eye contact with any of them, fearing it might provoke an incident. The entire time I have been here, only once have I ridden to work. Without a doubt, God had arranged my ride today, using my good friend, Uttam, whose friendship is even closer after this morning.

June 2013 - Staunton, Indiana

Three days before I left the States, Trinity, Joy and I drove to Illinois, to The Mound Cemetery to visit Steve one last time. As I walked to Steve's grave, memories swarmed through my mind.

Standing by his headstone, one can see for miles in every direction. Is this what I came to see?

Steve's mortal remains certainly lay at rest there, but they would be indistinguishable from the other "God-made" dirt which formed this sacred place.

Why did I come? Steve was not here.

He lives on in the spirit of every preacher who steps behind the pulpit Sunday after Sunday proclaiming the words God has put on their hearts to share with His people.

Now, my only constant kisses are the drops of rain I felt on my cheek that day. Or were they tears?

Two years have passed. Where did the time go?

It seems like only yesterday we were sharing extra value Happy Meals, swapping stories of how our day had gone, sharing conversations we had had with others, sharing a table together, sharing a home, sharing a bed, sharing a ministry, sharing a life.

After almost 40 years of marriage, so familiar with each other had we become, we even knew what the other was thinking. We completed each other's sentences.

Our hearts beat as one. Then, one of those hearts stopped beating.

The conversations stopped, meals were no longer happy, eating at the table became a quick bite while standing at the sink. The bed became cold. The home became a house.

It was as if two hearts had stopped that day.

When I heard him gasp his last breath, when I wiped away the lone tear that trickled down his cheek, it was no longer my husband sitting by my side. It looked like him but that soon faded. Only an empty shell was left. I could no longer "feel" him with me.

I looked up, wondering if he was watching.

Two years. It seems like only yesterday.

Two years. It seems like a million years.

A million years since sharing a meal. A million years since feeling his touch. A million years since seeing his smile, hearing him pray, discussing Scripture. A million years since sharing his life.

"I will give you a new heart and put a new spirit in you; I will remove from you your heart of stone and give you a heart of flesh." Ezekiel 36:26. (NIV)

The love I thought was lost, God is multiplying over and over in the people to whom He is sending me.

The more I love, the more I am loved.

My emptiness is gradually being filled with the joy of serving the Lord.

But today, I am remembering.

Love and Prayers,
Only me

September 2013 - Hong Kong and China

One of the attendees of the New Testament Church of Christ Hong Kong, that is the church with which I am working, lives in China. His name is King Kong. Kong has an excellent command of the English language, which he attributes to watching movies in English on television. He sometimes makes the four-hour round trip to the YMCA building in Hong Kong to attend our church services. King Kong tutors Chinese in English and had just taken on a new 9-year-old student. The father, Mr. Lee, owns and operates a factory in Shenzhen, China which is just across the Hong Kong border. His 18-year-old son is also struggling with English.

Mr. Kong suggested I come to China to have lunch with the family and interact with the children in English. I did so this week. I was glad Kong was there as the daughter had only had three English lessons and the son had forgotten most of the English he had been taught, never having a chance to use it with foreigners. Kong, trying to make a good impression with Mr. Lee, kept dominating the conversation I was trying to have with the son who sat by me.

The son was embarrassed to practice his English with the tutor present and the nine-year-old daughter, being a typical child with no interest, refused to even try. Thankfully, Kong had to answer calls on his cell phone, allowing the son and I to interact. To keep him from being so self-conscious, I attempted to make him the teacher instead of the student. I pointed to the tea in my tiny, handle-less Chinese cup and said, "Chai." Then said, "Tea." Pointing to the roasted pigeon, which was part of our lunch, I looked at him questioningly while shrugging my shoulders. The son gave me the Chinese word for it. I tried repeating it but failed miserably. The son said it again. Already sitting close to him during the meal, I took my glasses off, put my God-hand on his shoulder, got within inches of his mouth to see the way his tongue formed the word. The son was not embarrassed by my action but moved his hand away from his mouth for me to get a better view. When I thought I had it, I looked at the daughter and repeated my new Chinese word. Not satisfied with my pronunciation, she now began repeating the word for me, which I said after her each time. When she was finally satisfied with my Chinese, I pointed to the pigeon, said it in Chinese and then in English. To my amazement, the daughter repeated, "Pigeon" in English as did the son and even the mother! By then Kong was back, but my bond with the family had been solidified.

With a typhoon coming, it was beginning to rain harder out-side. Mr. Lee's factory was just down the road for him to return to work. Mrs. Lee was going to drive the tutor and me to the bus stop.

The others ran ahead to get in the car. As I started to follow, the son, who was as tall as me, put his hand on my shoulder. I turned around. His eyes were searching, as if he wanted to say something, but was struggling for the words. I gave him a big hug. He hugged me back. Then I took off running for the car.

I love wayside opportunities!

My last Sunday with the New Testament Church of Christ Hong Kong is not one I will soon forget! I was so humbled to receive the many gifts and kind words. Especially dear to my heart were the two shirts the church gave me. One had Scripture on the front and "We Love You" on the back. The second shirt that someone hand-carried from Manilla just for me was embroidered with their Philippine Islands! I was also given a book in which there were individual, personal notes from them to me and an album of laminated pictures of our times together. I was also given a glowing letter of recommendation, signed by almost EVERYONE IN THE CONGREGATION, to use for a future reference! In giving the gifts, church representative Vilma said, "Our hearts grow with yours so quickly." She then asked if they could renew my contract. (I had no contract. Vilma was jokingly referring to the contract Filipinos sign to come work in Hong Kong that is renewed every two years if their work is satisfactory.)

The Chinese Tai Chi exercise group with whom I participated every morning but Sunday treated me to dim sum my last day. (Light snacks with lots of chai hot tea.) I was not asked to come to Hong Kong to work among these Chinese ladies. It just happened (we know nothing "just happens") that I was invited to join in their daily outdoor exercising. I did not enjoy exercising, but knew I needed it. It got me out of the hot flat for a couple hours and made me EVEN

HOTTER, so when I returned to the flat it didn't seem so hot. Does that make any sense? The main reason I continued exercising was I loved the Chinese ladies with which I did it, even though most did not speak any English except Hello and Good-bye! Some of the ladies had been in the class for ten to fifteen years. Of course, they knew all the exercise steps by heart. I REALLY struggled to even keep up! I could either do the steps or do the arm motions but not both together. I finally learned to laugh at myself when I couldn't keep up with them. That made them smile too. Mrs. Du, who is married to an atheist Marxist, would run back and try to give me individual tutoring, but my jumbled steps sometimes threw her off too! Then everyone watching would giggle. Have you ever seen a Chinese lady giggle? It's contagious!

One exercise was so fast and complicated. I just sat down and watched them. During this one they exercised their hips. Seeing 40, 50, 60, and a couple 70-year-olds wiggle their hips was more than I could watch without laughing. I tried to muffle my laughter at first, afraid I would hurt their feelings or embarrass them, but I just couldn't contain myself. When I saw that the Chinese ladies were smiling too, I no longer held my laughter in. Before it was over, we were all laughing. Every time they came to that hip-wiggling part of the exercise, some would exaggerate their hip motions, which made it even funnier! That exercise is my favorite! (Perhaps because I don't do it!)

Hing, a 50-year-old mother who spoke no English told me through her 16-year-old daughter who had an excellent command of the English language that I was "Positive light in group. The center. It fun now." My last morning with them, Connie, a widowed Chinese lady in her early 50's, said she needed to be "more happy like you." I told her my happiness came after I became a Christian. "You happy after you found your God?" Connie asked.

Helen Jew, a Christian Chinese, born in the States, still exercises with them daily. Whatever seeds have been planted, Helen is there, perhaps God-placed, to water, cultivate and continue sowing. My last words to these caring Chinese ladies, who had taken me under their wing and allowed me to wiggle into their hearts, were the same words I spoke every time I left them after dim sum, "I love you," which they laughingly mimicked back with a deep Asian accent, "I love you."

This is just another of the many "wayside opportunities" God always allows me to enjoy those small daily happenings that make life so incredible, the moments that will never again present themselves for one to pass on to others, the love that has been so bountifully showered upon us. How many wayside opportunities have you taken advantage of to spread God's love? They don't just happen over here, you know.

October 2013 - Guinea, West Africa

I sent an e-mail to all 512 addresses on the MRS e-mail list telling about how the pilot light of our oven has to be lit every time we use it. Of course, it is located all the way to the back of the stove at the bottom. We actually have to lie halfway on the floor to light it with one hand, while pushing the oven knob in with the other and holding it for at least a minute or it goes out. Then, you have to start the whole process all over again! It's a real challenge for my God-hand. The oven knob is worn off and doesn't fit tightly enough to turn so we switch knobs with one of the burners until it is lit, then switch back, hoping we put the oven knob in the correct position to be able to adjust the heat to the proper temperature in the oven.

Two days after I sent that e-mail out, the pilot light stayed lit! We haven't had to re-light it since!

In that same e-mail, I told of sharing the mission house with three (soon to be five) other single, young ladies. One of us didn't get the Tupperware lid back on tight on the giant sugar container so we had gobs of tiny ants in our sugar.

Again, a few days after sending that e-mail, there were no more ants in the container! Whether they got their fill and left, or we ate them, I don't know. I DO know they are ALL GONE and I figure it is in direct response to your prayers!

Not only do I praise God for such small blessings that are felt in such big ways, but I am constantly thanking Him for YOU, knowing it is the power of your prayers that continually smooth the way for me wherever I am: physically, emotionally, and spiritually!

Thank you, Lord! And thank YOU!

December 2013 - Guinea, West Africa

My Hong Kong assignment was completed in September. I flew directly to Conakry, Guinea, West Africa to assist Pioneer Bible Translators, who have several missionary families on furlough in the States until the end of the year. I landed in the middle of Guinea's continued struggle to have parliamentary elections. Guinean parliamentary elections are to take place within six months after the swearing in of a new president. Their new president took office THREE years ago. There were 1170 candidates running for the 114 seats in parliament.

My duties here in Guinea are mainly to assist Pioneer Bible Translators' (PBT's) financial office, checking team reimbursement reports for proper supporting documentation, making and e-mailing reimbursement requests to PBT's main office in Dallas, Texas, assisting in reconciling weekly and monthly reports, and helping with the weekly cash count of all funds in the office. The Guinea frank is the currency used here and it is essential that PBT keep a sufficient supply of USD and GNP in the office. All 31 missionary teams, their ministries, plus all PBT interns coming to or living in Guinea, pass through our office to exchange USD for GNF or withdraw from their stateside work funds and living link accounts. I am also working on a newly-installed Excel inventory program for the auto shop on PBT's computer in which I hope to make 1900 entries before I leave in order to make it current. If I am successful, I've been told this will be the first time the branch has ever had an accurate accounting of all their auto parts.

The first month here I cooked a meal every day for a single, young lady missionary from Holland named Janneke, who suddenly fell ill while in the Christian Missionary Alliance guesthouse that shares this mission compound with PBT. Her mission society finally called her back to Holland on a medical emergency flight. She lost all energy, had trouble breathing, and was down to ninety pounds when she left. The area where she ministers as a registered nurse is in a valley that is constantly wet. Mildew abounds! The sun does not shine enough for her to hardly ever get washed clothes dry. She breathes mildew spores continually. Since arriving back in the Netherlands, her health has improved.

Conakry International Christian Fellowship meets in our mission compound every Sunday evening. (Steve preached for them a few times.) Missionaries of different denominations and humanitarian organizations take turns leading the service. Fifteen to twenty of the wives from the International Fellowship meet in our living room every Friday afternoon for Ladies Bible Study every other week. The off weeks, we use the two hours to pray. It is so uplifting to hear the heart-felt prayers of others and be encouraged through them.

I have never seen such brotherhood among believers despite denominational backgrounds. Perhaps, as one missionary wife observed, it is essential to survive on such a hard mission field. It is not uncommon to see different ministries share everything from strategies, to ministry resources, to home schooling books, to secular contacts, to best places to go for the best prices, to recipes, to local restaurants where one can eat without getting sick afterwards. It must tickle God's heart to see His children caring for and getting along with each other so well. I think Americans miss out on this because of all the luxuries with which they are blessed, perhaps relying on them instead of each other. If only they knew...

A young man called out to me as I was trying to find my way to a refugee church and an old friend Steve and I had made five years earlier on an assignment in Conakry. I turned around and tried to ask him of the Sierra Leone refugee family. He could speak some English, so for the next ten minutes, God helped us "communicate" somehow. I knew Joseph, a father and minister of the church had died, but I was inquiring about his family. They were still in Guinea, and I think they were still going to worship at the refugee church which is now conducted in French and English. Thinking I would attend church there, I tried to find out where they met but was afraid to follow the vague direction of one finger pointing "that way". I knew God's hand was in my missing the road to the church when the young man got out his cell phone and started to call Joseph's wife! He not only knew her but had her phone number! After five years and with over two million people in Conakry and I accidentally bump into a man that has the phone number I need! Coincidence? I don't think so! Who but God?!

I have acquired a variety of names during my three assignments this year. In India, the hostel children and cricket boys continue to call me Auntie, which is a sign of respect and endearment. In Hong Kong, the church referred to me as Sister Janeece when I was behind the pulpit teaching, but outside of the services, some Filipinos called me Mommy. Here in Guinea, the Guineans refer to me as MaMa whether it is here on the compound where they know me or in the market where they don't know me. My white hair is the main reason for this. Whether in Hong Kong, Africa, or India, white hair gains a person respect. I could be dumber than a box of rocks, but my white hair automatically ensures I am treated with respect. After the town hall meeting in the US Embassy in September one of the consulates took me on a tour of the embassy and its grounds. He called me a "TDY'er" meaning "temporary duty" in embassy lingo. Of all these titles, I think the ones I like best are Grandma and Mom, which I'm really looking forward to hearing again, just in time for my granddaughter's ninth birthday on December 13th. These past ten months have passed quickly, but I'm chomping at the bit to get home, even if it is only for seven weeks.

Janeece working on the mission computer after breaking her arm.
Kulpahar, India - 2012

2014

January 2014 - Terre Haute, Indiana

Excerpt from e-mail:

My Dear, Dear Friend,

I do so appreciate your concern for my well-being. I have considered your suggestion of accepting MRS' offer to begin paying me a salary but: *Our* mobile home was paid for years ago, as were our two vehicles. The land where the trailer sits belongs to a former deacon in the Staunton church who lets us live on his property in the woods free of charge as long as we keep it mowed. Now, I do not know how God did it, but Steve and I never lacked for anything we needed for the past 12 years of being with MRS and we never took a salary. For me to change now would be as if I did not believe God would or could continue taking care of me as He has always done. The moment I put our financial concerns into His hands and just lived as frugally was possible was the day I learned He CAN do it without me or my worrying.

Sometimes, I do look at the shiny new cars and big homes others have and think that would be nice, but then I would do nothing but worry while on the field. I'd worry about someone breaking into the house, worry about the car being stolen, worry that the bright sunlight was fading the car's paint. I have enough trouble reconciling all my physical blessings while working among people who feel rich just to have two sets of clothing to wear.

I have seen and helped too many little old people try to decide what few possessions they will move with them into a tiny assisted living apartment or into one side of a small room in a nursing home. Their life-time accumulation of things, once so important, was left to sit and rust or gather dust or be auctioned off at pennies on the dollar compared to what was paid for them.

The people to whom fancy cars and mansions are most important are people to whom I would never be able to measure up no matter what I drove or where I lived. They would not make very good friends for they would be too busy hiding flaws and being too concerned about how they were viewed by others. I am content where God has me.

I always think of the family our trio (Andy, you and I) went to eat lunch with after church one Sunday morning, back in the boonies of Kentucky or West Virginia. The kitchen was so small, only I was able to be in there with the mother. In the other room, the small table was right next to the bed with a pop-bellied wood stove that heated the entire home positioned at the end. Andy and you sat on the bed to talk with the father who had the only leisure chair, a wooden rocker, of course. I'm not sure if we sat on a bench at the table or on the side of the bed to eat lunch. Those are the only two rooms I remember, but the hospitality and love shown to us was greater than we had ever experienced anywhere else. The food cooked over a wood stove was so delicious! They didn't even have running water, yet I can't remember ever feeling more welcomed than there.

Thank you for your concern but I truly believe I am smack-dab in the center of His will for me and am not eager to make any changes. If I'm REALLY blessed, I'll be "coming home" soon anyway so I won't need any retirement!

March 2014 - Terre Haute, Indiana and India

I must apologize. Just before returning to the States in December after having nothing but hot, hot, HOT summer weather for almost the entire ten months of my three assignments in 2013, I told God I did not want to waste a prayer request (Can one ever waste a prayer request?!) but if He could see it in His heart to have a little snow while I was home, I'd surely appreciate it. I guess God has a BIG heart! Indiana had one of the highest recorded snowfalls in years! YIPEEEEE! THANK YOU, LORD!

Trinity, my granddaughter, and I took full advantage of every one of those "severe winter snow-storms," too! We had snow ice cream, went sledding, ate snow ice cream, tracked deer and rabbit paw prints in the snow, ate snow ice cream, put bread crumbs out for the birds, squirrels, and wild turkeys, ate snow ice cream, used a broom to knock down icicles for Trinity to catch to quench our thirst, and did I say, we ate snow ice cream?

The snow, which at one point was almost to my knees, was too deep to make snow angels in the open. The snow on the ground around us would fall on top of us. We had to make them under one of our giant, long-needle, pine trees where the snow wasn't as deep. Unfortunately, we both laid down in the snow at the same time to make our snow angels. BIG mistake! There was no one to help either of us get up without destroying our snow angel! No problem. We just made more! At one point, the snow was so deep, we had trouble pushing open the trailer doors. Trinity and I were snowbound for six days! Everyone was cancelling everything, including church, so we had our own. With the wind chill factor, the temperature dipped to 30 degrees BELOW ZERO for several days in a row. That's when my water pipes froze. But God took care of us, waking me up in the middle of the night with what sounded like a cell phone ringing. Seeing it was 4 a.m. and not hearing another ring, I snuggled up to Trinity to go back to sleep. Hearing it again, I got up and discovered the water had frozen. Going outside, I found myself standing in one and one-half feet of snow. I dug my way back to the trailer where I crawled under the trailer to plug in the heat tape and a space heater. Within 20 minutes we had water again! Talk about a kiss from God!

"The angel of the Lord encamps around those who fear Him, and He delivers them." Psalm 34:7 (NIV)

My seven weeks in the States passed way too quickly. I was not yet prepared to leave so soon, but thanks to so many prayers, so much love, such encouraging words, and actions by so many, by the time I got to the airport, I was ready. As I have said again and again, YOU are a big part of the reason I am here! I do not know how I could have left again so soon without your help in preparing me mentally, emotionally, and spiritually! I thank God for all of you over and over.

God did not wait to reveal His "angel unaware" that seems to always be just where and when I need one the most. Again, it was through my check-in ticket agent at the airport. When leaving the counter I asked his name. The ticket agent said, "Angel." Not believing my ears, I looked at his name tag. Sure enough, it was Angel. God did not even try to conceal His helper this time. It wasn't until two hours later that I discovered how much Angel had blessed me. When I started to go through security, I found I was already prescreened. I didn't have to take off my shoes, remove the laptop from my carry-on, display my liquids, get patted down, or even open my carry-on! I can't wait for my assignments to continue to see what else God has in store for me!

Isn't it something how God shows Himself to us even in our daily lives?! I was looking everywhere for a little coin bag I had packed to conceal money but just couldn't find it. I started to pray for God to help me do so when I decided I didn't want to bother Him with something so small and unimportant. Immediately, the thought came into my head where I had packed it. Sure enough, it was there. I just laughed and thanked God out loud, KNOWING it was He who planted that thought! I really think He was telling me that NOTHING is too insignificant to pray about, so I'm changing my prayer habits. I now pray about every little thing no matter how tiny I think it is. Yesterday I even prayed concerning the perfect shape of a tree I saw. Goodness! God is going to regret He ever put that thought in my head!

Last night, I came out of the bungalow to walk to the other mission compound. The girls were all still inside their hostel as study hours were not finished for them to be out playing. As soon as I went out the door, twelve small hostel boys (kindergarten to class two) came running to me from playing on the girl's swings. I am bonding more and more with the new younger boys who are not waiting for me to hug them. Now they run to me and start the hugging! As the boys are NOT allowed into the girl's compound, I was wondering why they were here, especially when I did not see an escort or chaperone. They asked if I was going to play cricket. When I said yes, they swarmed around me like a Queen Bee!

One morning, before the girls left for school, I was hugging them. As I turned to leave, a girl, whom I must have missed, hurried up to me and said, "Squeeze me too!" Sometimes, I kiss them on their head or cheek but missed one who told me, "I want kissie too!" I'm not kissing their heads as much after feeling something crawling on my face immediately after kissing a head. Lice are sometimes a problem for them because they have such long, thick hair.

Besides teaching the ladies weekly Bible study and interacting with the hostel children, I also work in the mission school library/office every day. The mission library has acquired more books that have to be processed. As I was walking to work this past week, I noticed many people with infirmities gathering at the roadside. Most were on crutches, but several were pulling themselves along the ground with their hands. A brightly colored, small, square tent with no top had been erected down a lane, just outside the wall of the mission compound. A loudspeaker was blaring in Hindi. I thought there was going to be a healing service of some type but was later told a politician was coming that afternoon. After his speech, he gave away adult-sized handicapped tricycles that were pedaled by hands instead of feet. With parliamentary elections this year politicians here in India are out "politicking." That evening I went to Phoebe (the ladies Bible study I teach every time I come to Kulpahar) I passed ten very happy individuals, who are now able to get around a little easier. I wonder who they will vote for?

I was being escorted back to the girl's compound by my interpreter, Jolly, after teaching Phoebe one evening. Our Hindu neighbors were loading stubble onto the back of an ox cart. The Hindu lady, who had been sitting in the cart, had to move for lack of room. She was watching me as we approached. I immediately went to her and gave the customary Indian greeting while patting her on the arm and taking hold of her hand. She smiled, showing terribly deformed, irregular teeth. Besides being dirty, her hands felt like they were covered in dried sand. I don't know whether it was from handling wet stalks of grain all day, or from mixing dirt with stubble and cow dung to make what I call cow patties These are used as fuel for the fire to cook their meals. Both the woman and the man driving the ox cart, who I assumed was her husband, looked like they had put in a long, hard day in the fields. Their clothes were almost as dirty as their hands. The pair of oxen, which pulled the cart, were also covered with partially dried mud, indicating they must have been out in the evening showers. Through Jolly, I asked if I could take a picture of the lady and myself. The man nodded sideways, the traditional Indian reply for yes. Just before the photo was snapped, I said to smile, which Jolly interpreted. The lady, in Hindi, said she did not smile because her teeth are not good. I immediately put my arm around her shoulder and hugged her. Instantly, a smile came across her face for the picture. In fact, when Jolly took a picture of all of us with the cart and oxen, she smiled again. Her husband was talking to Jolly through all of this. After we left them, Jolly said the man told him, "It hard to find rich, clean person who even talk to us. We are poor and dirty. They hate us... not she." I wanted to cry.

That Sunday, as I was walking home from church, I passed the man and wife on the ox cart going the other way. He stopped the ox cart, while calling to me in Hindi, motioning for me to come sit by him on the tongue of the ox cart immediately behind the oxen. The small cart was almost full of women and children that I assumed to be his family. I would love to have sat on the tongue of the cart but did not think I could climb up on it wearing my Sunday duds. I did NOT want to embarrass myself trying to maneuver in the eight inches of space between the cart and the hineys of the oxen. I also did not think it proper for me to be sitting by him, anyway. I sat down on the back edge of the cart when one of the children scooted over. The man nudged the oxen and off we went at a walk. I was enjoying the ride until the ladies motioned for me to hang onto the side of the cart, which I did. It was then the man put the oxen in high gear! We were bouncing down the road so hard in that wooden cart that I could not keep hold of my Bible, song book, coat and the cart! Thinking we were only going a couple feet, I just sat on the edge of the cart but was now close to losing even that with every bounce! I started saying WHOA-A-A-A, knowing they could not understand, but we were almost past the school compound with no attempt at slowing down in sight! It was then that the wooden ox cart wheels hit the three consecutive speed bumps (they call them speed breaks) positioned just inches apart outside the school gate. The aunties had tried for years and years to get them installed to slow scooters and motorcycles that have, on occasion, hit a school child. I had always thought of them as a blessing - not anymore! Steve once cracked a tooth on one of these very rough roads. I thought perhaps I was going to crack something too, but it would not be my tooth!

By now, the cart was coming apart, starting with the freshly cut, flimsy bamboo poles I was hanging on to for dear life with my God-hand. Just as I was ready to jump off, the cart slowed to a stop. I immediately got off before the driver changed his mind and started practicing his oxen for the Kentucky Derby again! The school chawkidars (guards) came over laughing and helped push pieces of the cart back together. I was now twice the distance from where I was going, full of splinters, but more than happy to be on my own two feet walking at my own speed - SLOW!

Following this assignment in India, I will be flying directly to Italy to be with Pioneer Bible Translators, ending 2014 with an assignment in South Africa. Lord willin', I will be back in the States this fall.

April 2014 - India

The second week of April I took the overnight Sampkranti train from the Kulpahar Station to Delhi. The purpose of this trip was to buy a guitar to be used in Kulpahar worship. After being told the price of the guitar I was interested in, I realized that for the amount I had set aside, I could buy two guitars. With not just one guitar but two to take back, I was anxious to return.

My return train trip *was* eventful! I was the only woman in the small twelve feet by eight feet cubical with built-in bunk beds. The only partition that separated me from my three other bunkmates was my closed eyelids. A grandpa sat across from me. When his son, daughter-in-law and granddaughter left the train after helping him on, the son touched his father's feet, then pressed that hand against his head and his mouth as a sign of respect. The Christians here do not practice this.

Grandpa talked up a storm for the first hour. Sitting with his legs crossed, he would pick his nose, then drop it on his ankle to inspect. I was eating the food Ruth gave me but was quickly losing my appetite by watching. In the middle of his conversation, Grandpa leaned over and tooted without missing a beat! Here I was afraid my sweaty feet would stink up the bogie (the train's car/carriage). It was then Grandpa reached over, using the hand that had been picking his nose and took a potato chip from the bag that I had offered him earlier. He asked me, "America chip?' When I replied, "No, India," he proceeded to drop it back in the bag. Needless to say, I was finished eating. My appetite was completely gone! Not knowing if Grandpa was trustworthy, I didn't dare leave my luggage there to walk to another part of the bogie for a breath of fresh air.

While making his bed with the two dingy sheets, blanket, and pillow provided by the train attendant, Grandpa threw all his belongings on my bed. I cringed. The "Don't ask - Don't tell" policy now made sense to me! The blanket I was given had the oily image of a body down the middle like the Shroud of Turin. The pillow had black hairs on it, so I KNEW they weren't from me! Nine hours was too long a ride to not use them! I tried to reason with myself that even the blankets on most airplanes, which are wrapped in plastic, have hair on them. That didn't make me feel any better, but it was so cold I thought icicles were going to form on my nose. I wondered what the unreserved bogies were like. One of the young men from the mission rode a train with a cobra in a basket that someone brought along to observe one of the Hindu holidays. With no reserved seating in those bogies, people push luggage through the train's windows and start climbing in the windows even before the train stops at the station creating a very dangerous situation for both those inside the bogie and out.

I thought it was going to be a long night, but I slept soundly, only awakening once to see our fourth bunkmate enter our cubical. He took his clothes off and hung them carefully on a peg so as not to wrinkle them, then slept in his underwear under his blanket. I reasoned with myself that he wasn't dressed any differently than our Hindu neighbor at Kulpahar who went everywhere in his underwear in the mornings and always wanted to talk or wave to me dressed as such. This is what keeps these mission trips so interesting! One NEVER knows what's coming next and it's so "faith-building" to see God get me through them! At least this time no one ate food in the upper bunk with crumbs trickling down on me or had food so spicy hot it made MY eyes water!

The train conductor came by to see our tickets. Running his finger through my hair, he said. "Your hair very fine." Although I had never seen this man before, I decided if he could run his fingers through my hair, I could talk to him about God. I inquired, "Do you go to church?" He responded, "I Hindu," to which I responded, "I worship Jehovah God." I was taken back when the conductor then said, "I a Christian. I know Christian B-I-G worship - twenty-five December - Christmas. I like very much." He then continued through the rest of the bogie, checking tickets. I never saw him again. I did learn something this trip. Snoring is the same in any language!

May 2014 - Milan, Italy

Finishing my assignment in India after the return of Auntie Sharon from furlough, I flew to Milan, Italy. There I was met by Pioneer Bible Translators. I worked with them last year in Guinea, West Africa. They had just moved one of their offices from Guinea to Breme, Italy. Not all of their boxes and trunks had been unpacked. The wife had fallen twice before leaving Guinea and her knees were now causing her much pain. A trip to the doctor revealed she had torn the meniscus in one knee and badly bruised the bones in the other. She was ordered to be on bed rest for one month. Keeping a missionary on bed rest is a little like trying to nail Jell-O to the wall - Impossible! God's timing for me to be there was perfect, as always.

Although I did not get to work directly with the people of Italy, I did get to weed, water and hoe in the PBT garden located just outside the front door. It was the first time in 12 years I was able to work in a garden. With the schedule of our MRS assignments over the years, we had not been home at the proper time to either plant, cultivate, or harvest our own garden. Now, the only home-grown veggies I get are the ones canned and given to me by Juanita, Steve's mom, who is no longer able to can like she used to.

God's continued watch-care over me was especially prevalent while traveling in Italy, such as missing a train whose departure time was moved up with no notification but catching another train just two hours later without paying one extra euro. (I'm sure it was all in God's plan as I was able to speak to an 18-year-old boy from Hong Kong concerning his salvation on the rebooked train.) Or, falling asleep on the train after a sleepless night, God awakened me five minutes before my stop. Or having other travelers (angels unaware, I'm sure!) help with my luggage when porters were unavailable. Or seeing illegal porters "shake down" another "lone traveler" sitting close by, but earlier, they had helped me with my luggage. Or waiting my turn at the train stop to fetch my bags from the luggage coach when an illegal porter, posing as a passenger, tried to walk away with MY luggage! (I let him carry my two fifty-pound bags out of the luggage coach and down the stairs before I stopped him. Teehee.) Who but God could arrange every little detail with such exact timing?!

God's watch-care didn't stop there. In February, just minutes before I was to leave home for the airport, I noticed my mission wedding band was missing from my finger. Steve and I never wore our original wedding bands on the mission field, having been warned they could target us as being rich. Instead, in South Africa, we bought cheap, three-colored, copper bands worth less than fifty cents each which we referred to as our mission wedding bands. I was devastated. I felt as if I had left Steve behind, that my last worldly connection to him was gone. With God's help, I got past the anguish that caused and resigned myself to the fact I would never find the band. I thought God was reminding me yet again that He was now my Husband. **Isaiah 54:5 "Remember no more the reproach of your widowhood. For your Maker is your Husband."** (NIV) I figured God was showing me I could now depend TOTALLY upon Him and not my memories. I didn't need a wedding band to keep Steve in my life. I was not to live in the past but in the present in both body AND mind.

Fast forward all these months - I just finished packing, preparing to leave Italy and fly to South Africa to begin my next relief assignment, when it happened. I was trying to push the plane tickets into my bag. They were not sliding in properly. When I pulled the purse wide open to see what the hang up was, I saw it - my mission wedding band! It was exactly one week before the third anniversary of Steve stepping into eternity. My mind had already been dwelling on it. God was helping prepare me, not to just get through the day again, but to gain strength from it. God was reminding me how day after day, month after month, year after year, He has taken care of me, protected me, led me, counseled me, consoled me, and now comforted me even before I felt the pain of separation.

God truly holds me in the palm of His hand. I continually feel His fingers around me and see them in my daily life. He even prepares me before He knows the going will get rough.

June 2014 - Kulpahar, India

Auntie Linda and Auntie Sharon, missionaries of the Kulpahar Church of Christ mission in India, are now the only mothers to 800 orphans here. When these orphans marry (sometimes through arranged marriages by the Aunties but only if the orphan approves of the match) and have children of their own, these children are the grandchildren of the missionaries. Think of all the grandchildren, 800 grown orphan children have given and continue to give these missionaries! Someone always needs to see a doctor, get medicine, have surgery, or requires an advance for bus or train fare and overnight expenses to get to a job interview. The financial obligations for a family with 800 children are staggering. This does not even take into account several of their children with physical and mental challenges who will never be able to live on their own outside the walls of the mission.

Praise be to God! All the orphan children become Christians which puts an even greater financial duty on the missionaries to educate "their" children through college. With India being predominately Hindu, Christians become targets and have to work twice as hard to accomplish the same as a Hindu because of this discrimination. To be educated is very important in India but especially so for the Christian Indian.

The mission no longer accepts orphans for adoption. The main reason is the change in government policies which would, in effect, allow government agencies control of the mission's children's hostels. Children could be taken from here and placed elsewhere. Our Christian matrons (house-mothers) could be moved out and others who were not Christian brought in to take their place. This would defeat one of the main purposes of the mission hostels which is to raise orphaned children to love and serve Jehovah God. Instead of orphans, the mission now accepts children as boarders who may have one parent, both parents, or no parents but live with a grandparent or uncle. Parents of boarders are always very poor Christians who ask (plead!) for the mission to educate their children. This includes furnishing room and board, books, school fees, any dental or medical attention needed, glasses, school uniforms, shoes, etc. In other words, the mission takes care of the boarder children as if they were their own while they are in the mission hostel. During long school breaks, the boarders go home unless parents ask the missionary to let their children stay at the mission and not come home for some reason. The only difference between the 800 orphans' care and the boarders' care comes after the child graduates from class twelve. At that time, the boarder is no longer the financial responsibility of the mission but returns to their own village family to continue their life.

With the new school year starting and five of the hostel boarders having graduated and returned home, the mission had room to accept new children as boarders. Six children, between five to seven years of age have just arrived: Hament, John, Taniya, Christeena, Isaac, and his sister, Sara. None of them speak a word of English nor understand it. Isaac and Sara were referred to the mission by a Christian preacher who knew the family. Their father can speak enough English for me to carry on a conversation with him, but this means very little, as I carry on "one-sided" conversations daily with many Hindus along the road, just as they do with me. Isaac's dad and I, however, do understand each other. Although both parents are alive, they are very, very poor and asked for the mission to accept their children as boarders while educating them for the next twelve years. The only clothes Isaac had were the clothes on his back. Neither child had underwear nor were accustomed to wearing it. While their parents were in the bungalow making final arrangements with Linda, Isaac and Sara would not sit on the chairs but sat on the floor the entire time. It was soon learned they probably had no beds on which to sleep either, as Isaac kept falling out of bed at night. Two beds had to be scooted together to keep Isaac from hurting himself in a fall.

That day in the bungalow the one very noticeable feature of Isaac was his blue eyes. They were glassy, not bright like a child's eyes usually are. The seemingly permanent look of hopelessness on his face was that of a grown man not a six-year-old child. I thought he was sick. I have seen Isaac almost every day, either in the opening exercises at the mission school or in the evenings while the Royal hostel boys continue honing my skills as a cricket player. That look of having given up long ago was constantly on Isaac's face. The first few days, I never saw Isaac smile once.

I have made it my mission to love on all these young boys every chance I get in the evenings, especially Isaac. I grab them up and give a big grandmotherly bear hug while kissing them on the cheek or head. Even though several of them do not understand a word I am saying, there is no misunderstanding my feelings for them. If they look especially down or expressionless, I continue making over them until I get at least a glimmer of a smile. That didn't come for almost a week with Isaac. Every morning while his kindergarten class filed into the chapel for opening exercises, his eyes would lock onto me the entire time. I always smiled at him and waved. Isaac would only stare at me with that expressionless look on his face.

One morning, while locked in a stare with me as usual, without his facial expression changing one iota, Isaac waved even before I waved at him! I felt like a parent who had just heard their baby say his first word... I was ecstatic! A few days more and Isaac was finally remembering how to smile! Such is the effect of the ministry of Kulpahar Mission on many children. Now, almost a month later, Isaac joins the others in taking his turn in coming to me for their evening "sugar lovin's" saying, "Good evening, Auntie" and then not moving until they get a bear hug and cheek kiss. That is definitely one of the favorite parts of my day!

Sonrise service is my favorite part of Resurrection weekend. Walking to the church in the dark, with only the stars and a full moon to light the way, gave me time to wonder, "When Jesus arose, who knew? Only God? Did anyone greet Christ as He stepped out of the cold, damp tomb into the darkness of the night? Were the angels there to offer a celestial fanfare worthy of the Son of God? Or was He by Himself in the garden as He was when Mary Magdalene stumbled upon Him, thinking Him to be the gardener? What did Jesus do waiting for Mary to come? Did He take in the fragrance of the flowers while the grass sprinkled dew upon His feet? Was He silently thanking His Father for seeing Him through, for being true to His promise, for bringing Him back to life? Or was Jesus remembering the pain and the hatred when He saw the scars on His hands for the first time?"

At the end of the Resurrection Sunday morning sermon, nine boarders in the mission hostel stepped out to confess Christ as their Savior. Four of them were boys I play cricket with almost every evening. Two years before that, I had played volleyball with them. We have had watermelon seed spitting contests together. They have "escorted me home" after our games in the evenings, night after night after night. We have celebrated victories together, had devotions together, and prayed together. I was SO thrilled, my heart almost exploded! They met in the evenings to be taught more fully before being baptized the next Sunday afternoon.

After the sermon that next Sunday, the invitation was again offered, and two more young people came forward! That day we had a total of eleven BAPTISMS! The day before Easter, the married son-in-law of my Phoebe translator was baptized. He had just been sprinkled previously. It was a rich weekend for the Kingdom!

On Mother's Day the Royal Hostel boys who were boarders gave me hand-made cards. Embarrassed by such an open display of affection, these high-school boys were telling me to read their letters later. One 21-year-old drew such perfect roses on the front of his card, I thought I could surely smell them! The boys who were boarders had no mothers present. My daughter was thousands of miles away. We filled each other's need for that one special moment. It reminded me of what was said to Steve and me by a young man from Zimbabwe who was a student in South Africa Bible Institute at Kimberly, South Africa. Steve and I were teaching a couple college classes there. That student made the statement, "You have children all over Africa, and now in Kimberly too."

When the older fellas came back from college for a visit over Easter weekend, they wanted to play volleyball, which we did one evening. I watched the first game to see how aggressive the game was going to be. A couple years at college had surely diluted the "win or die trying" attitude with which some used to play. I jumped in and played the next three games. My first game was not too bad. I should have stopped there. The longer I played, the worse my God-hand became and the more pain I experienced with it. Weak to start with, my God-hand grew even weaker the longer we played, and I became reluctant to even hit the volleyball. I quit after three games. It took almost two months for my God-hand to recover. Next time, I'll stop after the first game!

My last evening at Kulpahar Mission was spent playing cricket with the Royal Hostel boys, (the boys that are high school age and older). I was able to get a couple watermelons from the village. After eating the melons down to their white rinds, we had a seed spitting contest. I have had so much fun with these guys trying to teach me to play cricket. I actually do understand the game now and it's not half bad to watch on TV.

Usually when I leave India to head to my next assignment, the mission car with Sanjay, the driver, and Mark or Uttam take me to the train station. This time Auntie Linda said the entire Royal Hostel and a couple adults wanted to escort me to the train station to see me

189

off, which they did, except for three. They were in trouble for picking and eating kacha ulm (unripened mango) from Mr. Lal's tree without permission.

Here in Kulpahar, these hostel boys were the last "children" Steve ever mentored. This makes them even more special. They keep telling me they are now "my protectors." Most of the college-aged boys e-mail even though it is the same message over and over since their vocabulary of written English words is limited.

You should have seen the looks we got when 13 young men assisted one white headed old woman into the train. For lack of room, I finally stood outside the train while they stored my luggage, bedded me down, and got me all settled in the bogie. When the train finally pulled away, I left more than 13 boys standing on the platform. I left part of my heart, too.

June 2014 - Cape Town, South Africa

In June I arrived in South Africa during the beginning of their winter. One week in July it was warmer in Norway than it was there! Of course, not every day was that cold but enough to make me believe the Afrikaners who told me this was one of their coldest winters yet. Five weeks later, it was close to 90-degrees. I guess that is why most houses in South Africa have no furnaces. Electric or kerosene heaters are used to take the edge off the intense cold.

The hall where the Cape Town Christian Fellowship meets used two electric heaters, but we could still see our breath when singing. Many members brought blankets to wrap up in and wore woolen hats and scarves during the services. Having left my wool sweater on the plane when I arrived in India in February, I had no other winter coat. Aleta and Jerry Kennedy, whom I relieved in South Africa, met me at the airport with one of Aleta's winter coats. Goodness, did it feel good and warm!

I caught, contracted, picked-up, whatever, some kind of fungus in my ears in India the first of the year but didn't know it. The itching had been driving me crazy for seven months. None of my home remedies seemed to help, not even Avon's Skin-So-Soft or Vicks salve.

I finally went to an ear doctor in Cape Town who gave me some pills and ears drops that cured it in a week. While I was in his office, he also gave me a hearing test which I failed. He told me there was nerve damage in both my ears and I needed hearing aids. The doctor said I probably inherited the hearing loss from my Pop, who was very hard of hearing.

All this time I thought people were just talking softly, especially during our Wednesday night Bible study. It got so I would not readily participate in the discussions because I couldn't hear what most the others said. I was afraid I would repeat their words or talk about something that had nothing to do with the discussion.

As my hair grows thinner and my hearing diminishes, I remember the words of the Skin Horse in *The Velveteen Rabbit*: "Generally, by the time you are real, your hair has been loved off, and your eyes drop out and you get loose in the joints and very shabby. But these things don't matter at all, because once you are real, you can't be ugly, except to people who don't understand." Thank goodness, love is blind! I can't wait to be fitted with my new spiritual body which will be perfect in every way!

While at a wedding in India, the bride's father and two other men prayed. All three were praying in Hindi, so I had to keep peeking to

see when the prayers had ended. Uttam was standing by me. Uttam is a Kulpahar kid whom I LOVE to tease. I don't know how long the prayer had been finished when Uttam leaned over and whispered in my ear, while I still had my head bowed and eyes closed, "The prayer. It gone." Sometimes, I have a very difficult time maintaining control of my laughter around Uttam, especially when it is not the time or the place to be laughing!

On the ten-hour train trip from Delhi, India, to Kulpahar after the wedding, just before we reached our station, everyone was asleep but Mark and me. Mark is the young man from Kulpahar who I assist in the mission's school library most of the time. Like Uttam, he is also a former Kulpahar hostel child and is to get married next year too. We opened the train door so we could stand and let the wind blow in while watching the world go by. The first thing Mark said after opening the train door was, "Good morning, Jesus!" when he saw how beautiful the day was going to be.

My travel from the States to Kulpahar may be L-O-N-G and exhausting, but God never fails to shower me with blessing upon blessing in the most thoughtful ways. Truly worth the trip!

Having completed my assignments in India, Italy, and South Africa, I returned to the States the end of September, which was eight months after I had left. Coming back from my first "store-bought" haircut since returning, I passed two yard sales! It was the first time in THREE YEARS I have been able to go to a yard sale in the USA! They had just what I needed to take as a present for Simon and Priyanka's wedding that I attended in Delhi, India in October! At the first yard sale, I found glass tea plates that many Indians use to serve tea to guests. The matching glass cups I found at the second yard sale! Only God could have orchestrated such a find!

2015

February 2015 - Chinhoyi, Zimbabwe

Finishing the last of my three relief assignments for the year, I returned to the States the end of September 2014. Thinking I was home to stay until next year, I completely unpacked all my bags, something I've not been able to do for over two years. Two weeks later I received an e-mail from Andrew and Yolanda Burgess requesting my help in Chinhoyi, Zimbabwe for six months while they returned to the States to raise support.

Their mission of ministering to women and children is just starting in Chinhoyi, although it has been in the works in Yolanda's mind and vision since she was in my youth group in Masvingo 13 years ago. They needed me to be there in seven weeks! Two days before Thanksgiving I left the States for Zimbabwe, Africa.

One morning, after a heavy rain, Elizabeth, who lives behind the Burgess' was gathering termites that had been forced out of their holes by the water. I watched for a while and then helped. Unfortunately, most of the termites I gathered were roaches! This kind of termite only appears one or two times a year. They are not the small ant-like termites we have in the States. These termites are huge, perhaps half the size of a small bumble bee. Later that evening, Elizabeth appeared at my door offering eight of the termites she had fried in oil and salted for me to eat! Trying to find a way out, I told her I didn't know how to eat them. She picked one up and popped it into her mouth, showing me how! What could I do?! There she stood so proud of sharing this treat with me. I'm sure it was on her very best plate, too. Elizabeth pushed the plate into my hand, waiting expectantly for me to eat a termite in her presence. It was one of those moments when you KNOW you NEED to pray! You WANT to pray but have no idea WHAT to pray! God didn't let me down. He took away my thoughts of biting into the bloated belly of this dead termite and having it explode in my mouth with all kinds of undesirable flavors! I ended up eating all the termites on the plate and wishing for more! They were delicious and are loaded with protein, I'm told. And no, they didn't taste like chicken, but more like the juicy bite of a tender steak!

Termites are not the only "traditional dish" I have tried. The local grocery store often has a dishpan of maponi worms in their glass display case along with other prepared foods for sale. Week after week, I saw them being sold. Finally, I asked the man behind the counter if maponi worms were used in stews to add flavor. He said the maponi worm is first boiled, then fried and eaten along with sudza. For 43 cents, I bought nine maponi worms and some sudza to take home to try.

These were not as hard to get past my teeth as the termites had been, but they did not taste as good, either. Maponi worms are several times bigger and longer than the termites and much chewier but don't have nearly the flavor! It's ironic. I just de-wormed myself and now I am putting worms back inside myself on purpose!

The same grocery store with the maponi worms also had crocodile meat for sale. The first week here, I was invited for tea at a farm that raises crocs for a living. They get a good price for their skins and meat although I paid less than two dollars for four pieces in that store. Again, I questioned the Shona man behind the counter about how to cook croc. (His assistant is the one who instructed me in cooking maponi worms.) For the next ten minutes, I followed him all over the store as he collected spices with which to cook my croc and explained how to prepare it. I think I had part of the tail and back of the croc. It tasted like a pork chop and had the color and texture of one also. The croc was so good. I went back the next day and bought another package! ALL the workers behind the counter came out to inquire about my meal.

Not only are they teaching me to cook but to speak bits and phrases of Shona, too. Every time I shop, I greet them in Shona. They laugh and begin talking Shona back to me; then I laugh, not understanding a word they say! Now, even the manager is walking up to me so I can greet him in Shona, which varies depending on the time of day. Perhaps, I should accept the offer from the worker at the post office to give me Shona lessons, but then I would miss seeing the sparkle that comes into the grocery workers' eyes for that brief time they are elevated to the role of teacher.

May 2015 - Chidamoyo, Zimbabwe

While at Chidamoyo, I was put to work in the hospital looking for missing patient files. I don't know how many times I went through every file cabinet, every inbox, every outbox, every shelf, every nook, and cranny trying to find missing files.

One Sunday evening I attended the weekly church service held at the hospital for patients and family. The Shona singing was beautiful! By the time communion was served, the sun had already set, making it difficult to see. Sitting in an unlit hallway, I could not see which communion cups still were unused and thought I had chosen a full one. It was not until I tried to drink the communion and only a few drops were left in the bottom that I realized I was drinking from a cup that had already been used by someone else. I wondered if it was one of the AIDS/HIV patients but realized that most of the people I shook hands with and spoke to every day at the hospital probably had AIDS.

My thoughts reminded me of God's previous protection from catching TB after Steve and I transported a sick, elderly man to the hospital who was later discovered to have active TB. I thought of leaving Guinea six weeks before the Ebola outbreak was officially recognized as being there by the World Health Organization. I wonder how long Ebola had been in Guinea before being detected?! God protected me from Ebola before I even knew I was in the middle of the original outbreak! During my three-month assignment in Guinea with Pioneer Bible Translators, I was in the market, in church, and constantly among the people, shaking hands, and being hugged. We were ALL SWEATING because it was so hot! No one could have told who had Ebola by that symptom.

Just two weeks ago, I discovered the malaria medication I have been taking faithfully since I arrived in Zimbabwe last year is the one malaria medication mosquitoes have formed a resistance to here in Zimbabwe! If God protected me from TB, from Ebola, and from contracting malaria, I'm sure He Will also protect me from AIDS which we are constantly exposed to.

Cobra we killed outside the front door. Chinhoyi, Zimbabwe 2015

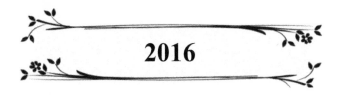

2016

April 2016 - Kulpahar, India and Chinhoyi, Zimbabwe

My arrival in Kulpahar, India was uneventful except for God waking me up just in time to get off a train. When I arrived I had just enough time to wash my face, change clothes, grab a bite of breakfast, and hurry to morning worship at Kulpahar Church of Christ.

Walking down the road to church, my Hindu neighbor saw me coming. She threw down the weeds, which were tied together to sweep the dust from the bare ground in front of her dwelling, to hurry to me. This is the family that has the rooster which loves to chase me. From her hand motions and body language when I crowed like a rooster and pointed to her other chickens, I am sure I will no longer need to keep watch when walking past. Although neither of us could understand the other's words, there was no misunderstanding the sweet look in her eyes. We had no lack of communication. She motioned for me to follow her and led me to the open fire where she had been cooking breakfast. There I met her sister, or maybe it was her daughter, that was visiting, I think. She was dressed in a beautiful sari and could speak some broken English, but her son spoke better English. He translated the rest of our chat.

The sister said she was moving there, pointing to the mission's church compound! "That's where the church is," I answered. "I am going there now." The sister got all excited as if she wanted to go. Since she was dressed as many would be at church, I invited her to come to church with me. "I want to meet Jesus!" she said. My heart melted. Then, I had second thoughts. If she is Hindu, and married or related to a strong outspoken Hindu, could I be putting the church in danger? It is against the law to proselytize. Therefore, when a Hindu wants to be baptized, some of the churches are having the candidate write an affidavit to that effect. This helps protect the church from unhappy Hindu family members or ex-friends who want to accuse the church of forcing them into this decision. (The same is true with Hindu-Christian marriages, only these affidavits are witnessed by government officials!) I thought perhaps I'd better check with others, so did not ask her a second time to come to church with me. I was later told it would be fine to invite her, but not to show a photo of Jesus, as we do not know what Jesus looked like.

My next "God-kiss" was from the chawkidars (guards at the gates) when they folded their hands in a prayer position bringing them up to touch their foreheads. Some cupped my hand in theirs which were so rough and grainy to the touch, an outward indication of the hard lives they live. As always happens, God had His angel unaware present who translated what one chawkidar said to me, "We all happy you back." And so was I!

I look forward to Sundays even though I can't understand one word of the service as it is in Hindi. I still enjoy worshiping with God's people, my siblings. Whichever Auntie plays the electric keyboard that morning always tells me if I'll know any of the songs so I can take a hymnal for words to all the verses. Otherwise, I sing the same verse over and over. Sometimes, I make up words to fit the meter of the song or sing Scriptures to it. I have my own worship and praise song service with Hindu music.

One morning I was walking back to the bungalow for lunch when I saw coming toward me a woman riding in an ox cart being driven by a Hindu man. It reminded me of the Hindu family in 2012 who insisted I ride to school in their ox cart just after I had broken my arm. I think they felt sorry for me. When they got closer, the wife pulled the sari cloth off her face, showing a big beautiful smile. It was the same couple! The Hindu husband waved for me to come to them and through gestures and pointing, insisted (again!) I get on the ox cart and sit right behind the team of oxen. He handed me the reins, which was a rope going through the oxen's noses. He prodded the oxen with a stick to make them start walking, and off his wife and I went with ME DRIVING THE OX TEAM. The husband stayed behind cheering! I don't know who was more excited that I was driving, him or me. To make a long story short, by the time I had driven the old, wooden spoke-wheeled, Biblical-looking ox cart back to the school, (which was the direction the team was headed when I got on), I had a following of bicycles, a scooter, motorcycle, tuc-tuc, and people on foot who had stopped to watch. Word of my coming had preceded me. A group gathered at the school gate to watch and cheer me on, or should I say, laugh me home! I felt like Ben Hur driving in the chariot race, only I was the lone chariot driver! I figured I needed to pull back on the rope to stop the oxen but didn't want to hurt their noses to which it was attached. I lifted up on the rope, so they could feel movement, while saying, "WHOA!" Of course, I KNEW the oxen wouldn't under-stand. They are Hindu oxen and I was speaking English to them! Don't laugh! The Hindu husband "spoke" to them (in Hindi, of course) and they stopped immediately! Even though it is against the law to proselytize, I would love to give a Hindi Bible on such encounters. I know that is impossible. I keep telling myself, if I can't speak to them about God, maybe I can show them God. Let them see the difference instead of hearing it - maybe that will have an impact too. At least that is what I'm praying, as total strangers continue passing me as I walk along that same road every day, with big smiles on their faces or waving and calling out, "Good morning, Auntie!" I continue praying for seeds to be sown and watered one wave, one smile, one cart ride at a time. **John 13:35 "By this will all men know that you are My disciples, by your love for one another."** (NIV)

April ended on a spiritual high as two Zimbabwean young men were added to God's family in Christian baptism at Hillside Chapel, the church I attend each Sunday morning here in Chinhoyi, Zimbabwe. A few Sundays later one of them asked to speak to me after the service. His father had a stroke and is paralyzed from the waist down. The young man must now drop out of school and provide for the entire family. He was in dire need of a job. With Zimbabwe's unemployment rate over 85 percent, a job will be hard to come by. That day alone, I was approached by two more young men asking for work. One wanted to buy food for his brother, who hadn't eaten in four days; the other wanted to continue his education. All were just young men, all three in tears. They come to my gate and plead for work to buy food, to bury their dead, to bring children from villages to town to attend parents' funerals. Some children beg food in parking lots. Adults try to sell items at most robots (stop lights) in Harare. Along the streets, people offer to sell me many things to have money for food to eat that night. I'm buying things I don't need, won't use, or can't bring back to the States, as a way of trying to give them the dignity of earning their living and not begging for it.

June 2016 - Zimbabwe

The government recently announced it will do away with the US dollar, which is now being used as the country's currency, and will print their own money. It will be called bond notes. Even now, Zimbabweans cannot access the US dollars in their bank accounts. When cash is available, people are only allowed to withdraw $100 per day and the amount keeps lowering. Foreign ATM cards are no longer honored. I have not been able to access MRS funds since the first week of May.

Past assignments in Zimbabwe have prepared me to plan for such events. Since I am flying to South Africa this month to begin my next relief assignment, I will be fine. I have never had trouble getting MRS funds with my United States ATM card through the banks in South Africa. (I just received word that the government may turn to the South African rand instead of bond notes. No one knows for sure, which adds to their daily stress.)

August 2016 - Chinhoyi, Zimbabwe

The community ladies club in Chinhoyi asked me to speak in June. Many of them are widow ladies whose families have left Zimbabwe to find employment in other countries. (The unemployment rate in Zimbabwe is 85 to 95 percent depending on whose report one uses.) Since they were wearing sandals, I noticed several of them had terribly long toenails. I doubt some can even see their toes. Were they able to bend down that far to clip them? I felt like I should ask if any wanted me to clip their toenails. I hate clipping fingernails for someone else, let alone TOENAILS! Some were in bad shape. I asked a nurse in a clinic close to me about sterilizing my nail clippers between each lady. She said to get WIRE CLIPPERS to do it as their nails would be thick because most of them would have a fungus. A regular pair of nail clippers wouldn't "cut it." She showed me what they used, so I went to the hardware store and bought a pair of "baby" wire cutters. The nurse also suggested soaking their feet before doing it.

Man! Just thinking about it! I'd rather FIGHT A COBRA than cut these toenails, but that inner "nudging" suggested to me I better listen. I got some rubbing alcohol. Over here, it is 100 percent not the regular 70 or 90 percent that we buy at Walmart. I want to wear rubber gloves, a mask, and a clothes pin, but I don't want them to know how much I'll detest every second of this... of even THINKING about this!!! Ugh! I've been praying for a better attitude. I'm sure God will help me correct it before doing this. I keep putting it off, although I've been collecting the supplies I need, so I know I'm going to do it.

I'll take the bottle of fingernail polish a mother of boarders in the Kulpahar mission hostel gave me in India earlier this year. I met her a couple years ago when she was visiting her two sons and daughter in the mission hostels. She is very poor but has the most beautiful smile. The Aunties provide transport for her to go to doctors when the need arises and also assist her with medical bills. I always give her hugs even though we can't converse in words as she only speaks Hindi. Her children all have her eyes and her beautiful smile! The new bottle of polish was a real sacrifice of precious money for her, worth approximately $1 USD. You can't imagine the multitude of feelings I experienced upon receiving such a heart-felt present.

I'll use the polish to share with the Zimbabwean ladies whose toenails I'll cut. I don't want the polish to dry up and no one get any good from her sacrifice. I'll take a photo of all the ladies that were blessed by her gift of love and send it to the Aunties to give her next time she is in Kulpahar visiting her children. Since she is always being on the receiving end of getting help, perhaps this will let her experience the other side, the blessing of giving to help others.

When I think of all the sick, deformed, blind, lame, leprosy bodies of filthy humanity that the royal Son of God touched without hesitation, I am ashamed for feeling like I do. I'm working on it. This will really be a stretch for me, but how can I do less?

2017

January 2017 - Kulpahar, India

Shortly after arriving in India, my return to the States was pushed back when I received a request from a missionary couple working in Prague, Czech Republic asking I come to help with their work. They will be returning to the states for the marriage of their daughter. Therefore, Lord willin' when I leave India, I will fly directly to Prague to begin my thirtieth assignment since MRS started fourteen years ago.

I was able to attend the nineteenth Global Gathering of World Convention for Christian Churches, Disciples of Christ Churches, and Churches of Christ held in Damoh, a three to four-hour drive from Kulpahar. Over 3,200 registered attendees all worshiped in a beautiful, GIANT, white tent that only held 3,000 people. Most were from India. The opening service was like that of ICOM in the states with an impressive "parade of the flags." Flags from most of the 29 foreign countries and 21 Indian states represented by those attending were carried in while we sang "He Reigns." It was beyond comprehension to realize that over 2,000 years ago the evangelizing efforts of just 12 men started all this.

Damoh is located in the state of Madhya Pradesh, which seems to be tolerant of Christians and was supportive of our convention, but in many other states Christians are severely persecuted. Even here in Uttar Pradesh, Christians better qualified for a job will be denied in favor of a Hindu applicant. During the World Convention several Christians, through Hindi translators, told of their persecution, which started in 2008 when a Hindu leader was killed by Muslims. Most were from the state of Orissa. Large groups of Hindu Extremists would enter villages asking Christians to deny their

Jesus. If they refused, they were killed after seeing their daughters raped and sons beheaded. Three-thousand-five-hundred families were displaced, 55 pastors killed, and over 200 churches burnt to ashes. Many Christians fled and could not return to their homes before doing five things: shave their heads, put a red spot on their forehead, (the symbol of Hindu religion), pay Rs5000 to a village leader (approximately $77 US, which is utterly impossible for most), perform a ritual of purification which included drinking and eating the urine and dung of a cow, and lastly, to kill a brother who is a Christian.

A middle-aged lady whose husband was a preacher said (through a Hindi translator) that when he left in the morning she never knew if they would see each other again. Through tears, she related that her husband refused to deny Christ, so Extremists not only killed him, but also killed her father with a sword, chopped off her mother's head, and 12 gang members raped her. She told us, "If you are not sharing Jesus, you have a problem!" Afterwards, when I hugged her, she felt like a bag of bones.

One man spoke, through a Hindi translator, of being told by his parents to take his wife and children and run when Extremists came to their village. Being old, his parents could not escape. He hid behind a tree and watched them beat his parents with swords, killing them. He wanted to come to the aide of his parents, but there were 50 Extremists. The son is now an elder in his father's place. He said, "No matter what happens, I will not leave Jesus!"

The last statement made to us by those whose testimonies we heard was to never pray for the persecution to stop, but that they stay faithful to the end.

April 1017 - Uttar Pradesh, India

I always look forward to Sundays here in Kulpahar, even though the service is entirely in Hindi. One week they sang the doxology with Hindi words, while I sang in English. I never knew the Doxology had so many verses. After two, I started making up my own words of worship and adoration. They didn't all fit the meter of the music, but they fit the meter of my heart and we were all in unison in our praise to Him that morning.

I noticed those who attend church sit close to the same spot on the floor mats almost every Sunday just as church attenders in the States also sit in the same pews. I remember the same being true in the church at Hong Kong. They sit in almost the exact same chairs each Sunday. Funny how different and yet how much alike we all are.

You'll never guess what I saw in a tuc-tuc one afternoon. (Remember a tuc-tuc is like our golf cart in the States but used as a taxi cab.) I saw a FULL-GROWN cow complete with horns! How in the world he fit is less amazing to me than how they got him in it! I guess where there's a will, there's a way.

The week preceding the ban on all meat being sold or slaughtered, the mission refused the goat brought in as it had been blessed by their Hindu god, Rahm, as part of (or in observance of) an annual Hindu holiday.

The hostel boys and mission personnel are anxious. For the last two months, they have talked about what may be coming, saying the government will not be kind to the Christians in India. From the pulpit, one Sunday in church, it was pointed out how times are changing. "We should be strengthening ourselves for what is ahead." I was told all this later as all church services are conducted in Hindi.

Police were at our Thursday evening communion service. Since it was dark outside the church, we didn't see them and only knew of their presence afterwards. Before Easter week, a local government office told the mission to turn in a paper listing all our church activities. They have never had to do that before but weren't surprised, as the newly elected Chief Minister we were told advocates for an "India Only For Hindus Only!"

On Easter Sunday, two armed soldiers walked into our church service during the sermon. With over 300 people in attendance, there was not much wiggle room. The women's side was packed. Hardly a space on the floor could be seen on which someone was not sitting. The men's side was not as congested. Extra chairs had been added to accommodate the older generation who were no longer able to sit cross-legged on the bamboo floor mats.

Stephen, a man from the mission, saw two policemen through the open church windows as they circled the church while toting guns over their shoulders. He immediately went outside. I didn't see them until all three reentered the church through the door only men use.

Stephen directed the policemen to two empty chairs on the men's side. I saw the first policeman had a modern-type gun that looked like an AK-47. The second had an older bolt action gun with a longer barrel. Both had pistols strapped to their sides. When they sat down, I could only see the muzzle of the bolt action gun pointing straight into the air. I assumed the butt end was resting on the floor by his feet. It must have been quite uncomfortable sitting in the plastic chairs with their ammunition belts on as well as their neatly pressed, hot, brown uniforms. It was 108 degrees outside and even hotter inside. They reminded me of the photos I have seen of the Brown Shirts who served Hitler in World War II, adding to thoughts running through my imagination.

Jolly, who also serves as the Hindi translator for all my Phoebe Ladies Bible Studies, was only five minutes into his sermon. If he saw them enter, it did not show in his face or in the tone of his delivery. From the reaction of the people sitting close, one would have thought the armed men were merely some in the community arriving late to the service. A new grandbaby continued to be passed around. A little boy continued to move from his mother on one side of the church, to his father on the opposite side.

I immediately thought of the e-mails received that morning in response to a hurriedly written one I sent the day before about policemen circling the church with guns on Good Friday saying they would return. I knew I was seeing in action the prayers of those who said they were praying for us. Everyone remained so calm.

I began to pray fervently for Jolly, realizing this may be the only time the one Muslim and the other a Hindu man would ever get to hear the gospel. Anti-conversion laws, in place in six of the 29 states in India, prohibit Hindus from converting to Christianity. In other states, as here in Uttar Pradesh, it is even illegal to speak to someone of Christianity unless one is answering a religious question that was asked.

The longer Jolly preached, the faster, louder, and more confident he became. In the States, this usually happens when a minister is really getting into his sermon, becoming empowered from a greater force than himself. Even though I could not understand a single word, I was being so blessed seeing such an immediate answer to my prayers and many others' prayers!

When the sermon ended and we started into the communion service, I became uneasy. I remembered what someone said of being glad we did not serve communion during our Good Friday service because of the possible reaction from the policemen who were circling the church and listening that morning. While continuing to pray, I suddenly thought, "How many times have I taken communion with no thought whatsoever of getting into trouble for doing so?" Then I thought of all the people in America going through their communion service with minds not focused on the sacrifice of Christ, but rather their pending Sunday lunches or afternoon plans. Even more painful was the thought of those intentionally absenting themselves from the service for no reason except they chose not to be there. My eyes filled with tears.

I shall never view communion service the same, thanks to what was happening at that very moment. I've always heard that persecution of the church strengthens the body. We weren't even being persecuted, yet already there is such a deeper meaning of communion. "I am overwhelmed" doesn't begin to express my feelings. Some things are too deep for words and are experiences that can never be poured into the mold of speech. Such was today.

As four Royal hostel boys and two men from the mission wove their way through the congregation with the bread and the cup, the policemen looked on with great interest. I continued to pray intensely as the servers came closer and closer to the row where the police were sitting. I asked God to give the servers the courage that I lacked. I wondered if the policemen would try to partake themselves. What would the servers do? What would the police do if by-passed? The policemen didn't try. Even more prayers were answered.

Sometime during the last communion prayer, the two policemen slipped out as quietly as they had entered. I wondered if they would be outside waiting. They weren't, but I was one of the last to leave after greeting so many with the traditional "Happy Easter" greeting on Resurrection Sundays.

It wasn't until later I learned that one of the policemen told Stephen, they were there to protect us from any trouble that outside religious factions might bring. I guess with us as a minority religion, we were a possible target of "India Only For Hindus Only!" campaigners. I am in awe! What seemed to be a threat was actually turned into an opportunity for God's Word to be heard by two who would never have entered a Christian Church service otherwise. Only our living God could do that, not any of the thousands of stone idols worshiped here in India.

I have begun my new adventure to the next assignment. Eleven hours after leaving India I spent my first hour just sitting in a hot tub to bathe. It was my first bath since leaving the States in January. I've been bathing out of a bucket, taking turns standing with my feet soaking one at a time in the bucket while bathing out of it. I'm getting quite good bathing this way and can probably bathe with less water than the average American wastes letting it run while brushing their teeth.

May 2017 - Prague, Czech Republic

I left India the end of April and arrived in Prague, Czech Republic on May Day. I did not know the missionaries, Jim and Laurie Barnes, who I was relieving. Having only seen photos of them in their e-mailed mission newsletter, I walked right past Jim, who met me at the airport.

Public transportation is good in Prague, so much so that the Barnes have not owned a car in the entire 20 years they have ministered here. After taking a bus, switching to a tram, then walking a bit, Jim and I arrived at the Prague Christian Library. Located above the library is the Barnes' flat in which I will be living for the next few months.

I had been told Prague was a beautiful, old city and one of the few that had escaped being bombed during World War II. I wasn't prepared for what I saw. Gothic and baroque architecture abounds. Every trip on a tram or bus is like riding among the photos in a colorful fairy book hundreds of years old. The city is so inviting, so warm and friendly. I cannot say the same for its inhabitants. I've found most people on the street and in the shops are not friendly at all. I guess it is customary here to maintain a certain amount of distance from those you don't know very well. This may be due to the 40 years of Communist occupation, when neighbors were forced to spy on each other. After spending more time and being seen more frequently by Czechs, they are a little more open. Having said that, I am reminded of the Czech men AND women who immediately get up and offer older or disabled people their seat on trams and buses. Complete Czech strangers help mothers carry their strollers up and down bus and tram stairs. People having trouble with crutches or walkers have several people come to their aid almost immediately. I've never seen such on-going offers of help by young and old alike in any other country I have ever been in.

At a fast food stall I ordered goulash and dumplings, a delicious Czech dish. The lady taking my order was very impatient, to the point of being rude. With neither of us speaking the other's language, I pointed to the pan of goulash. Unable to finish all of my meal, I went back up to ask if I could take the rest with me. The same lady was there. With crude hand signs, smiling big, rubbing my stomach, licking my lips then pointing to her, I indicated it was good, thank you. By pointing to the goulash, then to her, and a few other gestures, I asked if she made it. Shaking her head, yes, she smiled while scraping my leftovers from the plate into a box. Before handing the box back to me, she put two more ladles of fresh broth on my left-overs. Every time I see her now, which isn't very often, I wave. She smiles and waves back. I think I've made a friend, and I don't even know her name.

Saturday, in the midst of hundreds and hundreds of people, my wallet suddenly went missing just minutes after I was bumped into by a man walking by. I immediately thought "pickpocket," but my wallet was in my hand, or so I thought. After looking for it in vain, and retracing my steps, I tried to remember exactly what was in my wallet: my ATM debit card, (which is my only access to MRS funds), driver's license, Czech transportation card (good for my entire stay in Prague), medical insurance card, family photo, and cash. I had just withdrawn crowns (Czech's currency) to pay registration for a week-end retreat with the International Church of Prague where I attend. I went to a police van just a block away and asked if anyone could speak English. "A little," the lady officer replied. While talking to her and her partner another young policeman came over who spoke better English. After repeating my story a second time, he told me a woman had it. "It police station" pointing up the hill. I wanted to kiss him. Now, I understood why I wasn't shaking on the inside, which happens when things like this occur.

When I asked him to call the station to see if they did indeed have my wallet, he just looked at the lady officer. Thinking he didn't have a phone, I handed him my cell phone, which has a Czech sim card in it, and repeated, "You call, please." In broken English he explained the police station was only 500 meters away. (Just a tad farther than the length of five football fields.)

"You go.... Get.... You go.... there," pointing up the hill. I got my map out and had him show me exactly where it was as I still cannot understand the Czech pronunciation of most street name which are sometimes not pronounced anything like they are spelled. He wrote the address on a scrap of paper I had and off I went. Little did I know what was supposed to be a ten-minute walk up the hill to get my wallet and a ten-minute walk back would turn into over a three-hour ordeal.

The police station was not well marked. Stopping to ask directions while showing my scrap of paper with the address, I was redirected back down the hill. It was a pub. As no other store was open, I entered the pub hardly able to recognize the waitress through all the cigarette smoke. Waiting for her to finish serving beers, a couple at the bar kept motioning me to join them.

All I could think about was how Shadrack, Meshach, and Abednego came out of the fiery furnace not even smelling like smoke, but I'd probably be smelling like the bottom of an ashtray by the time I left this place.

Luckily, (and we know luck had nothing to do with it!) the waitress spoke enough English to point me back from where I'd come. Turns out, I was just one block from the police station when sent back down the hill to the pub.

Now, which door is it? The first door I tried led into a very derelict series of flats, so I tried door number two. It was locked. Heading back up the street, I saw two policemen come around the corner. Running as I hollered to them, one finally heard and turned around. I handed him my scrap of paper which was nearly torn in two by now.

He pointed to the door I had just tried. "It's locked," I said.

"Push buzzer," he instructed. I resisted asking him to come show me. I should have. There must have been 12 buttons I could push, so I just started pushing them one at a time.

After pushing the last button on the bottom row, I heard a voice, but passing cars made it impossible for me to even know what language he was speaking. I pressed the button again and began speaking while holding the button down. Since there was no response, I pressed the button a third time. After hearing the voice respond, I let loose of the button and spoke with the button up, then waited. Nothing. A fourth time, I pressed the button. I heard a buzz, so hurriedly pushed the door. It opened! Thank you, Lord!

Entering the room, it was empty except for a man sitting against the wall. After five minutes a young bald-headed policeman entered with an empty form asking me all sorts of questions. He finally pushed the form at me to fill in. It was written in English so no problem, until the cop tried to read what my God-hand had written. I think he was already aggravated from the button incident. I understand now why the young policeman just looked at the female police officer when I asked them to call this station. Neither of them wanted to talk to him! This is when he began giving me a writing lesson on how to make my letters the correct way, like the Czechs.

My long home address didn't help matters. It took him four tries to get that correct. Frustrated, he called for a translator.

Three and one-half hours later, I left the police station - with no wallet. They did not have it.

I went straight home, called the bank (by Skype) and cancelled my ATM card. (I still have my personal ATM card I can use.)

In my devotion the next morning, the Scripture I read said, **"...and joyfully accepted the confiscation of your property because you knew that you yourselves had better and lasting possessions." Hebrews 10:34.** (NIV)

Isn't it amazing how God ministers to His children?

Later that day, I had to take a different route to church as there was a city marathon which was going to shut down much of the tram's regular schedules in our area. Instead of taking the tram, I took the metro to the Adlen metro stop where I switch to a bus that goes past the International Church of Prague I attend. The bus has a scheduled stop at the church's front door.

The building is owned by a Seventh Day Adventist Church that meets there on Saturday night. On Sunday morning, the International Church of Prague meets there. Sunday afternoon, it is the meeting place for a Russian church.

This will be the only time while I am in Prague this alternate route will have to be taken.

Five minutes before heading out the door for church, I got a telephone call on my cell. (I actually had it switched on for this sole reason! My name and cell phone number were in the wallet.) The call was from a policewoman who said they had my wallet, for me to come get it. I got excited but squelched my excitement remembering I had heard this before.

It was another battle trying to get the name of the police station and its address because it was not the same station where I had been but quite a distance from there. The policewoman did not speak good English and was not a very good speller of Czech street names either! Finally, she told me to just ask any person in yellow where the police station was located AT ADLEN!!!

Adlen is the bus station I was using this morning due to the marathon. It was only six or seven blocks from where I had to switch from metro to bus and even closer to the store where I intended to get groceries. God even placed a pair of officers there who were randomly stopping vehicles and "just happened" to be at that corner. One spoke broken English but enough to recognize the misspelled street name of the police station. He gave me directions and even pointed it out on my map. Ten minutes later I had my wallet in hand with hardly anything missing!

Needless to say, there was a time or two I could easily have been overwhelmed, but God knows just h-o-w f-a-r to stretch us. Each time, it's a little further, a little further, a little further. Before you know it, your spiritual muscles are so much stronger.

Who but God can use pain, discomfort, adversity, and even death to make us stronger. He uses it to make us into overcomers, like His Son.

Thank You, Lord, for this adversity, but thank You even more for helping me through it!

June 2017 - Prague, Czech Republic

On June 13th I experienced another God moment. You know the kind. The one that sneaks up on you and is almost past before you recognize it. The husband of Carol, a dear lady from home, had recently lost his fight with cancer. I shouldn't say "lost" because being a Christian, he actually won.

Excerpt from e-mail to Carol's church in the States:
TO: Women of Grace Sunday School Class, Union Christian Church, Terre Haute, IN

Howdy,

I've a favor to ask all of you. Please try to help Carol focus, not on the life that is now gone, but the life she was blessed to share for so long with her husband, Norm.

Her heart will be empty because she can't see him, but she still has all the love they shared, all the memories. I guess that's another way God blesses the one who remains... the memories. I think it is God's way of helping us to let go while still hanging on.

Right now all those memories are probably bringing more hurt to her heart, but one day those memories will put a smile there instead.

All those trite phrases that "He's in a better place now." or "He's not suffering anymore." are all true, but it doesn't address the pain here and now Carol is being swallowed up in. Remind her it's fine to shed tears that he's gone, but she can smile, too, because he lived!

Isn't it just like God? Here I am thinking up ways to support and encourage Carol through you, when today is also the day Steve stepped into eternity six years ago. In encouraging her, I just encouraged myself....

It's not such a "hard" day after all. What a mighty God we serve!!!
Love & Prayers,
THEE & me

July 2017 - Prague, Czech Republic

In Prague, I attend the International Church of Prague where the library has a display of books that we set up and take down each Sunday. Every Sunday visitors are asked to stand to introduce themselves. My first Sunday, there were people from New Zealand, Canada, England, Africa, Netherlands, India, Mexico, Cameroon, Holland, Pennsylvania, Louisiana, California, and of course, me from Indiana. ICP's minister is from the States. He and his wife returned to the States for a few weeks leaving two men in the church to fill the pulpit in his absence. The sermons were so down to earth, so helpful, so filled with Scriptural wisdom that I know the words they spoke were whispered into their ears by God. I was almost sad to see the preacher return, though his sermon last week was definitely inspired and surely fed us well.

2018

January 2018 - Terre Haute, Indiana

One of my first Sundays back in the States, I arrived early for Sunday School. I saw a tall, dark, cylindrical shaped tower sitting on the table. I had seen Sirius advertisements showing the tower answer questions and play music just by a person speaking a command to it. So, while others were getting coffee, I started asking the Sirius tower questions to see if the commercials were true. I began with, "What is today's date?" The tower gave no response. I rephrased my question but still no response. It was then one of the ladies who had come up behind me said, "That's a coffee mug." I've been gone too long.

April 2018 - Kulpahar, India

I have thanked you many times for your prayers. I am again certain it was because of those prayers and God's faithfulness that in February I arrived safely at my destination here in India. I wasn't even checked in at the Indianapolis airport when the ticket agent alerted me to my flight being delayed to the point I would miss my next two connections. He then proceeded to reroute my entire itinerary before I even began my journey. The only part that did not change was my arrival time in Delhi, India at 2 a.m. Unfortunately, there was no one at the Delhi airport to pick me up as prearranged. Even in this, God provided. On the plane a little voice in my head told me I might not be collected at the airport which gave me time to prepare a Plan B - just in case. At the Delhi airport, I walked the length of the exit twice rereading all the hand-written names on pieces of paper and cardboard being held up by drivers of pre-booked taxis, rental cars, hotel shuttles, etc., but did not see my name. I saw an Indian just finish a call on his cell phone, so I asked if I could make a local call using his phone. He spoke English (Thank you, Lord!) and even dialed the number for me. I woke "my ride" up. He thought I was flying in the next day. Again, God provided. The man whose phone I borrowed, owned a taxi and offered to drive me to my lodging in Delhi but for a terribly inflated price knowing my dilemma. I thanked him but refused, telling him what I would pay. He said no. I walked away pushing my overloaded luggage cart with three big suitcases weighing a total of 164 pounds, plus another 55 pounds in my airport purse and carry-on which were balancing precariously on top. The airline did not have a maximum weight limit for carry-ons of which I took full advantage! It wasn't long before the man came after me, agreeing to my price. Afterwards, while reflecting on the day's happenings, I realized that when I came out of the airport and no one was there, going to Plan B was as natural as taking the stairs when the elevator is broken, an inconvenience but nothing more. Either I have become a calloused traveler, or God's arms were wrapped around me so tightly they served as a cocoon to shield even my fears. I know which one it was.

The five donated balls from the USA were definite hits. The hostel girls got a rubber ball and basketball. Not only do they play with them every evening during play time but also every morning while waiting for the bell to ring for them to line-up and walk to school. By then, most of the girls are hot and sweaty.

Only a few days had passed before that rubber ball had a "puncture," as they call it. I took the ball to the men who do the hostel laundry. We aired the ball up first (put gas in it as Mahima, one of the hostel girls, says) then submerged it in their wash water to find the hole. As fast as the air was coming out I'm surprised we couldn't see it with the naked eye.

Just outside the compound wall is a Muslim-owned tire stall where I headed next. When he saw the ball, he shook his hand, which meant no. While rubbing the surface of the ball, he started speaking in Hindi. Although, I couldn't understand a word he said, I knew it was because of the textured surface on the rubber ball. A patch would not hold.

Now the girls are so used to playing with the ball deflated, I don't think they would have liked it inflated again anyway. They don't have to chase after the ball when someone misses catching it, and they can get a better hold on it to throw at each other. They use it to play a game called Tee-Poh, which they love! It is a spin-off of our dodge ball. I have seen as many as fifteen girls of all ages playing it at the same time. The flat rubber ball is a perfect fit. It's interesting how the girls prefer the flawed rubber ball since they are able to do more with it with less resistance.

I sometimes think God also prefers the flawed, for when His purpose is accomplished, there can be no doubt it was done, not by any action on our part, but only through His power in and upon us.

I just can't get over how 12 men could have "turned the world upside down" even within their lifetime! We now realize how powerful their work and preaching were having SEEN WITH THEIR OWN EYES! They bore witness to Jesus' miracles. They saw the changed lives first-hand. No wonder uneducated fishermen, a hated tax collector, and the rest could change the entire religious world and become the foundation of the New Testament church with Christ as the chief cornerstone!

Can you imagine what the people thought after having to bring unblemished animals to the temple to sacrifice all their lives and now being told they never needed to do that again? They would never need an earthly high priest to be their mediator? The old covenant, written on tablets of stone, had been replaced by a new covenant written in their hearts? In fact, they could completely do away with the altar, the golden lampstand, the showbread, the entire Holy of Holies and Ark of the Covenant!

I wonder when Jesus died and the veil of the temple was ripped from top to bottom, do you think the temple leaders tried to sew it back together and continue with their worship as it was before Christ's death?

Every Sunday during communion, I think about how mightily God worked through twelve men as ordinary as you and me. If God was able to work so powerfully through twelve FAT men (Faithful - Available - Teachable) just think what an entire church of FAT people could do today!

Now you know why my favorite response to the question, "How are you?" is, "I'm FAT and sassy!

June 2018 - Kulpahar, India

There were five of us from Kulpahar on the same train to Delhi with 15 people at the Kulpahar train station to get us and our luggage on board during the three-minute stop. Although we were on the same train, we were not in the same carriage. I shared a carriage with two men and a mother and daughter.

Once again, the Indian driver that was to meet me at the Delhi train station was nowhere to be found. About that time Armand and Sallil had disembarked from their carriage, which was just down from mine, and were walking by with their luggage. Armand bartered with the coolies for me to bring the price of Rs1000 (approximately $16 USD) per bag to carry my luggage to the car park down to Rs200 (approximately $3) per bag.

There was no trouble getting a local street taxi which was even less than the driver who was to meet me was going to charge. Thank you, Lord! Of course, only two of the four doors worked and when we got to my lodging, it took the taxi three tries to get the power to drive up the hill. I thought the security guard was going to have to push the taxi. Sallil rode with me to my lodging using the GPS on his cell phone to give directions to the taxi driver. I thanked Armand and Sallil profusely and then thanked God for making it so easy for me this time.

The next night I boarded an Ethiopian Airline plane for my second assignment in Africa. Upon entering the plane, the aroma of urine just about knocked us down. I've been exposed to my share of bad smells but NOT ON A PLANE where we would be breathing the same air over and over! I know they filter the air but just the thought of breathing that air for five hours only added to the experience.

Before we taxied to the runway, two crew members walked down the aisles in the cabin continuously spraying a can of something. I don't think it was for the smell but to fulfill regulations since some countries require the disinfection of inbound flights with an aerosolized spray while passengers are on board. Countries do this to eliminate any threat to their public health, agriculture, or the environment.

This was an old plane as evidenced by the stuffing coming out of the seats. I was afraid to sit for fear my seat was saturated with urine. After five hours we either got so used to the smell of the recycling of that tainted air over and over and over during our flight, that we didn't notice the smell again until exiting the plane when we got our first whiff of fresh air. So much for the claim of the quality of recycled air inside planes. I pity the crew who works this plane regularly.

I need to add here my connecting flight was also on Ethiopia Airline. I dreaded having to get on another Ethiopian airplane, but it was 100 percent better! No stuffing coming out of seats, no smelly cabins, and the food was delicious! We did hit major turbulence during our meal. I thought we'd all end up wearing supper instead of eating it. It seemed forever before we got to calmer skies. The last time I was in turbulence that severe was in 1976 when Steve and I flew to India to try to relocate as career missionaries. There was political unrest and the foreigners where we were had three days to get out of the city and fifteen days to leave the country. Years later, we were told, had we bribed the government official, he would have renewed our visa stay.

The missionary I am relieving said they have always had good experiences with Ethiopian Airlines and have never experienced anything like that on any of their flights. At least the crews of both planes I was on were polite and professional.

Would I ride Ethiopia Airlines again? Given the baggage allowances and extra leg room in economy class, yes, I would. But Ethiopia Air would not be my first choice, especially since it goes through the Addis Ababa airport. Up until now, I have only been scared in one airport, a little one in Beirut, Lebanon on that trip to India in 1976. Our plane made a quick stop to pick up passengers and refuel. When we landed the sole runway was lined with military tanks. The airport was crawling with fierce-looking soldiers all armed with new AK-47's. Not thinking, I took a photo of one of them. I immediately knew that was not a smart thing to do! I thought he was going to grab me and take my camera. I took off, almost running, and immediately got back on the plane.

The Addis Ababa airport in Ethiopia has not expanded to keep up with the growing number of planes coming through. It is over-crowded with not enough knowledgeable ticket agents or up-to-date flight schedule boards.

The first time I had a connecting flight at Addis Ababa, I found a corner where I could keep my back to the wall and used a newspaper to hide behind while pretending to read it. For all I knew of their written language, the paper could have been upside down!

That airport was chaos! Mostly men shouting in a language I could not understand. The tone of their voices I did understand, and I did not want to be anywhere near them. There was an elderly woman in a wheelchair who asked if I would check the flight schedule boards to see when her flight left. I would wait until the mob thinned out before quickly running to look for her flight. It never showed on the board and neither did the employee who was to push her to the gate. She missed her flight.

When a ticket agent would come, he was mobbed by passengers trying to find what gate they needed. I actually saw him point in the opposite direction and when the mob rushed to that gate, he made his escape. By the time the passengers realized no one was there and returned, the ticket agent was gone.

This year I did not have such a long layover at Addis Ababa air-port. We must have arrived between planes from other major airlines as it was not as crowded or chaotic. I think I was even in a different wing of the airport. I caught my connecting flight with no problems. Thank you, Lord!

August 2018 - Kulpahar, India

Over and over I witness God's perfect timing. Such was my going to Kulpahar, India, an assignment added at the last minute. I had balked at including this third assignment as it meant my overseas work would be extended to almost a year. I would not be returning to the States until January of next year, 2019. I have never before been gone this long but only do so with my daughter's blessing. She says, "Just be sure to come home, Mom!"

I now see God's hand in those plans because while I was in Kulpahar, Auntie Linda fell and broke her hand. Having a cast on one's hand can greatly hinder what one is able to do. I was glad to be at Kulpahar to help her like they helped me when I broke my God-hand several years ago. The same village doctor that put the cast on my arm did Linda's. I was surprised he remembered me. It was not long before Linda was finding ways to do with one hand what had once taken two. This offered me an opportunity to drive in India while acting as Linda's chauffeur, even if it was only from one compound to another. Driving around the goat herds, dodging the water buffalo, tuck-tucks, bicycles, motorcycles, scooters, pony tongas, ox carts, and women carrying L-O-N-G pieces of firewood on their head made driving much more interesting than in the States.

I love teaching Phoebe, the weekly ladies Bible study. I teach in English with Jolly translating into Hindi. Because of their spiritual maturity, I can delve deeper into the Scriptures, not just what the Scripture means but the "whys and wherefores" behind it. Using Scripture and personal knowledge, (observed and experienced), these ladies came up with over 20 solid reasons to answer my question about why so many godly parents in the Scriptures had such ungodly children. We brought it forward to present day asking why faithful workers in the church have children who have abandoned their first love. I find that the levels of spiritual growth of ladies in various countries are as different as the cultures in which they live.

In some countries I am ashamed of my spiritual depth compared to theirs. This is especially true where governments disregard the good of the people for personal gain. The more hopeless the external living conditions, the deeper their faith seems to be. I guess that's nothing new as this is what helped the Christian faith spread, when persecution forced them into the "utter most parts of the earth."

Since 2010 I have been choking down the food of India trying to learn to like it. I can now honestly say, I love Hindustani food, well, not all of it. It only took me three years to be able to say that about chicken feet. Either I'm getting more set in my ways regarding what I eat, or it took my tongue longer to get used to the hot spices of India. Either way, I thank You, Lord, for making it a bit easier over here.

The day before Kulpahar Christian School was to begin, I helped sort and distribute books to some of the students. The school has just over 400 students from the villages, and most are Hindus and Muslims. Christians form a small percentage in comparison. Yet these Hindu and Muslim parents sign consent forms permitting their children to attend chapel every morning (called opening exercises in the curriculum) and Moral Education classes that use the Bible from which to teach. In this class, students are required to memorize Scripture verses as well. One parent when criticized by another Hindu for sending his child to a Christian school, said his son was a better child at home from the training he was receiving so why shouldn't he send him? KCS is making a difference, one child at a time.

I had the privilege of attending another Indian wedding ceremony. Mr. Bhagat, the mission's auditor for many years, has one child, a son, who was to be married. Several in the mission received wedding invitations that were carved out of wood and hand delivered in wooden envelopes. The invitation indicates the caliber of the wedding and the extravagant setting in which it was to be held. No expense was spared. Guests received a full-size winter bedspread and box of sweets. Guests, including me, were housed, along with Mr. Bhagat, in a luxurious (by India's standards) hotel close to the wedding venue, which was a three-hour drive from Kulpahar.

Being a Hindu wedding, it took a full two days to complete which began with a final ring ceremony on Saturday. Traditional events were also held all day Sunday, culminating with more wedding customs at night followed by very late suppers. I have never seen such pomp and fanfare, or ornate gowns and suits with the toes of men's cloth-like shoes curling up to a point, like a genie's slippers. It was like being in a Bollywood movie of India. The opulently dressed wedding party paraded around accompanied by beating drums, blaring horns and innumerable cameras taking pictures. Even a drone was filming from overhead.

The groom arrived riding in a regal horse-drawn cart covered in lights and surrounded by family dancing and swaying to music of bugles and drums. All the way up the driveway they danced, stopping and starting to allow ample time for merry-making. It looked and sounded like the "Light Parade" at Disney World and had that intensity, as well. I was standing on the sidelines taking photos with countless others when the groom's cart passed, then stopped. A man who I think was Mr. Bhagat's brother danced my way. Out of all those people standing there, it was my hand he took! He slowly led me toward the middle of the gaiety, dancing the entire time. I was hemmed in by the masses with nowhere to escape. Audibly I was saying, "Oh, no! Oh, no! What do I do God? What do I do?" The music was so loud, no one but the Lord and I could hear my embarrassed pleas.

Fearful if I jerked my hand from his grip I would offend, but even if I got free, there was no place to go. He led me to where the women were dancing in this "parade." Upon seeing me, the women immediately formed a circle around me continuing to dance while urging me to do likewise, not in word but in actions. Everyone was almost shoulder to shoulder…me …alone in the middle. By now I was laughing. It was either laugh or cry from overwhelming embarrassment. My emotions were screaming at me to do something.

It was now Mr. Bhagat, father of the groom, the man who invited us, the man who was paying for our hotel room, the one who was providing all our food, who had given all the gifts. THAT Mr. Bhagat made his way over and began dancing behind me. The look on his face clearly revealed he was very pleased I, a foreigner, had joined in celebrating his son's marriage.

I need to include at this point: I don't dance. I haven't danced since one time in eighth grade. But as I had not seen any lewd movements or inappropriate dancing, I joined in, for all of two minutes! I pointed my index fingers to heaven in an up and down motion taking turns of pointing one finger higher, then the other higher, back and forth. At the same time, I swayed my weight from one foot to the other foot like I do with the African women while singing in the township churches, keeping rhythm with the beat of the music.

Little did I know how God would later use dancing as an opening for me to talk with these Hindu ladies, sisters of Mr. Bhagat (?), to describe a Christian wedding, the symbols (unity candle, communion, cross, etc.) and meaning behind it like they were describing this Hindu wedding. Pagans and a Christian, each speaking of their religion, them listening with a positive frame of mind, all because of a couple minutes-worth of being WAY out of my comfort zone. Who but God could pull that off?!

The wedding continued most of both nights. A giant buffet-style supper was served each evening, with appetizers, fruit, desserts, drinks (no alcohol), etc. It took 22 big tables to hold the feast.

My only regret is that Mr. Bhagat was not a part of the conversation on Christian marriages nor did I get to speak to him afterwards. When we finally called it quits in the wee hours of the third morning (Monday), they were still not married.

September 2018 - Zimbabwe

In most of Africa, people refer to the flowers and plants, etc., in the yard as their "garden." Where I am living, the missionary's garden is just starting to bloom as it is now summer here in Zimbabwe. The Burgess' garden consists of two lemon trees, a peach tree, several palm trees, bamboo, and a moringa tree I planted as a seedling two years ago. (It's over 15 feet tall now!) They have a variety of other plants and trees, even a clump of sugar cane, which won't be ready to cut until around April. It's just as well. When I start chewing on a stick of sugar cane, I slurp and suck and chew until every ounce of sweetness is gone, then spit out the pith, grab another piece, and start all over again. My face ends up as messy as having eaten a juicy, half-mooned shaped piece of watermelon down to the white rind.

In the tops of three of their palm trees, a bunch of weaver birds are building their nests. The male weaver is beautiful with a bright yellow breast. He is about twice the size of a sparrow. The female is a paler burnt-orangish color. During mating season, the male builds a nest to attract the female. If she likes it, she helps him finish it and then moves in. If she doesn't, she tears it down. If the nest is too old, it will not attract a female, so the male tears it down and starts all over again.

It must be mating season as freshly built nests seem to always be littering the ground under these palm trees. Oh, the noise! Mercy! They must "whistle while you work," as the seven dwarfs would say! It's not a pretty sing-songy type melody but a busy obnoxious chatter, chatter similar to a squirrel taunting a dog while chattering at him from the safety of a tree branch just above the dog's head.

The nests they weave (hence their name) are so sturdy even the strongest wind of a mighty storm cannot pull them off the branch. The entrance is a tunnel-shaped hole located at the bottom of the nest which makes it hard for intruders to enter. The male uses the younger, long, tender grass-like leaves off the palm trees which nearly stripes them bare. The nests usually face the west to catch the warmth of the last rays of sun.

I've seen these weaver nests built in huge colonies on telephone poles in South Africa. They look like one GIANT bird's nest that almost covers the entire top portion of the telephone pole. Snakes love to raid these nests as it is like a smorgasbord buffet for them slithering from nest to nest.

I am headed to Harare, the capitol city of Zimbabwe, this weekend to meet a dear lady I served with on one of Masvingo (Zimbabwe) Christian Church's music teams. Gill was the pianist. She is bringing back an inverter the Burgess's sent to South Africa for repair. The World Health Organization has declared a state of emergency in Harare due to an outbreak of cholera. The mismanagement (corruption) of city funds has left the city unable to repair broken sewer pipes. Raw sewage is running down the streets in one Harare suburb. Bole holes (wells) are being contaminated. Over 20 people have died.

As conditions in Zimbabwe continue to deteriorate, supplies are limited. Not only are supplies being limited, but prices have sky-rocketed. Trying to get sugar, cooking oil, bread, and refined table salt, I went to a store located in the middle of Chinhoyi, where I live. It had over two hundred Africans pressing to get in and wasn't even open yet, although it was supposed to have been opened two hours earlier. Word got out they had cooking oil. Fifteen police came with two vicious dogs which snapped and barked to make people line up properly. The Zimbabweans would scream and run, only to return when the dogs were gone and police had their backs turned. I watched from a safe distance.

The store kept its doors closed, but police let five to ten people in at a time. Eventually, they began to trickle back out carrying one bottle of oil and two loaves of bread. It was then I realized there was no way the store would have enough for everyone who had been standing in the hot 95-degree sun for hours to get the same. I could only imagine their reaction to hearing there was no more stock. I knew it was time for me to leave.

I realize my skin tone alone draws attention no matter what I do or where I go. This is true in India also. So, I have always been conscience of taking extra precautions. I am not foolish enough to pray for God's protection while walking in front of a bus. I realize I must do my part in staying safe, but I also know nothing I do can really protect me from someone who is determined. Only in God's intervention is my true safety. I cannot be scared of what might happen, nor live in fear of all the "what ifs." God did not give us a spirit of fear but of power and love.

Gideon's 300-member army was extremely outnumbered, and yet they attacked the Midianites and won. With a trumpet or torch in one hand and a pitcher to cover the torch in the other hand, some of those 300 men didn't even have a hand free to carry a weapon. Was that foolishness or trusting in God's deliverance after following what God told them to do?

I'm not claiming to be a Gideon, but God did not lead me overseas to do His work had He not intended to protect me. That's why I sign most of my correspondence, "THEE & me." If something happens, I mess up doing my part to keep safe, God can still turn it around for His glory, if it is His will to do so. If not, I know He will be by my side as I go through it. Either way I'm protected from it... or through it... because God is faithful.

The next day the supervisor in a store across town was allowing people to buy up to three bottles of cooking oil with their purchases. When the Africans began buying three bottles, keeping one then increasing the price of the other two and selling them in front of his store, that policy changed. By the grace of God (and my white hair), they let me buy three bottles. I felt guilty for having that many, so I gave one bottle to a Zimbabwean. I gave the second one to Elizabeth, who still cooks for her ex and kept the third bottle to cook lunches for the 12 to 15 African ladies every Wednesday after our Bible lesson. There was a time I would have hoarded the oil away and it was tempting. I wouldn't have to worry about sourcing oil again for quite a while if I did. However, I'm out of Mazoi, which is a liquid concentrate that is mixed with water for a fruity drink. It was one of the first items all the shops sold out of as the Africans love it. Mazoi and biscuits (cookies) are what I serve both ladies groups as a snack. When a lady at church heard I was looking for Mazoi, she GAVE me a bottle of it and would NOT take any money for it. How could I do less with the cooking oil?

It's really odd how something that simple can change your entire perspective for the day. I didn't even mind the bottle-neck traffic of everyone trying to get fuel, or four lanes of traffic on a two lane road, or people not obeying any traffic laws. I didn't mind everyone driving wherever they see an opening to advance forward, even driving on the wrong side of the road until meeting traffic coming the other way, then there's no place to go as others followed the "wrong-lane" driver so no one can back up and we all just sit there - baking in the sun, burning what precious fuel we still have in our tanks. Driving in the USA will be so boring compared to this!

November 2018 - Zimbabwe

This Sunday is Veteran's Day, a holiday that here in Zimbabwe will not be celebrated. Most Zimbabweans have never even heard of Veteran's Day let alone know why it is such a revered holiday in America. For those of us who had loved ones fight in past wars or "skirmishes" and were blessed enough for them to return home, Veteran's Day has a special meaning.

In 2011 while on assignment in Hong Kong, I was able to visit the area in the Philippines where my father had been stationed during World War II. I saw the huge cannons left behind on the island, the rusted artillery, the stone walls and buildings dotted with pit marks caused by bullets and shellings. As I walked along the halls turned into barracks which housed American soldiers, I wondered if it was here my Pop slept. I felt close to him, walking where he had walked, seeing what he had seen even though it was over 75 years ago, before I was even a twinkle in his eye.

I saw the whitish-colored stones with bright spots of red lying on the ground. We were told the stones were not marked like that before the war. They thought it was the effect of falling residual debris from the air after so many repeated shellings of the island while the occupation of the island went back and forth between the Allied

Forces and the Japanese. The US State Department said the war "resulted in the death of over 4,200 Americans and over 20,000 Filipino combatants" in the Philippines alone. "Over 200,000 Filipino civilians died from violence, famine and disease." How ironic the red spots on the stones looked like drops of blood.

I didn't know much about WW II except what was taught in history class in high school. Even then, more time was spent on the Civil War and Abe Lincoln. My father would sometimes tell of a fellow soldier in his unit that was exactly like Gomer Pile on TV or talk about volunteering to lay communication lines that ran through fields of pineapples. They would get in the middle of one of those fields, cut open a ripe pineapple and for a few minutes, while sucking on the juicy, fresh pineapple, forget they were in the middle of a world war. Those pineapple fields are still there today.

Pop never talked about actual combat. I guess those who served in hand-to-hand combat wanted to forget the horrors they were forced to witness or sometimes cause.

I walked along the war memorials erected for those who fought, some giving the ultimate sacrifice, on foreign soil, for a people they had never met, who spoke a language they could not even understand. I wanted to tell everyone, "My Dad was one who came! My Dad helped defend your country!"

The most sacred memorial was the Manila American Cemetery, better known as the "Philippines' Arlington." Over 17,000 are buried here with row after row of pure white gravestones filling the 152-acre cemetery. The Filipinos do not take lightly the sacrifices that were made on their behalf. It is even seen in the rules for entering the cemetery: No food. No dogs. No exercise clothes.

This past year, 2018, while on assignment in South Africa, I was one of the speakers for a "Celebrate Ladies!" day outside of Cape Town.

I hadn't been there 15 minutes when a lady, definitely Asian, walked up to me and boldly stated with a deep accent, "I'm from North Korea. Are you scared?" Then she laughed. I didn't know if she was joking or not. It was then her husband, Paul Kim, stepped forward and introduced himself.

The Kim's were originally from North Korea but to escape Communism fled to South Korea. From there they came to Johannesburg, South Africa. With tears in his eyes he said, "I want to thank you. Your soldiers saved my country." By now he was almost crying. "I am so thankful. You pulled my country from Communism. It my duty to thank you."

From there he proceeded to speak of the talks that were taking place between North Korea and South Korea. "North and South Korea talks, not from bottom of heart - hiding behind Kim (Kim Jong Un, President of North Korea) "Hide behind him... Those who chase American soldier out are wrong. It bad. Not thanking for favor. It my duty to thank you."

Would you help me deliver Mr. Kim's message to the veterans you know? "It my duty to thank you."

People sometimes ask when I am going to retire from doing missionary relief work. - I have no idea. Since God started this ministry for us in 2002, I guess I'll keep at it until He shows me it's time to stop. I figure He'll do that by missionaries no longer asking me to come or my health failing. My health is fine, but I'm finding it takes me longer and longer to do less and less. Steve and I used to clean missionary's gutters and wash all the outside windows. I don't even attempt that now. (Of course, with the water rationing still in effect in Cape Town, I had an excuse!) However, it made me wonder if retirement was getting near since I had no future requests after this assignment ends next year.

One week after "wondering" I received a request to relieve a missionary couple who gave me the exact dates they wanted me to come in 2020! One week later, another request for help next year, 2019, with a note, "We'll take you whenever we can get you." I had to laugh. It was almost as good as getting a Post-it-note straight from God!

I see God's hand almost daily here in Zimbabwe.

If it were not for how much my faith grows and is strengthened while in Zimbabwe, I would surely be tempted to pass on assignments here. But it's the hard times, the power outages, the not finding fuel until your tank is almost empty, rejoicing in finding a bag of sugar on a grocery shelf that makes one realize our joy does not come from external circumstances. Our joy is from within. It is that joy which allows the man with no savings, and no home of his own to know he is the richest man in the world as he looks into the eyes of his children.

"The joy of the Lord is our strength." Nehemiah 8:10 (NIV)

No wonder I feel so close to the Lord in Zimbabwe.

Thanksgiving 2018 - Zimbabwe

Earlier this week I went to Lomagundi College to help a class of 18 eight-year-olds learn more about India. Their teacher had gone WAY BEYOND the call of duty to make learning about foreign countries an almost-true-life travel adventure. The children made their own passport which had to be stamped with a visa before being allowed to visit the classroom which was decorated like the country they were visiting. Either a sweet, beverage, pastry, or savory morsel eaten in that country (or close to it) was served at each destination. The children were only allowed a five to six minute "visit" in each country. The teacher asked me to return that Thursday to talk to her students further about India and its people.

My first MRS assignment this year was four months in India. I had some left-over money which I will take to show the students while wearing my punjabi suit which is a common outfit worn by the ladies in India besides their saris. When I counted my change, I found I had 18 one-rupee coins which look almost exactly like Zimbabwe's one Zollar Bond coin, just enough for each student to get to keep one. I also have enough individually wrapped hard candy to give each student a sweet from India made with masala, a spice much loved in India.

It was not until I went to reserve this day on my calendar that I saw it is Thanksgiving that day. I had to chuckle. It's just like God. He always keeps me busy on the days that could be a little tender for me. I will be thoroughly enjoying myself with the children. I always leave there "walking on the clouds."

Thank you, Lord for "directing my path...."

Some of the older hostel volleyball boys. Kulpahar, India 2014

2019

January 2019 - Zimbabwe

When I arrived in Zimbabwe on September 2018 I made friends with Wes Jr., Western and Elizabeth's son. Wes's parents work for the missionaries and live next door. Sometimes when he heard my voice, he would come crawling as fast as his little hands and knees would take him. A couple months later, his first steps were taken walking to me.

One morning in January, Elizabeth cooked porridge for their breakfast over an open fire like always. As she was pouring it into the bowl, Wes got his hand in it. By the time she got to my back door, the skin was just hanging off his hand. The clinic didn't open for another 30 minutes so I immediately put his hand in cool water. He stopped crying for a minute, then started again.

I drove Wes and his mother to the clinic where we were the first to be seen. Of course, they couldn't treat Wes until we bought the medicines and bandages, etc., and brought them back. We took the list of necessary items and were able to get them all in the first pharmacy at which we stopped, a miracle in itself as empty as many shelves are in pharmacies. Taking them back to the clinic, Wes was finally treated, and his hand wrapped. He has to go back every day to be checked and the bandages changed.

Wes's hand seems to be healing with no scarring and doesn't seem to hurt now, but he won't keep a bandage on it. The lighter discoloration of skin may be a permanent reminder, but he will not have any webbing between his fingers because of the burn. It could have been much worse. Thank you, Lord.

At this moment, I'm not sure when I'm heading home. I know what my ticket says, but current government decisions have riled the people. (Almost tripling the price of fuel yesterday for one thing.) As I type, riots in Harare and Bulawayo have caused schools to close, businesses to shut down and all traffic to be off streets. It was intended to be a peaceful demonstration rebelling against the government, but people are dead, others injured. Demonstrations are to continue tomorrow and Wednesday.

The US Embassy just sent out a warning about people fighting in fuel queues so don't get in one. How in the world do they think we can get fuel if not join a fuel queue?!

The army is shooting. People are burning cars and police stations, throwing huge boulders and rocks at any vehicles on the road. I'm to go to Harare on Thursday to renew my visa one last time and then to the airport to pick up the missionaries I'm relieving. I wasn't to be home until the 30th. The missionary's plans changed at the last minute because of the "increasing challenges" here in Zimbabwe.

The road to the airport, the *only* road to the airport, is closed with a heavy military presence. All roads to Harare are closed at present, and the toll gate through which I must pass to get to Harare has been burned down, one man shot and killed, and others wounded. That's the only road from Chinhoyi to Harare.

I've been told through texts, "they," whoever "they" are, will let you go through if you pay. I have no doubt "Europeans" get charged double and triple anyone else. I'd sure hate to lose my passport to them and would only carry my copy if I didn't have to renew my visa. I MUST have my original passport to do that.

Goodness, I didn't intend to talk your leg off. But I want someone there to know what's going on here and know if anything happens, it wasn't me!

Don't panic if you don't hear from me for a while. The government may shut down the internet, but it is probably just a rumor, like the International Airport being closed, which wasn't a rumor. I'm just so thankful I don't live in Harare or Bulawayo for the next couple of days!

The two nights before leaving for Harare I woke up making a mental list of all the precautions I could take and how to implement them. It was that "little voice" telling me all this. It reminded me of the top security man in Chinhoyi whom I called to see if it was safe to go. Although the demonstrations were to only be three days, Monday through Wednesday, talk on social chats before the internet was taken down said it was extending to Friday. The security man was in Harare and able to give advice for safety. The earlier I traveled, the safer it would be, but that was changing hourly. I had already decided to leave at 5 a.m. for that very reason (per the "little voice") and go straight to the airport (normally a one and one-half hour drive) even though the missionary couple wasn't due in until 5 p.m. that night. Rumor said the airport was open and safe.

At 5 a.m. it was dark. I had to wait until 5:30 a.m. to leave. By then it was raining, which makes driving on Zimbabwe roads even more hazardous. I wondered why God saw fit to add rain to the equation but figured He had His reasons. I had been told rocks placed in the road were not allowing traffic through at Hide and Seek Mountain Road, over which I would travel. Scoundrels hiding in the ditches often use this method to get a vehicle to stop and then they hijack it when the driver gets out to move the rocks or "smash and grab" while the driver is trying to turn around in the road. Whether the rocks had been put there to force people to observe the three days of totally shutting Zimbabwe down in protest of the government's neglect and financial abuse of its people recently, or by scoundrels with criminal intent, I didn't know. The rain would certainly help curtail the latter. Ahh, the rain. Now, I understand, God.

There were hardly any vehicles on the road. Many more people were trying to hitch rides than usual, probably because the kombies (taxi vans) weren't running. Mobs were still stoning and burning vehicles working during these three days. I felt bad driving past all these people, but I've pretty well stopped giving rides since picking up a young man on my way to church only to learn that he had just been released from prison the night before.

Two nights ago in Chinhoyi three businesses that were opened during these three days were looted and stripped of everything. With no social networks, I only learned of this by word of mouth. You know how distorted that information can get. I tend to think part of it was true because of the heavy police presence in Chinhoyi when I drove out this morning. A police truck was even parked in the middle of our deserted main street. It gave me an eerie feeling as he started to follow me with his lights off. I wasn't scared, just anxious to find a safe place to hide my passport so it wouldn't be confiscated. He stopped following me at the edge of town. The only other problems I had was at Hide and Seek Mountain Road trying not to hit any of the baboons in the middle it!

It was just as I got to Harare that I realized that since the government had shut down the internet in the entire country of Zimbabwe, the GPS on my cell phone would not work. Since most street signs are missing, getting lost would be inevitable. I hadn't thought of this, but God had. At that exact moment, Lindale, a second-generation missionary born in Zimbabwe, called my cell. She sat in Chinhoyi looking at her map and gave me directions as I drove.

I was surprised to see the toll booth that I thought had been burned down during the demonstrations. A video of it from a distance was sent to all of us on social network, again before the government took the internet down. The toll booth that burned and people who were shot were on another road. At the toll booth I had to go through, armed soldiers were stopping all vehicles coming from Harare and searching all loaded trucks going into Harare. I was in the mission truck in order to have room for the missionaries' luggage, yet I was not stopped or pulled over. In fact, their system was off-line so I didn't even have to pay the $2 toll. Thank you again, Lord.

Traffic increased at the edge of Harare, but it was too early to know if the three-day demonstration called for all of Zimbabwe was over or had been extended as rumored. It looked like a normal day, that is until a truck-load of African men with some in the open truck bed, drove up beside me. The one closest shook his finger at me, saying something while giving me a terribly mean look. Even though I've seen fiercer looks when my daughter was a teen, it was effective. I had to keep reminding myself, God has not given me a spirit of fear, but of power and of love, and a sound mind.

Last night, for a very short time, someone must have flipped the wrong switch because the social network was on in Chinhoyi where I live. It was on just long enough for over 300 WhatsApp texts to download. Among those was a voice WhatsApp text from the States that read aloud several Scriptures about fear and God's protection. I was remembering those Scriptures now. It wouldn't surprise me in the least but that God, Himself, flipped that switch.

I headed to the airport using the route an unknown taxi driver in Harare by the name of Farai (friend of a friend of a friend) texted me they had been using safely. (Even though our internet is off, and all social networks disabled, we can still call and text each other by cell phone. Here in Harare they can send and receive e-mails as well. (We can't in Chinhoyi.) By texts, I had set up Plan B with Farai to pick the missionaries up in case the road from Chinhoyi to Harare was blocked and I had to turn around and go back. He would take them to a B & B I had booked just hours before our internet was turned off.

By now my "spirit of fear" had been conquered seeing a few car taxis, kombies and many people who appeared to be going to work. I decided to see if the fuel station from which I can usually get a few liters of petrol was open. It wasn't open yet but would be opening soon, and the queue of vehicles was almost a km long! I was in the mission truck whose tank must be larger than their personal car because the fuel gauge was still on "FULL" after driving the one and one-half hours to Harare. With help, we syphoned diesel into the truck from the gerry can whose fuel I sourced last month. Another God-filled, God-directed adventure. We filled it to the point of being able to see the fuel!

I felt like I had enough fuel to travel to an area in Harare that has many shops and stores all together and still have diesel enough to drive back to Chinhoyi. Stores were beginning to open, which meant business as usual! One would never know the crisis we are passing through by seeing the normal, everyday activities beginning to unfold before my eyes. I pulled into a parking lot where I talked to the guard. He told me to park there in the shade and he would protect my truck. By the time I found a coffee house open (and WITH WORKING INTERNET) my heart could hardly contain my gratitude. I don't know how long I sat in the truck. I was just so, so thankful and kept telling Him so!

How timely is the verse you chose to send today - of all days!

Philippians 4:7 "And the peace of God, which transcends all understanding, will guard your hearts and your minds in Christ Jesus." (NIV)

For once again the "powers that be" here in Zimbabwe have betrayed the very people whom they were elected to serve. Most of the population will suffer immediately because of that lack of responsibility. I can hardly imagine, how much and yet they remain upbeat (for the most part), going about the everyday tasks they are still able to do.

I often think how blessed... How so, SO blessed I am coming from such a rich and privileged country as America even though we rely more and more on possessions and people and bank accounts. But then I see the way the Zimbabwean people cling to their God despite the huge everyday obstacles they face, and see these challenges just pull them closer and closer to the One who gives them true inner peace, "which transcends all understanding by guarding their hearts and minds in Christ Jesus."

I wonder... Perhaps it is I that comes from a third world country....

These are the times I love. I don't cherish going through them but love seeing His hand at work putting all the pieces of the puzzle together.

Sometimes, I actually feel His presence.

Please especially remember the missionary couple I'm relieving. They have been in the land of milk and honey for six months and then return to all these "challenges!" Even though Yolanda was born and raised in Zimbabwe, it will still feel like they have been thrown into the deep end of the pool, I imagine!

July 2019 - Terre Haute, Indiana

Over the past 17 years of relieving missionaries on foreign fields, I have served in many capacities: adjunct instructor at a Bible Institute, teacher of youth groups, Sunday School classes, women's groups, religious classes in a secular private school and in orphanages, speaker at Ladies Days and retreats. I've co-led seminars on parenting, marriage, raising children, how to teach Sunday School, preparing lessons and devotions. I have prepared payrolls, paid weekly salaries, and bills, fed and walked dogs, visited in homes and hospitals. I even passed a surprise audit of a mission's financial records in their office by that country's government officials. A hospitality ministry found Steve and I not only ferrying missionaries to and from the airport but hosting overnight guests 24 nights in one month alone only one of whom we knew. On one assignment, working with a church of all ladies and one man, I even found myself behind the pulpit a few Sundays. But none of the duties or responsibilities I have had during any of my past 32 assignments was like the one I just completed in Hungerford, Berkshire, England.

This was an assignment for which the Lord started preparing me almost half a century ago, 46 years to be exact. It began shortly after Steve and I graduated from what is now Kentucky Christian University and started a full-time ministry with Surprise Christian Church in Surprise, Indiana. Shortly thereafter, I was hired by the local hospital in Seymour to be a CNA (certified nurse's assistant), working on the surgery floor for two years. Thus, my preparation began.

In April 2019, I received a text from Yolanda Burgess in Zimbabwe. (Yolanda and Andrew are the missionaries I just finished relieving in Chinhoyi, Zimbabwe in January of this year.) Her mother, Vanessa, who lives by herself in Hungerford, two hours from London, had just been diagnosed with lung cancer.

I first met Vanessa in 2002 when she brought Yolanda to the missionary's house that we were relieving in Masvingo, Zimbabwe, for a youth group outing. Yolanda was still in high school and a member of the youth group I taught. It was the very first time Steve and I had ever gone overseas to relieve missionaries Ben and Karen Pennington. We were friends with the Penningtons and thought assisting these missionaries was a one-time event that would end in five months. (It hasn't ended. Seventeen years later, I'm still being contacted to relieve missionaries.)

In high school Yolanda's dream was to go to Bible College in the States and return to Zimbabwe to start a ministry to women and children, which they have done. She was such a good student that upon graduating from Boise Bible College she was offered a full scholarship from two different colleges to earn her master's degree.

The doctors in England informed Yolanda's mother, Vanessa, that if the cancer was confined to her lung they would be able to operate to remove it. If it was also outside the lung, there was nothing they could do for her. A test was performed which would show the location of the tumor. The doctor told her if she was a candidate for surgery, it would be performed two days later. The test results would be back the next week.

The Burgess' scurried around in Zimbabwe, packing, getting permission to leave their mission work while attending to Yolanda's mother. They arrived in England in time to be with Vanessa when she received her test results. They would be able to do surgery but not until the middle of May at the earliest. Yolanda tried to get the surgery moved up to the original date in April but with socialized medicine, Vanessa never saw the same doctor twice.

After a month, the surgery still had not been done. The Burgess' could not stay away from their work any longer. Heartbroken, Yolanda tried to find someone who could assist her mother through this. The cost was exorbitant because not only would the person need to help with cooking, cleaning, and laundry, but also assist Vanessa with bathing, dressing, etc., AND be a CNA with surgery patient experience to help with Vanessa's therapy, changing bandages, and after-surgery care.

I texted Yolanda I used to be a CNA who worked on the surgery floor, if that would be of any help to them but it was MANY YEARS ago. Yolanda texted me asking if I could be in London on May 15th. Thirteen days later I headed out on a wing and a prayer that it would be like riding a bike and all come back to me when I got there. Besides, I thought, would God have worked on putting a plan together for almost 50 years had He not intended to bring it to fulfillment?

God fulfilled and I remembered!

Vanessa met me at the gate at Heathrow airport and drove us on the two-hour trip to her home at Hungerford. We had three days for Vanessa to quickly acclimate me to all the ins and outs of Hungerford which even has round-abouts on "T" road junctions!

A friend drove us back to London where the hospital put Vanessa and me up for the night in an adjacent seven-story hospital unit set up with dormitory-type rooms, shared bathrooms, showers, and small kitchen. This is offered free to all patients living far from the hospital who have early morning check-in times for their surgeries.

Entering the hospital early the next morning, it was over four hours before they finally came to take Vanessa to surgery. We did not get to speak to the surgeon, only to his assistant, who they call his Registrar. The Registrar usually attends the surgeries but sometimes preforms one while the doctor oversees. As England has National Health Care, no cancer patient pays any medical bill. I was told the taxes that are withheld from everyone's paycheck are quite exorbitant to pay for free health care.

Vanessa asked me to keep 23 people updated while she was in the hospital. My concern was the massive 16-18 hours per day power cuts in Zimbabwe that would not only challenge our internet updates with Vanessa's Zimbabwe family but add to the anxiety of separation already being felt by Yolanda and her Mum during this time. I had hoped to Skype Yolanda when the doctor came out after the surgery to let him speak to Yolanda himself. That was a joke! Doctors don't come out after surgery here, or at least not this surgeon at Guy's Hospital in London!

The Registrar said the surgery would take four hours. It had been six hours. Family were texting, asking for updates. The waiting room for family was so hot, I sat outside the room. It was then I saw the Registrar walk by in his surgical greens. I jumped up and ran over, asking if it was indeed him. It was. He said Vanessa came through the surgery fine and was resting comfortably. I asked, when I would be able to talk with the surgeon. (I was listed as "next of kin" on hospital records.) He said probably not until tomorrow when Vanessa would be awake to hear. I asked, "What am I to tell her children in Zimbabwe and Australia? We can't leave them hanging." He told me about the surgery. I was just so thankful I recognized him since it was seven and one-half hours before Vanessa came back to the ward. It would have been seven and one-half hours without an update if I hadn't recognized the Registrar. Thank you, Lord, for help with all these "little things."

I had very little time with Vanessa before visiting hours ended. She was not feeling well at all and was nauseated the entire time. It was past 8 p.m. before I got to the train station called London Bridge Station just a couple blocks from the hospital. If it sounds familiar, there was a terrorist attack at that station two years ago. Eight people were killed and 48 seriously injured when three men drove into pedestrians before starting to stab them in Borough Market, which is where I walked for a bite of lunch that day.

I had no idea what train tickets I needed and only knew the name of the train station where I should end up. It was to be within walking distance of the room that had been offered for me to use at night while Vanessa was in the hospital. A friend of Vanessa's was part of a Christian chat group on WhatsApp. She had asked if anyone had a room I could use. Caro answered the appeal.

Before going to the hospital, we drove by the house in which I was to stay. The further we drove into London, the more Vanessa kept repeating, "This is not a good neighborhood. This is not a good place. You are w-a-y too far from the hospital. No! You mustn't stay here. I won't allow it." We pulled up to the house, which was connected to others along the block, and knocked on the door. As soon as the door opened and I saw the lady, all concerns melted away. I could see God in her smile.

Caro greeted us with a big hug and told me that the first time I came to the Brockly train station she would pick me up and drive me to her house so I could see the way I would be walking each morning and each evening. Caro said it was a 16-18-minute walk. I found it to be closer to 25-30.

God must have sent His angel to help me in the form of a Nigerian train ticket agent. Even though there were three other people in line behind me, he still closed his window and came from behind the counter to walk me through using a vending machine to load the proper number of British pounds on the correct sections of my "oyster" train card. This would allow me to take the bus, train, or tube as transportation for the next four days. It was great because I found a bus that took 15 minutes off my walk time when it was threatening rain, or I was too exhausted to walk the entire way home. I usually left the room where I was staying by 6:30 a.m. and returned around 9 p.m. which was still light enough to see without a flashlight. I was not out after dark.

After two nights in the hospital, they wanted to release Vanessa but kept her one more night for which I was thankful. Vanessa just had half a lung removed. She did not act, feel or look like she was ready to be released. At home, the seepage on the dressings I changed continued longer than either of us thought it should. Vanessa ended back in a different hospital for three more nights. After these set-backs, she finally began to improve.

Vanessa saw her surgeon the next month. He released her to start driving. She drove us to church that Sunday. Now that Vanessa was able to drive and take care of herself, I boarded a plane for home the next day.

I am very glad to have this time at home until my next assignment. I hadn't noticed how travel-weary I was becoming. God did. It's so good to physically be with the ones I can just talk at overseas. As an added bonus, I got to celebrate (again) my February birthday and Christmas on July 4th this year. I was given those gifts while sitting with my family on the golf course in Brazil, Indiana, waiting for the fireworks to begin.

I have been asked to have an hour workshop at the 2019 International Conference of Missions (ICOM), formerly known as the Missionary Convention. It will be two weeks before Thanksgiving in Kansas City, Kansas this year. I will be telling of the services MRS offers to the overseas missionary while on furlough. Lord willin', a seed will be planted for others to start similar ministries for relieving missionaries on furlough.

I have found this ministry, which God started for Steve and me more rewarding than my pen can write. Two years ago in 2017 an interview for LOOKOUT magazine was done. (The complete interview follows.) I was asked what was the most rewarding in this ministry to which I replied, "The people!" Many, many people I talk to overseas, we cannot understand one word the other is saying, yet we stand in the road, or on the sidewalk and take turns jabbering to each other using hand gestures, facial expressions and body language to convey our encrypted messages. Although I may never see that person again and couldn't pick them out of a police line-up, I will never forget the smile on their face or the twinkle in their eye the moment we are able to communicate without under-standing a word the other said. An indescribable bond begins to form with each meeting. Their smiles become broader as they begin to cross the road to meet me, hold my hand, stroke my arm, pat my back, and eagerly introduce me (I assume) to the other ladies with them.

So many of the Christians, and others, with whom I work or have made their acquaintance not only open their homes to me but their hearts. A cleaning lady in India with whom I walked with on the road when we happened to be there at the same time, invited me to her house for tea, or at least I thought. Neither of us could understand the others language but again we had no trouble communicating. I had one of the older English-Hindi speaking hostel girls accompany me to the lady's home. She was our translator for the entire evening. Even with the meager salary of a cleaning lady, she had many Indian sweets and samosas in addition to the tea. The entire extended family was there. I felt so humbled to be her honored guest and pleased to be able to pray over the tea in a state with an anti-conversion law which does not allow teaching any one about Jesus or God without being subject to arrest or being thrown out of the country.

In Hong Kong, the Chinese ladies with whom I exercised early each morning, took me to lunch along with a daughter who served as our translators. Again, I was able to pray before the meal and for every additional dish that was served as they thought that is the way it was done. I didn't have the heart to say no when they asked me to pray again... and again... and again....

When I buried my love six-feet under, in a small, country cemetery on top of a hill, I thought I would never feel love again. God is giving that love back through the people to whom He is sending me.

This year before blowing the candles out on my birthday "pie," I was told to make a wish first. I couldn't think of anything for which to wish. God has given me more happiness through serving Him than I could ever have imagined. All of my heart's desires, and more, have been fulfilled. There is nothing more for which I pine.

My prayer now is to finish strong....

Philip being buried in the watery grave of baptism by Steve the Sunday after Steve helped bury Philip's sister in an earthly grave. Johannesburg, South Africa - 2003

Oliver - mission hostel baptism at Kulpahar, India - 2014

Ox cart owner, wife and children. Kulpahar, India - 2014

Hostel boys teaching Janeece to hit a cricket ball - 2012

South Africa Bible Institute students enjoying our Friday evening
homemade spaghetti dinner.   2006

Wrapped up in blankets for church service. It was colder inside than it was outside.
Cape Town, South Africa 2014

Baptism in children's pool. Fairview Christian Church, Hong Kong 2011

An Interview With Janeece England

Original interview of Janeece, by Laura McKillip Wood for Lookout Magazine article 2017. Updated responses as of 2019.

1. *Tell me about your Missionary Relief Services (MRS) ministry. What do you do? Do you work with an agency of some sort or are you independent?*

Actually, it's not "my" ministry but one the Lord prepared for my late husband, Steve and me. We just stumbled into it, with our footsteps being divinely directed.

Our first relief assignment was in April 2002 when Ben and Karen Pennington asked if we would come to Zimbabwe to assist the nationals with the mission work for the five months they would be on furlough.

In Zimbabwe, Steve helped with the preaching, met with the village preachers, paid salaries, kept ministry bills up to date, etc. I taught the high school Friday night youth group, led the weekly ladies' Bible study, and sang with the praise team. We both assisted with their Holiday Bible Club (like our VBS), held a marriage seminar, parenting workshops, conducted classes on how to write devotions, prepared and taught Sunday School classes, and made hospital calls. Whatever duties of the missionary that were not done by the nationals, we did.

Since then, we have served on other assignments as interim instructors at Bible Institute/extension classes, hospital chaplain, counselors, Sunday school teachers, youth leaders, special function speakers, community ladies' Bible study leader, speaking at week-end church rallies, and ladies' retreats, and financial office personnel. We have updated library accession records, filed, taught nationals to plant and tend gardens, over-saw the building of a domestic quarters, (They taught me how to lay bricks!), paid contractors, took care of pets/guard dogs, taught Scripture classes in a private boarding school and orphanage, and tutored one on one, to name just a few of our ministry duties.

Two days before we were to board a plane to fly home in 2002, a fellow missionary in South Africa e-mailed Ben asking if he knew of anyone who could help with work for six months while they were on furlough and Missionary Relief Services, an independent agency, was born.

The elders of the Church of Christ oversee the ministry with their minister of 35 years, Bob Wickline, acting as our forwarding agent.

Towards the end of our second assignment, Steve e-mailed our forwarding agent to ask that he keep his ear to the ground for possible churches looking for a minister. We never knew where or even IF there would be a next MRS assignment but relied totally on God's guidance. Often, it was within the last days of the ongoing assignment we received an e-mail from a missionary requesting our assistance. The last three years I have had three back to back assignments each year, flying from one mission directly to the next.

I completed two relief assignments this year, 2019, in Zimbabwe and Great Britain. Lord willin', I will complete my 35th and 36th assignments next year with relief assignments booked through 2021.

Since God established this ministry, I will rely on Him to "tell" me when it has ended, which I assume will be when missionaries no longer ask for my assistance or I am physically unable to continue.

2. What are your main goals in ministry?
MRS is a mission to the missionary. Simply stated, MRS's main goal is to relieve the missionary not only of the physical duties on the field, but to perform those duties so thoroughly as to relieve him from worrying about the mission or the security of his house, car, and possessions during his absence. This will allow him to focus on

his work at hand and perhaps actually get some R & R while on furlough.

3. What do you find most challenging in your work?
Feeling I don't belong here in the States or overseas. Thankfully, in all the beds, in all the countries of all the people in which I have slept, I have never awakened overseas wondering where I am. But I come home, fall asleep in my own chair, and wake up wondering, "Where in the world am I?"

I take consolation in the fact that my citizenship is neither here nor there but in Heaven.

4. What is most rewarding?
The people with whom I work are the most rewarding part of our ministry. Seven years ago, I thought I would never feel love again when I buried my love six feet under in a small cemetery on top of a hill. But God is giving that love back through the people to whom He is sending me. Many, many people I talk to, we cannot under-stand one word the other is saying, yet we stand in the road, or on the sidewalk and jabber to each other using hand gestures, facial expressions, and body language.

5. Tell me about yourself. Where did you grow up?
I was born close to and raised in Oblong, Illinois, which I refer to as "the Promised Land." I met and married my husband at Kentucky Christian College, now Kentucky Christian University (KCU). Of the 39 years we were married 30 were in the located ministry and the rest in mission work. We were blessed with one daughter, Rebekah Joy, her husband, Jake Liles, and a granddaughter, Trinity Jade.

6. How did you decide to go into full-time ministry?
I think every Christian is in full-time ministry. Mine is just specialized.

Since the age of 11, I always wanted to graduate from Bible college, marry a preacher, and be a missionary in Africa. I was 51-years-old when God answered that prayer. It was mostly due to the influence of a preacher and his wife. She was my Sunday school teacher for two years. Sunday school teachers should never dismiss the impact their lessons and life can have on a student.

7. How did you decide on this particular role?
As I said before, God is the one who led me in this ministry. Steve and I were just going to help one missionary couple for five months. Seventeen years later, I'm still doing it.

8. What has been your favorite place to work? Why did you enjoy this one?
Oh, my goodness! That's difficult to choose just one. The people, not the location, make places "my favorite." It seems wherever I am is my favorite place to be.

9. In what countries have you served?
We assisted with missionary work in Mexico, St Croix, India, and Jamaica before MRS while in the located ministry. As a relief missionary, I have helped in Zimbabwe, South Africa, Tanzania, Italy, Guinea, India, China, Czech Republic, Great Britain, and Hong Kong.

10. What advice would you give to someone contemplating intercultural work for the first time?
A. Remember, you are there to evangelize, not Americanize.
B. Our way of doing things, in or out of the church, is not always best overseas.
C. Watch and follow the national's lead if it is not unscriptural.
D. See and listen with your heart. I often feel they teach me more than I teach them.

11. Where do you see yourself in ten years?

Lord willin', on the other side of the clouds worshiping at His feet! God has given me more happiness through serving Him than I could ever have imagined. All of my heart's desires, and more, have been fulfilled. There is nothing I lack, nothing more for which I pine. My prayer now is to finish strong....

Janeece with the Indian woman who was embarrassed of her smile. 2014

Janeece driving the ox car in India. 2016

"Challenging" conditions in Zimbabwe take their toll even on the children. 2005